An Inspiring Academic Journey

About the Author

Prof. Ganapathy Palanithurai, Rajiv Gandhi Chair for Panchayati Raj studies, Department of Political Science and Development Administration, Gandhigram Rural Institute—Deemed University, Gandhigram is an academic activist working with academic community, civil society, policy community and political community to impress upon them the importance and need of democratic local governance in India to enable the poor to lead a decent dignified human life. All his academic, research and outreach activities are being supported by an array of funding agencies namely the World Bank, the UNDP, the UNICEF, the Hunger Project, SDC, DANIDA, Action Aid International, the Ford Foundation, Population Foundation of India, the Rajiv Gandhi Foundation, Toolkit Foundation—Netherland, Ministry of Panchayati Raj and State Planning Commission. He was a visiting Professor in Cologne University, Germany. He has to his credit seventy three books, 126 research articles, 112 popular articles in popular newspapers, 83 monographs published in a span of three decades. He is the coordinator of UGC-SAP and UGC innovative programme. He held several administrative positions like Dean, Faculty of Social Sciences, Dean, Student's Welfare, Member, Syndicate, Member Senate, Member, and Academic Council in Gandhigram Rural Institute. He was and is member of many advisory committees of the Government of India and Government of Tamil Nadu pertinent to local government and rural development.

An Inspiring Academic Journey

By
G. Palanithurai

CONCEPT PUBLISHING COMPANY PVT. LTD.
NEW DELHI-110059

ISBN-13: 978-93-86682-69-7

First Published 2018

Published and Printed by:

Concept Since 1974

Concept Publishing Company Pvt. Ltd.
A/15-16, Commercial Block, Mohan Garden,
New Delhi-110059 (INDIA)
T : +91 11 25351460, +91 11 25351794
E : publishing@conceptpub.com, *W* : www.conceptpub.com

Cataloging in Publication Data--Courtesy: D.K. Agencies (P) Ltd. <docinfo@dkagencies.com>

Palanithurai, G., author.
An inspiring academic journey / by G. Palanithurai.
pages cm
Includes bibliographical references.
ISBN 9789386682697

1. Decentralization in government--India--Tamil Nadu. 2. Local government--India--Tamil Nadu. 3. Rural development--Government policy--India--Tamil Nadu. 4. Education, Rural--India--Tamil Nadu. 5. Palanithurai, G. 6. College administrators--India--Gandhigram--Biography. I. Title.

LCC JS7025.T36P35 2018 | DDC 320.8095482 23

To

The Divine Mother

Preface

This book is not an empirical analysis of issues connected with decentralization of powers. It is an account of my personal experiences as an academic activist involved in the process of decentralization of powers in India. Having been very deeply involved in activities ranging from policy making to grassroots level action, I have had the privilege of observing many facets and phases in decentralization. My friends felt that the inspiring journey of mine as an academician has to be recorded and made available for the young social science teachers in higher learning institutions in India and against this background they asked me to write some of the interesting stories about the initiatives of decentralization of powers in India. For long, I was mulling over the idea of writing this book. But I found time now to do it.

Obviously, stories of the academicians journey in decentralization is different and it is inspiring that might interest a reader, but for someone who has closely observed it—often as part of it—it is quite stressing to narrate especially because of the controversies involved. However, I realized that a book with such stories can serve two important purposes: (i) put across how an academic can play an active role in the transformative process of a society; and (ii) documenting the self-satisfying experiences of 'involvement' which most others, perhaps, have not had or have not bothered to have. These motives prodded me to take up this task. I believe this will be of use to the young academics who join academic institutions in social science faculties. Being an academic should not end up as transferring the notes of the teacher into the notes of students without getting into the heads of either. If you delink yourself from the society, your notes are no longer relevant to the classroom.

As a young faculty member in Annamalai University I gained a perception that teachers in higher learning institutions have two obligatory functions, namely (i) teaching, and (ii) research. But I used to ask my teachers Dr. S. Bhaskaran and Dr. A. Shanmugam: how a teacher can connect to larger communities. Their reply was: "act on your own and there is no barrier for your community service as there is nothing inbuilt in the university system to reach out to the communities". Later, under the leadership of Dr. S. Baskaran and Dr. A. Shanmugam we started "Village Welfare Society" and worked for some time. The instinct of connecting ourselves with larger communities was with me and it was tuned by my teachers. But, when I joined the Gandhigram Rural Institute (GRI)—Deemed University in 1991, I realized that outreach programme can be part of our academic activity in the university system. That is Gandhigram gave me the insight that outreach programmes (extending the activities of the university beyond the campus to benefit the larger community around) are viewed as integral activities in a university system besides teaching and research. I was fascinated to plunge into action. I always hold this view that Dr. S. Bhaskaran trained me in research; and Dr. A. Shanmugam trained me in teaching. In 1991, I joined (as a Reader) in the Gandhigram Rural Institute (GRI) after seven years of teaching and research experience in Annamalai University. GRI carries the legacy of Gandhian thinking, perspective and actions, and so I landed here with a lot of aspirations, and hope to involve myself in community service as well.

I joined as head of the Department of Political Science and Development Administration (When I joined it was Politics and Development Administration). I was given the responsibility of looking after Gandhian Thought and Peace Science unit also. I knew that I was neither an expert in development administration nor in extension activities. All that I had was an unwavering interest to learn and contribute. I wanted to start my outreach activities as the little voice inside me was driving to get down 'doing' rather than talking. In a conversation with the then Managing Trustee of Gandhigram Trust late. V. Padmanabhan, I took into my head that my department in GRI was started with the objective of preparing a cadre to work in rural areas to strengthen grassroots institutions and to improve the services of the public institutions at the grassroots level. We offered an undergraduate programme on Development Administration. I prepared my mind to contextualize the programme by giving new thrust to New Panchayati Raj System. Because, I knew that this subject would gain importance in the years to come.

I thought that there would be much scope and future for local self-governance system, and so, I was planning to introduce a master's programme on this subject. Hence, I made up my mind to work on this area and started my teaching, research and outreach activities in the domain of Panchayati Raj. After I joined the department, I discussed with my colleagues about the proposal of strengthening the academic programme of the department in this area and they evinced interest. But, they also cautioned me that Panchayati Raj had already reached the lowest ebb in this institute and nobody wanted to teach this subject and moreover in many of the programmes this subject was removed from the scheme. At that point of time my intuition prompted me to plunge into action by taking up that subject with new vigour and new perspective.

In the beginning of 1990s the whole world started moving towards globalization and decentralization. Against this background I firmed up my decision of specialising in decentralization and decentralized governance. Against this perspective I started my work on decentralization of powers and Panchayati Raj in India. From 1991 to 2017, I have been in the subject and involved in various activities in association with the federal government, state government, donor agencies, bilateral and multilateral agencies, civil society, academic and research institutions, political parties, NGOs and media.

There is another purpose for writing this book. In the beginning I said that the untold stories of the process of decentralization of powers are going to be discussed and explained in this work. I am of the strong opinion that our academics are happy 'doing the teaching in the classroom', rather than 'being involved in the transformation process of society'. They do not actively involve in outreach activities to enhance the quality of development process.

I believe that many of the ills in Indian society, politics, administration, governance are due to the poor quality of man power at work, and the blind-spots created by information asymmetry that shadow the reality. Massively these problems could be tackled through outreach programmes/direct interventions. Unfortunately, our intellectuals in the portals of the higher learning institutions choose to turn a blind-eye to such problems because: "they are mandated to teach, they are busy teaching ….or simply they are busy being busy." Clearly, there is space for the academics to act in the public sphere, but they do not seem to use that space for reasons, perhaps, they know best. I could use that space to the best of my satisfaction, and involved myself in human endeavours in the larger society.

When I set out, I did not realize that this involvement would open up in a serial taking me across levels. The outcome is fulfilling and satisfying. I have recorded all the events and incidents with an objective of motivating young scholars in social science to prove the point academics involving in community outreach activities is possible, and mutually enriching. This put me to great stalwarts I never imagined I shall be working with. These connections also enabled me to realize the mission I took up. I have covered in this work, whatever I have done—awareness creation, capacity building, research, policy advocacy, publication, media networks and other activities—for strengthening Panchayati Raj System in Tamil Nadu. All these were carried out roping in support, and collaborating with individuals, organizations, and many agencies. I started working with one panchayat, and today there is almost no panchayat functionary in Tamil Nadu who does not know me. I started this work with Rs. 200 given by our institute. Now, the Rajiv Gandhi Chair for Panchayati Raj Studies at GRI handles projects in millions with research, training and capacity building agenda.

This is a demonstration of commitment of an academic. In the whole of my journey we have developed the department infrastructure that benefits the students and research scholars. As a mark of recognition, the UGC has elevated our department by giving Special Assistance Programme (SAP) in the domain of grassroots governance. Further, the UGC has given Rs. 41 lakh to evolve an innovative masters' programme on 'governance and development'. Subsequently, our Department has been allowed to move to the second stage of the SAP by the UGC from 2015 to 2020. We are in the remote village in a backward district Dindigul, Tamil Nadu. Yet, we have also opportunities and potentials. If they are used, the socio-political and economic transformation would get momentum. Utilizing the potentials depends on both the academics as individuals and the academic institutions effectively. I have written this book to demonstrate to the younger scholars that without the demand of the institution where we work we can act voluntarily on our own and deliver something meaningful to the society. This can eventually make us inevitable individuals to the institutions, friends, policy makers and larger society. Reading this book, if a few teachers get prodded to involve in community service, I would consider this book a great success.

G. Palanithurai

Acknowledgements

In public space if something happens, one should not claim that he or she has achieved or he or she is responsible. It is only a self-deception. It is always a collective effort. Whatever little bit I have done in public space to transform something it is because of the support and service rendered by many individuals and institutions. Moreover, in academic institution, when an individual is working consciously and continuously with a sense of commitment in the public space, no matter if it means 'contributing' or not, it certainly means he or she is 'gaining'. The gains may be name, material, elevation, improving infrastructure and enhancing his or her own capacity. It is unfair to claim that I have contributed rather it is to be stated that I worked in the domain along with others.

Against this background I look back my activities for a while and realize the fact that many have contributed substantially for my academic, research and extension endeavours. The contributions may be in the form of ideas, moral support, financial support, administrative support, enabling facility, carrying out activities in the field as per my request. Lots of individuals and institutions have contributed towards the successful conduct of many academic research and outreach activities in the domain of Panchayati Raj.

Late Mr. V. Padmanabhan, the Managing Trustee of Gandhigram Trust had initially put me in the track by his constant interaction with me. He called me many times and discussed with me the genesis of Gandhigram and the Gandhigram Rural Institute. He unresistingly discussed with me the strengths and weakness of both Gandhigram and the Gandhigram Rural Institute. He positively advised me to work on Panchayati Raj. Since, I evinced keen interest on this subject whenever I organized any programme I used to inform him. He participated in all our programmes on decentralization and Panchayati Raj. He never participated as VIP in the programme. He was there as a participant and contributed substantially on the subject under discussion from his rich experience. Until his demise, he continued to extend his support to all our activities. I pay my tribute to him.

Secondly, some of the vice-chancellors of the Gandhigram Rural Institute gave special attention to our department to strengthen our academic programmes, research and outreach activities. Of them I have to mention Late Dr. T.R. Natesan. When he was the Vice-Chancellor he allotted a separate building for our Department and sanctioned two more staff to our department. He was instrumental in creating the Rajiv Gandhi Chair for Panchayati Raj Studies in our Department. We have introduced an innovative M.A. Five Year integrated programme twenty years back. When no one imagined in Tamil Nadu a five year PG Programme can be offered in our university system. We have proposed the programme despite serious apprehensions expressed by academics in our institute. He stood behind us and got it passed in authoritative bodies. Hence, it is my duty to thank him for the visionary support extended to our Department despite opposition of many of our senior colleagues in this institute.

There was yet another individual Dr. N. Markandan who was with me in Panchayati Raj team for all our activities. Later, he became Vice-Chancellor of our Institute. He helped me to consolidate and expand my department and Panchayati Raj activities of the Rajiv Gandhi Chair. He acted as facilitator for all our activities. Whenever I organized Panchayati Raj Programme he was with me as a senior colleague and he participated in all our programmes whenever we organized the programme whether in the institute or in the villages or anywhere in the State. Till today he visits our Department and participates in our programmes. He deserves our mention here as he holds our work on Panchayati Raj close to his heart.

Another humble individual, my colleague Prof. V. Ragupathy, my first Ph.D. student, from day one when I joined the Department till today he is working with me as Lakshmana to Rama. A devoted and deeply committed individual for public cause and more specifically on Panchayati Raj, he was with me as part and parcel of my team. He was and is always next in command and a very unassuming individual. He has his deep vision on Panchayati Raj and his support to all our activities. He in fact freed me from many of the routine works from the Head of the Department and enabled me to devote my attention on research and outreach programmes. He indeed helped me to maintain harmony in the department throughout my career. Moreover, he inherited the legacy of his uncle late Mr. G. Venkatachalapathy first Development Commissioner of Tamil Nadu and a prime contributor for strengthening Panchayati Raj in our State. Dr. V. Ragupathy has lots of insists gained from his uncle and substantially contributed for all our activities. I have learnt the art of serving others with love and affection from him. He is such a person working with me for Panchayati Raj activities.

Dr. K.S. Nakkeeran, who worked with me when I was in Annamalai University and jointed with me in the Gandhigram Rural Institute later. He looked after the student discipline and classroom activities when I was totally involved in project and research activities. Managing more than hundred students and taking them to file periodically with limited member of staff are not easy matters to deal with. He did all the works with a sense of dedication and commitment. He in fact took pain to correct many of the students who deviated from the mainsheet academic activities by carefully analyzing their socio-economic background. I owe a lot to him for his painstaking work he has done to the department. Prof. A. Celeni Rani and Dr. S. Hoakip are copy look teachers, discharged their duties with a sense of dedication and for which I have to register my deep sense of gratitude.

I had more than twenty five staff, both at the senior and junior levels and of them a few are remarkable persons in the fieldwork. Dr. M.A. Thirunavukkarasu is still with me not as a regular staff but as a freelancer since he takes lot of consultancies and he contributed immensely in Panchayati Raj activities of the Rajiv Gandhi Chair. Likewise Dr. G. Uma, now she is working as Assistant Professor in Indira Gandhi National Open University (a central university), has untiringly worked with me both as a field staff, and as my associate in my programmes and projects. She also worked as a research scholar under my supervision for her Ph.D. degree. Her devoted work has substantially helped the chair to grow from strength to strength. There are two other researchers Dr. R. Ramesh and Dr. J. Vanishree, former is working for an Ethiopian University, and the latter is working as Assistant Professor in IGNOU worked in my research activities. I must say that they are the role models for young scholars in terms of their search for knowledge. They worked with a sense of passion and commitment to enhance the quality of research. There are three other individuals who worked with me in computer section. They are Mr. S.P. Ramesh and Mrs. Punitha Lakshmi and Mrs. Rajalakshmi. They were really creative individuals and hence they have contributed immensely in report preparation, and designing reports. It is immensely satisfying to see that all our works on Panchayati Raj are useful and carry the name of Gandhigram across districts, states, and institutions.

In the same way they are other individuals who worked with me in the field and in designing and carrying out various field programmes. They are Mr. K. Tamilarasan, Dr. D. Devaraj and Dr. M. Gurusamy, who put in their best to deliver a meaningful work. They deserve mention here. There is yet another individual Dr. G. Umashankar who worked with me in the initial stages and contributed in his own way for the projects and for the Rajiv Gandhi Chair for Panchayati Raj Studies. Dr. P. Sathyaraj and D. Sivakumar worked in UGC SAP Project in the first phase and they continued to work with me in other projects professionally. D. Sivakumar too working with me till date in the IRMA Project with a sense of dedication. I compliment both of them.

In this context, I have to mention the role of my teacher Dr. S. Bhaskaran. He taught me, apart from research, providing the right kind of leadership, which enable me to provide the same to my Department and the Rajiv Gandhi Chair. He demonstrated how a teacher can be a role model in working with others instead of ruling others and saying: 'get going' is leadership; Dr. S. Bhaskaran heading a team democratically, and to say: 'come along'.

I led a team by allowing them to work freely without any domination and allowed them real freedom with the self-respect without interference by others. At the same time facilitate and make sure each one gets due recognition and rewards. It is always a "Win-Win" formula I have adopted. This I have learnt from Dr. S. Bhaskaran. He is a democrat in all his actions. I have also learned another virtue from my teacher Dr. A. Shanmugam. How one can conduct himself or herself in all our actions in academic life ethically? This is an art I learnt from him. Equally Dr. R. Elango, former Dean of Arts and Professor of Economics of Annamalai University is a model researcher and teacher. Though his discipline was Economics, I was constantly in touch with him to have my academic work enriched and research meaningful.

There is yet another unit which deserves my mention here—my family. My wife Mrs. Mala a devoted wife, a mother, a daughter-in-law took care of my family, which allowed me to pay undivided attention on my academic, research, and outreach activities. She is a *karma yogi* in one sense. Likewise my daughter Mrs. P. Senthil Vadivu and my son Er. P. Aurobindh both did their work successfully moved their career on their own and never they took my time. The entire family unit allowed me to work 24 × 7 in Panchayati Raj domain.

Apart from all in our Institute many worked with me. All Vice-Chancellors, Registrars and officials in the office have supported me to carry out all our activities successfully. Hence I pay my tribute and thank all of them.

G. Palanithurai

Contents

PART–II
Curriculum Vitae of Prof. G. Palanithurai

Publications

Part-I

Profile of Prof. G. Palanithurai

1

My Research Programme

Ph.D. is methodological thinking of an issue that combines rigour and reason. At present universities have become Ph.D. thesis production factories. In higher learning institutions research ventures are undertaken and they lead to Ph.D. thesis production. If anyone asked a question: 'Beyond Ph.D. what?' They draw a blank. I am able to guess two reasons why they draw a blank. For one, most young researchers walk with a foregone conclusion that Ph.D. is the pinnacle of knowledge; secondly, whatever tables, graphs etc. they produced, they were churned out of software tools such as SPSS, STATA, SAS etc. The researcher made nothing out of 'the results'. The thesis is beautiful, no matter if it is not meaningful. The researcher made nothing out of it, except his/her Ph.D. degree. It is a computer game meant for smart-researchers. The computer game grinds the data down to a powder—no matter if it is coarse. The tragedy of university research today is that it is very uncommon to find a hard-core researcher. We have only smart-researchers and over-smart ones. They hire statisticians to put on show statistical gimmicks at a technically acceptable significance level, without getting into their head what the results 'mean'.

In the way social science researchers work, there has been a visible shift in the past decade—from undertaking socially relevant research for knowledge production to research that employs quantitative tools for sophistication. Sophistication for the sake of it and no matter if they do not make sense to a pragmatist. Computers—the researchers' treadmills—have eased research with sophisticated software tools most of them available for free download. The good news for today's researchers is obtaining a Ph.D. is no more a longing.

It is no more a dream. It is just a matter of 'hiring a statistician' who can mill about your data in anyone of these softwares—SPSS or whatever. Software tools mill around any data in whatever form "the statistician one hired thought it could be presented". The researcher has no idea what has come out of it. The result: the 'results' seem to have come out from a 'treadmill'—no discussion, no argument, no eloquence in the expression. What go missing are all the essential features that give soul to a thesis. Often, the presentation is good but the palatability is not. Computers helped prove your point. But, the big question is: does your thesis prove useful? Precisely, in our obsession to "using software tools to report a certain significance level", we are losing sight of the "real meaning and eloquence in the argument". This makes the definition 'a thesis is an argument' no more valid. I find the data undergo change, but the researcher does not. It is machine-driven research and not researcher-driven. Eventually, I find a 'survey report' though not a thesis. Surely, I do not find 'researcher in the person'.

Taking socially relevant issues to the heart and work for a solution is becoming outdated. A thesis must be pleasing to the eyes; it does not have to impact on your heart, not even in your mind. Social relevance as the decisive factor in knowledge production or knowledge transmission is archaic. This is the depressing reality we witness today. Personally, I am of the strong opinion that by involving oneself in Ph.D. level research, one must gain not only knowledge and insight, but also sensitivity, sensibility and commitment. I cultivated methodological thinking and proper perspective to research only from my research supervisor Dr. S. Bhaskaran.

When I joined my Ph.D. programme as per the advice of my teacher Dr. A. Shanmugam of Annamalai University, I registered under Prof. D. Balasubramanian of the History Department. I joined in Ph.D. programme with an assurance from Dr. A. Shanmugam that after the arrival of Dr. S. Bhaskaran from the U.S. he will prevail upon him to take me as a Ph.D. Scholar. I had not even completed six months in Ph.D. programme Dr. S. Bhaskaran came from the US and joined the Department of History in Annamalai University as a Reader. For many of the students Dr. S. Bhaskaran was a demigod. He was a model teacher and researcher. In the next day of his arrival I met him in the Chidambaram Railway Station. I told him that I have joined Ph.D. Programme with the assumption that I can pursue Ph.D. programme under his supervision. He immediately told me that he will help me in this regard. It was a great day for me.

I was in a jubilant mood and I went to Prof. D. Balasubramanian. The moment I met he told me that Dr. S. Bhaskaran has come from the U.S. and he will be a suitable guide for you. Then I requested him to help me. He immediately responded that he would talk to Dr. S. Bhaskaran. The very next day Dr. S. Bhaskaran called me and informed that Dr. A. Shanmugam had written a letter to him when he was in the U.S. and he requested him to take you for Ph.D. programme after rejoining in Annamalai University. Further he told me that Prof. D. Balasubramanian also requested me to take you for Ph.D. programme. But before taking a final decision he asked a question to me. The question was why do you want to do Ph.D.? I said, "I would become a scholar in a particular field." He immediately responded that it is difficult but certainly possible. If you are willing to undergo a difficult process you can come to me for earning a Ph.D. degree. He further told me that Ph.D. is not something you are 'given', it is something you 'earn' through determined work. Getting Ph.D. is very easy in Indian academic setting and earning a Ph.D. degree demands passing through a struggle. I responded that I am ready to undergo any difficult process, and I meant it. Then I was transferred to Dr. S. Bhaskaran for Ph.D. guidance.

I was the first student of Dr. S. Bhaskaran. Within a few days we finalized the syllabus for course work. At present UGC is insisting on course work for Ph.D. Programme. In 1980 I did course work under the supervision of Dr. S. Bhaskaran. After the course work was initiated, I became like an undergraduate student as he had to start from fundamentals of the concepts related to our subjects on which I prepared assignments. I never experienced such a rigour in my life as I experienced in my course work for earning my Ph.D. degree.

Dr. S. Bhaskaran, with his US exposure, wanted to shape young Indian researchers to do socially relevant research that would be useful for India's development. With this spirit he came from the US despite he had several offers to work in the US itself. With a sense of dedication he started the work of preparing young scholars from the school in Social Science in Annamalai University in 1980s. For three years I worked just like a graduate student and I was always preparing assignments, submitting the same to him and participated in all the discussions. I had to write monthly tests in his house from Morning

10 to 1.00 pm. He evaluated the assignment papers. One could see his meticulous care in evaluating the papers prepared by me. I preserve all those assignment papers still with me.

Before I completed my course work, my friends working in other departments started writing their thesis. Once course work was over, my supervisor asked me to prepare a research proposal for my thesis. I prepared it and submitted to him. He in fact sent it to his friends for critical assessment of the proposal. Quickly, I got back their comments and a few books. In their review they have indicated the gaps and to fill up the gaps in the proposal, I was asked to read the books they had sent to me. I read the books. A few weeks later, I felt I gained some clarity, and so, I improved my proposal, and resubmitted. After his approval I started collecting the relevant material, analyzed the same and wrote up the thesis. I had done all the works from data collection to submission of my thesis within six months time. In the whole process of the course work I was asked to read series of books, articles monographs, working papers, classics, on Political Economy, Political Sociology, Comparative Politics, Political Analysis, Political Geography, Governance, Administration and so on. Dr. S. Bhaskaran made me to learn and he took part as a co-learner himself.

Dr. S. Bhaskaran constantly, reinforced the idea of how self-learning can elevate a person's intellect. He made me understand that earning a Ph.D. degree was only the first step, and a kind of grounding to getting down to do serious research with confidence. From data collection to report writing all the activities that a researcher has to do were put across to me not in a teaching-mode but in a learning mode. I learnt a whole array of techniques such as: how to review a book or article; how to write an article; how to make effective presentations; how to handle theories in research studies and so on. But, the whole process was not in a teaching mode but in a learning mode. I was shaped to make research as a way of life. There were several occasions I can quote how I struggled in my research.

Once a book was given to me in the course work and I was asked to review the book. I felt I had done a good job. The book was Karl Deutsch's "*Nerves of Government*". I read the book and wrote a review. My guide told me that the review was not up to his expectations. He asked me to read it again. I prepared the review and re-submitted. His remarks this time was that I could not establish my grip over the subject on which the book was written. Third time I reviewed the book and submitted the review. I was told that I have gained something correctly from the book and not fully. Then, I did the same exercise fourth time. He appreciated me that I have established my grip over the subject. Undergoing that exercise, namely reading, re-reading and repeated reading of the same book for the fourth time was almost a suffering.

One day he called me to review Gunnar Myrdals '*Asian Drama*' and more specifically to single out the methodology part of it. Within fifteen days I had completed reading the three volumes, and had done with the write up. After reading my write up, his comment was: 'criticality in the review was insufficient'. Subsequently, I was asked to make a second reading and rewrite my review. In the second reading, I had indicated the gaps in the Asian Drama in terms of the methodological nuances. After seeing the review he gave a small write up done by an American economist on Asian Drama. I found many of the points which I have made in my paper are in the review done by that American scholar. Dr. S. Bhaskaran told me that I have the capability to do higher things. Really I found this kind of exercises taxing, but empowering. When I look back now, I feel such suffering made me the researcher I am today. On all the occasions he indicated that how I was picking up and moving forward in enhancing my capacity.

The amount of freedom I enjoyed working with Dr. S. Bhaskaran was unfathomable. I always had a feeling that I was working for my Ph.D. in an American University. The amount of work he put me through was always voluminous. At every step he pointed out very minutely how my capacity was being enhanced because of my rigorous research work. At the same time he made it a point that unless I reach certain stage in building up research capability. I shall be permitted to submit my Ph.D. thesis. I was permitted to write my dissertation and get Ph.D., only when I had reached some level, I realized that it was actually the *Gurukula* system in practice. Ph.D. scholars have to be groomed and shaped through a process of determined work. He unequivocally made it clear that learning does not take place without hard work and struggle. If I am able to do all my academic activities vibrantly and tirelessly it is because of research process that Dr. Bhaskaran saw me through.

2

Linkage with Political Parties

Honestly speaking, I did not know how 'policy advocacy' works at all? Now everywhere I find a course on policy advocacy. There are NGOs known for their Policy Advocacy works. But I have involved myself in policy advocacy work for long without having a professional understanding of how it works. I did my research leading to Ph.D. degree on "*The Role of Political Parties in Tamil Nadu Legislature*". During those days (1980-84) I met many political party leaders, Members of Legislative Assembly, Members of Legislative Council, and Members of Parliament. They were all purely academic and research-oriented contacts. Subsequently, I did a project on "Role Perception of Legislators" for Indian Council for Social Science Research (ICSSR). This work demanded conducting an extensive survey among the members of Legislative Assembly. Nearly 178 members of Legislative Assembly were contacted for an extensive interview. This experience made me wonder how weak our members of Legislative Assembly were. They were far short of the competence needed to perform their roles and responsibilities.

My Ph.D. thesis, as well as the report submitted to ICSSR got published. Poor performance of the legislators and the poor role perception of the legislators have been captured and analysed in these two books. The contact I had established during my Ph.D. days continued even after my Ph.D. research. Many of the occasions I closely moved with the political party leaders. I moved closely with P. Nedumaran when he was in the Congress Party and subsequently also. I also moved closely with G.K. Moopanar. Along with them I moved closely with the leaders of the left political parties. These contacts helped mutual learning. But, after the enactment of the 73rd Amendment to the Constitution of India, I used all my political contacts for doing policy advocacy for decentralization of powers. In Tamil Nadu pushing decentralization posed its own risk and difficulties. Though, the AIADMK had enacted the conformity legislation, it did not conduct the election. We did several programmes to exert pressure on the government to enact conformity legislation and subsequently for conduct of election. We failed miserably. But during 1996 general election to Legislative Assembly we found an opportunity to influence the political parties. Tamil Manila Congress has incorporated the Panchayati Raj as one of the aspects in election manifesto. The DMK also included in its manifesto the New Panchayati Raj. Left political parties had always been voicing their concern towards the Panchayati Raj System.

I used to interact with the left political parties closely as I have more friends in the left and this relationship I had continued from my university student days. When I was the secretary to the Research Scholars Association in Annamalai University, Annamalai University Teachers Association launched a major struggle against the University administration where I was a part. While we were in struggle it was the left political parties that supported for the cause of the teachers and I played a considerable role in this struggle and I was in jail for more than a month for the cause of the teachers. From that period onwards I maintained a close link with the left political parties. Moreover, while comparing all the political parties; I feel that the left political parties are not corrupt and always working for the cause of the poor. Even within the left, Marxist Communist party is fine model for taking up the people's cause with a human perspective. Periodically, I prepared working papers just like working papers in Western universities and gave them to the political parties. Even I have prepared newsletters and circulated to political parties and media for wider dissemination and political action.

Representatives of Political parties who are looking after Panchayati Raj used to contact me constantly for my opinion on major issues of Panchayati Raj System. I also maintained regular contact with them and fed them the needed information support for them to take a stand on various issues. In my opinion on Panchayati Raj System consistently the left political parties voiced their concern for more powers to Panchayats. Equally the PMK voiced their concern for Panchayati Raj in Tamil Nadu. When Tamil Manila Congress was functioning under the leadership of G.K. Moopanar it voiced its concern for Panchayats. Later I found neither the Congress nor the

Dravidian Political parties showed genuine interest in Panchayati Raj in Tamil Nadu. It is also a known fact that Dravidian Political parties have taken a principled stand that they are fighting for more powers to State. And when they are not getting powers from the Centre how Panchayats would be strengthened by taking away the power of the States.

It is a pity that the Indian National Congress in Tamil Nadu never showed any interest whatsoever in Panchayati Raj. Even this party never organized their own party local leaders meeting. As long as G.K. Moopanar was alive, whenever any serious local body issue arose, I went to him and offered information briefs. He used to seek a lot of clarifications. After getting clarifications he used to issue a press release. It had its own impact in the government. Even before meeting G.K. Moopanar I used to prepare note on the concerned issues and hand over the paper to him. He knew the whole story of Panchayati Raj. From the days of Nehruji, Kamaraj to Rajiv Gandhi he had a deep understanding of Panchayati Raj. I made it a point that whenever I write any book on Panchayati Raj in Tamil, it was to be released by G.K. Moopanar and the same to be received by the left political party leaders. He was extremely happy to release my books. Never had he projected me as a party man. He projected me as an expert in Panchayati Raj, which made me feel comfortable to move with any political party. I moved with all political parties on issues pertaining to decentralization of power. I enjoyed the liberty of attending the political party inner circle meetings of both left parties to brief them on critical issues of local bodies and decentralization of powers. In the same way, I moved closely with PMK founder Dr. Ramdoss. He issued press releases and directed his party members in the legislative assembly to speak on the issue with the sense of commitment. In my opinion, left political parties have consistently spoken on this issue.

Apart from briefing I actively participated in the Panchayati Raj functionaries meet also. The two left political parties periodically organize local body leaders meet for orientation. Almost in all the meetings, I participated and delivered lectures. They want my perspective, views and solutions to critical issues. In the same way the PMK organized local body leaders meet and I have attended the meeting also. I expressed freely my opinion about the functioning of the local bodies and how government is performing their role in strengthening the Panchayati Raj System. Many times I was critical of the state government. On many occasions I was critical of the role of the state government, and during those periods the higher officials were not comfortable and they asked me not to criticize the government. Since, I was a member of the many of the committees of the government I was asked not to comment. I was inducted as a member of the committee as an expert but officials are not comfortable when I expressed my views which are contradictory to the views of the Minister of the government. They expect that I had to play the role of a party man. This is the political culture in Tamil Nadu which created many problems to me.

Despite the opposition of the higher officials I have expressed my opinion freely. Apart from myself I have prepared the elected representatives of the local bodies to approach their own party for redressal of the issues akin to local bodies. It is only the left political parties consistently helped the local body leaders when they faced problems. PMK also lent helping hand sporadically. Neither the Dravidian parties nor the Congress have done any such training for local bodies. The leaders of the parties which worked for the Dalits have never done any substantial work in this regard. But they have to do substantial work in local bodies as Dalit leaders face volley of problems in local bodies. For the Dalit Panchayat leaders it is only a few NGOs that consistently worked. But, then they also faced volley of problems in collecting data and doing policy advocacy. In the left political parties, they have earmarked persons to look after the local bodies. They have to prepare the local body leaders to work effectively in the local bodies. They had to earn good name for the party and they had to fight for powers to local bodies. For all such activities, the party representative who was working for local bodies had to take steps. Further, they have to brief the members of the Legislative Assembly about the stand they have to take in the Assembly on the local body issues. Apart from the left, political parties of Tamil Nadu have done only lip service to new Panchayati Raj System. At national level I worked closely with Rajiv Gandhi Foundation. Ever since I started participating in the foundations programme, I met Smt. Sonia Gandhi on a few occasions in the Rajiv Gandhi Foundation, New Delhi. I interacted with her on a few occasions mostly on Panchayati Raj. She was very keen in getting details about Panchayati Raj. Later she became the President of the Indian National Congress. After UPA won the election I wrote a letter to her about the victory she won and the steps to be taken in governance she promptly replied to my letter.

3

Voluntary Contributions for Extension

In 1992, I mooted a new idea with some of my colleagues in GRI. It is on the possibility of appointing a field worker who is ready to contribute voluntarily to organize meetings in rural areas. His job was to create awareness among the villagers about the new Panchayati Raj System. Mr. V. Ragupathy, Mr. S. Narayanasamy, Mr. William Bhaskaran and I had decided to contribute a small sum of Rs. 100 from our salary to pay for the field worker. Incidentally a good friend of mine Mr. Alwar Reddiar, properitor of Arya Bhavan Hotel in Dindigul agreed to contribute Rs. 300 every month towards this cause. We appointed one Mr. M. Ponnusamy as a field worker, who agreed to carry out this task for an honorarium of Rs. 700 a month. His work was to organize two kinds of meetings in the villages. One was awareness creation on Panchayati Raj to the general public. And the other was orientation of youth and activist involved in Panchayati Raj activities. Indeed his duty went beyond these tasks.

The field worker had to mobilize support from some individuals and organizations to organize such programmes in the villages. We found even this simple awareness programmes involved expenditure, and that amount had to be mobilized. For all our programmes donations came in the form of kind. Many offered food, snacks, public address system, transportation, printing of leaflets and pamphlets etc. For about two years we organized such programmes extensively in the rural areas of Tamil Nadu. While doing such a kind of activities, we found active support came from well meaning NGOs as well. Many of the NGOs started forming network and organized such awareness programmes in their villages. We extended our support to them in the form of information-provision and knowledge-sharing.

We used to prepare pamphlets for them and participated as resource persons in the meetings they organized. Apart from the awareness creation programmes, we started imparting systematic training programmes to the NGO staff, who later involved themselves in Panchayati Raj activities.

A team got formed in GRI, and members of this team started looking at me for any ideas on Panchayati Raj System to get on stream. The team consisted of the following persons: Dr. N. Markandan (Then he was heading the Department of Extension and later he became the Vice-Chancellor of GRI), Dr. T. Karunakaran (Then Director of Rural Technology Centre, subsequently became the Vice-Chancellor of GRI), Dr. S. Narayanasamy, and Dr. V. Ragupathy.

Padmashri V.P. Anna (V. Padmanabhan, Managing Trustee of Gandhigram Trust) who happened to read a newspaper report in *The Hindu* on the work of this team on Panchayati Raj System, enquired me about the goings on. I explained to him 'how we work' including how the logistics is arranged. He appreciated our work, and as a mark of encouragement he participated in some of the programmes we conducted later on.

Then he called up one-day and put forward the idea of developing a perspective paper for the Panchayati Raj activities in Tamil Nadu. It occurred to me too that it was very important in the domain of Panchayati Raj. He had also pointed out that a perspective paper of that kind should be acceptable not only to the Gandhian circle but also to the World Bank. We were fully aware that it was at that time the World Bank also started showing interest in decentralization of powers. I developed a perspective paper with Gandhian ideology of *Gramswaraj* in the backdrop. Thinking through that paper and putting down ideas for giving shape to that paper was an eye opener for me. Shri V.P. Anna participated in many such programmes and gave the perspective of Gandhi on *Gramswaraj*.

Panchayati Raj activities of GRI got spoken about widely in the state especially because of the voluntary involvement of some of the faculty members I mentioned above, and not upon instruction by the authorities of the Institute. We were exploring a way to connect ourselves with the community, and we found Panchayati Raj as the best carrier given the conditions at that time. The idea clicked because we laid hand at the right issue at the right time. More than anything else, our whole-hearted commitment to establishing a local self-governance system in the State was carrying our activities forward.

This created a ripple effect bringing in the ideas and blessing of great people, one of whom was Padmashri V.P. Anna.

I seem to have taken a digression, let me call back our Mr. M. Ponnusamy (the volunteer we had appointed). He was also contributing extraordinarily organizing village level meetings. He mobilized the villagers for the meeting and resources for organizing such meetings. Really, he carried out activities with a sense of commitment and dedication. And I observed that he almost forgot about the honorarium promised to him and started committing himself for the cause along with this team in GRI, which we never expected. His contribution towards the activities of Panchayati Raj at that point of time was remarkable. Having developed this art of mobilizing people for meeting, he joined in a political party later on and became organizing secretary of the party. Perhaps, his involvement with people and the learning he gained listening to and discussing with resource persons of varied stature made him the person he turned out to be. His tireless work for the Panchayati Raj in Dindigul district deserved mention.

In the whole process, the name of Gandhigram Rural Institute got floated around across districts and thereby the authorities started giving some kind of support to all our Panchayat Raj activities. The 'outreach component' of the Institute got its meaning reinforced. There were four newspapers that continually gave wide coverage of our programmes. That made me think how media can be put to profitable use, if only we know how to project developmental activities find place in newspaper reporting. These newspapers are: *The Hindu* (in English), *Dinamani*, *Dinathandi* and *Dinamalar* (in Tamil). I preserve all the paper clippings and it has come to seven volumes now.

4

Writing Letter to Opposition Leaders

I joined Gandhigram Rural Institute (Deemed University) as Reader in Political Science and Development Administration and I found the department offered an undergraduate programme. It was B.A Development Administration—first of its kind in the country. Somehow, I felt that the programme did not deliver any professional content—neither the quality of the programme was good nor the quality of students come to the programme was good. In plain language, candidates who got rejected admission elsewhere got admitted in Development Administration. Barring a few students from Kenya and Sudan all other students from India except Kerala were not serious about what they were doing. We were three teachers, Mr. V. Ragupathy, Mrs. Celine Rani and I. Our office was a small room of 10 × 10 size—no clerk, no attender.

I joined the University on 1st April, 1991 and for about four to five months I was not given any responsibility and the Dean, Faculty of Rural Social Sciences, was in charge of the Department. In one of the heads of Departments meeting someone raised: "why Dr. G. Palanithurai was not considered to take charge as Head of the Political Science Department. The then Vice-Chancellor D.K. Oza a former I.A.S. officer, appointed me as Head of the Department of Politics and Development Administration." There was yet another unit "Gandhian Thought and Peace Science" attached with our Department. Three lecturers and one Research Associate were in that unit.

After taking over the responsibility I determined to give new face to teaching, research and extension activities of my Department, and so I moved in an entirely different direction. I had taken cognizance of the fact that the University was not free from the usual tensions and grape-wine that any bureaucratic organization faced. Here I found it went to the extent of making even normal functioning very difficult. The then Vice-Chancellor took notice of the Institute receding from its outreach activities and he insisted that the university has to reach out to the larger society through its extension activities. It was a problem for every Vice-Chancellor as there was no clear-cut mandate or methodology for rural extension. But, I had deep urge and faith in extension and outreach programmes, yet I knew I was not an expert in extension.

While I was in deep introspection, it occurred that decentralization of powers was going to be an emerging subject. I had discussions with my colleagues. They subscribed to my ideas. We finalized that we had to work on 'decentralization' in all our academic programmes.

Against this background, I took an initiative to conduct a signature campaign in support of decentralization of powers. When I did that exercise Sri P.V. Narasimha Rao was the Prime Minister, and he committed himself in bring out an amendment for decentralization of powers. I got the signatures from prominent public personalities starting from the Managing Trustee of Gandhigram Trust. After securing enough signatures I have sent to the then opposition party leader Mr. L.K. Advani. He promptly replied to my letter. While getting signatures from prominent public personalities, my colleagues expressed apprehensions that that was not the responsibility of university teachers, nor a mandate of a university. But, I look back now, going to the public space for socially relevant action started only from writing letter to the opposition leader.

5

Supportive Department

I was heading the Department of Political Science and Development Administration, Gandhigram Rural Institute, for about 17 years since 1991. Initially, it was a two-member Department attached with the Dean's office. I joined in 1991 and I was appointed as Head of the Department in 1991 itself. At that point of time I was with Mr. V. Ragupathy and Mrs. A. Celine Rani in the Department. These two lecturers were working with me. I was a Reader and heading the Department. I really enjoyed the whole period in working with them as they were always supportive in all my activities. First I asked them to register for Ph.D. and they did it along with teaching. They completed their Ph.D. programmes. They had registered under my supervision. Mr. V. Ragupathy has got a rich background in decentralization initiative in Tamil Nadu. One reason was that his uncle was the first Development Commissioner who took initiatives for the first wave of decentralization in Tamil Nadu after Independence. For many of the occasions he was a source of inspiration. He was always with me in my room assisting me, and at times guarding me also. He is a creative and committed individual and hence whatever assignment I took he lent his shoulder to lighten my burden. Without his support I could not have completed all such project activities. Whatever gap is left in all my activities, he filled up silently. Nobody can understand the relationship between me and my colleague Dr. V. Ragupathy. He embodies love, affection, care and assistance. If I am able to play around comfortably in research and outreach activities, in a way it is because of the ease he renders being with me, ready to offer a hand wherever required. At present he is heading the Department and he is leading the Department as I led in the same way with the same methodology.

I kept one important principle for the functioning of the Department that is a conducive atmosphere should prevail in the Department, and everyone should really feel that they are comfortably working. When I create opportunity I entertained in my mind that everyone should work as I do. If they made use of the opportunities I created, I was there to facilitate. Otherwise I removed it from my mind. But, I was firm that the minimum expected responsibilities one had to discharge and had to be discharged. There was no compromise on it. I come to the Department morning 8.45 am. But I never expected that everyone should come to the Department around the same time. It was usual I left for home (from the Department) only after 7.30 pm. I never expected that everyone to stay on working until that time. But I saw to it that everyone should be in the department between 9.15 to 4.45 pm and discharged their responsibilities. In this regard till date everyone follows the norm. It is more a cultivated self-discipline. I organize programmes such as training, workshops, seminars, and symposia periodically. I involve them and assign responsibilities. They discharged responsibilities perfectly to my level of expectation. Credit and recognition was being given to everyone who involved in my programmes. I believe in creating a 'win-win situation' as one of the principles of success. It has always been teamwork, and I provided only the leadership. In the course of involvement, I have observed enormous amount of capacity has been built up in every individual who committed themselves to be a part of my programmes.

Department activities are being shared among ourselves. Workload management, conduct of classes, conduct of examination, student activities, student discipline, student placements, student internship, student camps, outreach programmes, dissertations, library maintenance and research activities are shared. For all the activities, I provided only guidance and leadership. As a mark of recognition of activities of the Department, the UGC through its five year plan sanction accorded for additional appointment of one Reader and two Lecturers. Subsequently, we became six in the Department. Amongst us, it is the informality and our friendship in assisting each other could be noticed more than the difference of opinion or politicking. Any differences of opinion, which is normal to humans, are sorted out through open dialogue process. At times, some of my colleagues remark negatively of the freedom I allow to staff—be it regular or project staff.

My giving freedom to staff, my nature of forgiving people easily, being free, being soft, and being compassionate is viewed as 'letting people uncontrolled'. I, for one, believe that people deliver their best when you demonstrate that you trust them, and when you express through unspoken language that "the more the freedom you want to enjoy, the more responsible, you must behave". I want you to enjoy freedom in your work so long as you demonstrate you know the real meaning of the concept of 'freedom'. I have never ever spoken this to my staff. But, I am sure I have got across this message to them. They behave responsibly which turns out to be a good work culture. And they enjoy real freedom as well. My evidence for this is: the quality of results I witness, and how the Department has grown in the last two decades.

Whether they are students or research scholars or project staff or teaching staff I give full freedom because I entertained a notion that democracy will bring more dividends than regimentation. As a result in the Department everyone has extended full support to me and my activities. If I do not allow freedom to my staff, then what democracy am I talking about? But, one cannot expect the same kind of support as extended by Dr. V. Ragupathy. Because everyone has his or her own perceptions and conditions and accordingly they will extend their support.

Absolutely none has given any trouble to me. If a staff created problems in the Department whether he/she has contributed or not the Department is bound to suffer a lot. But, nobody creates problems deliberately. Even if students—out of ignorance—created problems, our teachers resolve them even without my knowledge. Later I come to know what cropped up and how it was resolved. In such a way they extended support to me. This is part of our work culture and how we are functioning. But, although my staff have extended support to me, the level may vary from individual to individual. It is not only the teaching staff, but also the project staff, research scholars, students and non-teaching staffs extend support in all possible ways to the activities in the Department.

There may be yet another reason for such a kind of co-operation. Primarily everyone is seeing the growth in increasing infrastructure, project activities and getting opportunity for career building. While seeing the growth of the department everyone is tempted to extend their support. Further, no one is at any loss at any point of time. I saw to it that their career progresses without any setback. As and when they complete the mandatory requirements, they are elevated to the next cadre. I have faced many problems in the University because of academic politics but I never face a single problem in my Department—all of them are with me in their true spirit and commitment.

6

Awareness Creation

Once the 73rd Constitutional Amendment was passed, and later it was given presidential accent, I started awareness creation programmes in the villages, for which I sought the help of many. There were several NGOs who helped us to reach out to communities in the rural areas. Printed pamphlets prepared by me were distributed in the villages. I approached the All India Radio and they recorded several of my talks and broadcasted them several times. Even now they are using. I have written several popular articles in Tamil newspapers especially *Dinamani*, *Dinamalar* and *Thamil Ozai*. Later, all such articles were edited and published by New Century Book House, Chennai. I had mentioned earlier that for awareness creation we employed one Mr. Ponnusamy. Mr. Ponnusamy had the ability to mobilize resources for such village meetings. The village meetings were of two types. One was workshop type meeting, mostly organized in NGO premises for the whole day. Second one was, three to four hours, meeting usually held in some common ground in the villages. Since, we had established contact with the newspaper staff-reporters from many newspapers they used to attend our meetings and cover the whole exercise. Newspapers gave extensive coverage to our awareness programmes. In fact, these paper clippings piled up into four volumes.

Newspapers reportage added strength to our programmes. Like it carried the name of the Institute across, it carried my name as well. In many of the occasions, newspapers published Panchayat-related question and answer columns in the newspapers with my photo. Several hundred meetings were conducted in the rural areas. In our team we had Dr. N. Markandan (Later he become the Vice-Chancellor of Gandhigram Rural Institute) Dr. V. Ragupathy (My first Ph.D.

student, who is now Professor & Head, Department of Political Science, GRI), Dr. S. Narayanasamy (Professor and Head, Department of Gandhian Thought and Peace Science) and Dr. T. Karunakaran (later he became the Vice-Chancellor of Gandhigram Rural Institute) and all the above members participated in all village meetings and workshops.

Here I have to mention another person who was inspiration for such meetings in the villages Padmashri. V. Padmanabhan, (affectionately called: 'VP Anna') the then Managing Trustee of Gandhigram Trust. He attended many of our village meetings despite his poor health at that time. He advised me that this was the most important extension work that I had to do on behalf of the Institute. Whenever he organized such meetings in the service villages of Gandhigram Trust, he asked me to participate in all those meetings. Here I have to mention that the team worked with me for this cause spent their money for all their travels to participate in village meetings.

There were NGOs also constantly organized such meetings as per our request. CHERU of Vadamadurai in Dindigul district, Peace Trust of Dindigul continuously engaged not only in their areas but also in other areas with their affiliates. For all such meetings these organizations spent their resources. At that point of time I had no project on Panchayati Raj. By using our own resource we have done such exercises.

7

A Bus for Awareness Creation

The Government of Tamil Nadu, even after enacting legislation did not evince interest in conducting the election for local bodies in 1994. In order to draw the attention of the people to this fact, I wanted to do an innovative programme. At that point of time, I did not have money to take up any campaign. It occurred to me that NSS could be used for this purpose. I approached the NSS Coordinator Dr. N. Narayanasamy. Both of us designed a programme for ten days. We called it: 'Bus for Panchayati Raj and Peace'. Part of the expenditure was met by the NSS and the rest was from some local donor organizations.

We took twenty students from NSS and a team of teachers who had reasonably good knowledge on Panchayati Raj. From Gandhigram to Chennai we travelled by bus. The idea was to stop the bus wherever we find a gathering of people, and address through loud speakers. We had passed on information about 'Peace Bus' to many organizations on the way to Chennai. Therefore, several organizations had arranged meetings on the way. We delivered our message in village meetings, road side meetings, hall meetings, meetings with university students in different places. We created awareness on Panchayati Raj. Several universities helped us by arranging accommodation and food for our students and staff.

We carried printed notices, pamphlets and leaflets on Panchayati Raj and distributed among the public throughout the tour programme. All the notices, leaflets, pamphlets and other reading materials were written up by me and some NGOs contributed substantially for printing them. Local organizations and interested individuals had arranged meetings. Finally, we reached Chennai and submitted a memorandum to the Governor of Tamil Nadu insisting that the government conduct the Panchayat elections. The Governor of Tamil Nadu met our team had a mini workshop in Raj Bhavan. We submitted the memorandum to the Governor Mr. Chenna Reddy. He explained that the Government has to act only on public pressure and the civil society has to exert pressure on the government to conduct the election. He asked our students what he can do as a Chancellor of the Tamil Nadu Universities. One student replied: "as a Chancellor, he can pass an order to the universities to the effect that NSS unit can devote one full year for awareness creation among the public about the New Panchayati Raj System". He appreciated the student who gave the idea, and he assured that he would consider the idea.

To our joy, we found within a month's time he passed an order that every university with NSS unit to conduct awareness programme on New Panchayati Raj System. Several Universities after receiving the order approached us for ICE material in New Panchayati Raj. We shared our material with them. They multiplied them to their requirements. We visited several universities in that year to participate in the programme organized by them on Panchayati Raj. The NSS unit of our university took keen interest and found a lot of meaning in supporting this programme. Dr. N. Narayanasamy was known for his innovative programmes and he still is a committed person on Panchayati Raj. The innovative ten-day bus *yatra* took the name of our university across, and it helped establish working-links with many development organizations throughout Tamil Nadu. We got extensive media coverage. Lots of news items appeared in the vernacular and national newspapers. Our University got appreciation from the Governor of Tamil Nadu.

The *Bus Yatra* drew a close with a valedictory meeting in Gandhi Mandapam where we had invited Gandhian Industrialist Pollachi Mahalingam. He delivered the valedictory address. When he came to our programme, he showed a lot of interest in getting to know the activities we had done on Panchayati Raj. He appreciated us and assured us of any help from his side for Panchayati Raj Activities. Later he wrote an article in his popular magazine. He devoted a section appreciating our activities, and my role in Panchayati Raj Activities in Tamil Nadu.

8

Creation of Rajiv Gandhi Chair for Panchayati Raj Studies

In India we have Rajiv Gandhi Chairs in select ten universities with the liberal financial support of the Central Government through University Grants Commission. These Rajiv Gandhi Chairs were sanctioned during UPA-I regime. The reality is only a few of the Rajiv Gandhi Chairs are in operation/functional today.

The Rajiv Gandhi Chair for Panchayati Raj Studies in Gandhigram Rural Institute was created not for availing a provision made available by the Government. It was created in the year 1996 itself by Gandhigram Rural Institute. I, in fact, prepared a proposal for the establishment of a Chair in the name of Rajiv Gandhi that too for Panchayati Raj Activities. In order to recognize a leader who gave vision for the new Panchayati Raj System in India, it was decided to give his name to the chair. Further, it was designed to have the chair as a model centre for specialized research, policy advocacy on Panchayati Raj issues. Further, it should act as a training centre to train grassroots level leaders as transformative leaders. Bearing these in mind, I prepared the proposal and sent it to the Central Government for financial sanction. The authority to sanction such proposals rested with P.V. Narasimha Rao as Prime Minister and Mr. Arjun Singh was the Minister for Human Resource Development during that period. Since, there was no reply I approached Rajiv Gandhi Foundation and it was headed by Smt. Sonia Gandhi. Rajiv Gandhi Foundation accepted our proposal and sanctioned the Chair. Since I was part of Panchayati Raj activities of the Rajiv Gandhi Foundation many of the advisers of the foundation knew our activities in Gandhigram on Panchayati Raj. The sanction accorded was only for three years. While sanctioning the proposal an undertaking they demanded from the authorities of Gandhigram Rural Institute that the newly created Chair would continue even after three years.

The then Vice-Chancellor Dr. T.R. Natesan gave an undertaking that the chair would continue its Panchayati Raj activities even after the expiry of the three-year period. Rajiv Gandhi foundation had given financial support only to cover the salary of a research professor. For all other activities, it has to rely on the funding of other agencies. The then Vice-Chancellor filled up the position of the chair professor through official selection process of Gandhigram Rural Institute. I was selected for this post and I was given the responsibility of heading the Department of Political Science along with carrying out the activities of the Chair. The then Vice-Chancellor Dr. T.R. Natesan asked me to strengthen the Chair by its activities and for which I had to prepare proposals and got them cleared by the funding agencies. In the meanwhile the funding from Rajiv Gandhi Foundation got disturbed, during the period when Congress was not in power. I went to G.K. Moopanar and explained the problem faced by the Chair because of paucity of funds. He asked me to approach C. Subramaniam in this regard. I went to him and explained the same to him. He knew very well about my Panchayati Raj Studies. He said without any reservations that the Congress Trust would give funds to the Chair. He asked me to submit a letter. I came to the University and wrote a letter to C. Subramaniam through our office. Immediately I got reply and funds to run programmes. I continued my activities on Panchayati Raj. Later, I got funds from various agencies for programmes of varied nature, all centring around Panchayati Raj and Rural Development. Gradually, funding agencies started giving funds for various kinds of activities. The activities of Rajiv Gandhi Chair got stabilized and go on. The Rajiv Gandhi chair stands on its own by its performance. After ten years we made an evaluation of our performance. We published a document based on our evaluation. Till today I maintained a good relationship with Rajiv Gandhi Foundation but I am not getting funds from it. It is appropriate to mention an event here. When BJP was in power Mr. Venkaiah Naidu was the Minister for Rural Development. In Rajiv Gandhi Chair we organise annual Panchayati Raj women leaders meet in Gandhigram. During that period I invited him to be the chief guest. Promptly he had agreed to participate in the programme as he had committed to participate in an international conference in an engineering college in the nearby city Dindigul on the same day. On the day of the programme he finished his responsibility in the international conference and reached Gandhigram around 11 O'clock. It was a very big crowd. He spoke for one and half hours in the women Panchayat leaders meet. He openly interacted with women Panchayat leaders. During the meeting he asked me personally who created Rajiv Gandhi Chair in the Institute. He raised this question with the thinking that it was created by some Congress men. I replied that it was created by us. He further asked me why it was created. Against I replied that we wanted to recognise the service rendered by Rajiv Gandhi to constitutionalise the Panchayati Raj System. He told me that Vajpayee as Prime Minister appreciated openly in a meeting Rajiv Gandhi for his initiative to constitutionalise the Panchayati Raj System. He appreciated me and he told me that whenever Rajiv Gandhi Chair needs any help, it can approach the Ministry, it will help. In such a way he commented our activities in Panchayati Raj. The Panchayati Raj activities of the Rajiv Gandhi Chair are in our website. (www.rajivgandhichairgri.org).

9

Tsunami Reconstruction

When Tsunami struck the coastal Tamil Nadu, I was in Gandhigram. I contacted Dr. Kubendran an old project staff, who worked with me in DANIDA Water and Sanitation Project. He was in Tiruvarur then. I asked him to visit immediately the tsunami hit areas, and send a report. He visited the areas and sent a few photographs immediately by email. I got oral permission from my Vice-Chancellor to pay a visit to Tsunami hit areas. Next day I hired a taxi and visited the areas in Nagapattinam district. I was there for two days and met many affected families. I had intense interaction with them in the relief camps; I met the district administration, the media, civil society, traditional community leaders, officials, and a few donor agencies.

Massive relief operation in an unprecedented scale was on. But what I could observe was community being treated as 'passive subjects'; and the neglect of their role in the relief and reconstruction process. All humanitarian assistance was based on externally identified need, manifesting the community as alms takers with no voice or choice, if I can use a crude word for that. To a painful extent, I could witness in the relief rehabilitation and reconstruction process the neglect of the involvement of the affected communities. Not only the neglect of the communities but also the constitutional governance institution the Gram Panchayats. It is not only the neglect of the involvement of the constitutional Panchayats, but the whole activities were designed not based on demand. There were a series of supply driven activities. In my two days of interaction with everyone affected in Tsunami what I found was the community and Panchayats being neglected—relief operations treating the community, as helpless subjects, looking for alms.

I interacted with community leaders and Gram Panchayat leaders about the possibility of preparing a long term reconstruction of village development plan with the participation of all communities and to carry out the activities with the active support of all stakeholders. Interestingly, some of the community leaders informed me that in the first two days it was only the community managed affairs on their own. Hundreds of dead bodies were removed and buried; and the same way dead animals. They had managed on their own. The third day onwards the scenario has been changed, when many external aid agencies landed there. I prepared a detailed note on the Hunger Project Country Director Rita Sarin on that missing aspect and the power of the communities and potentials of the constitutional Gram Panchayats in transforming the villages and the lives of people in the villages through the reconstruction process. She had agreed in principle that we can work through the Panchayats. Later, I got a communication from the Country Director of the Hunger Project that the SDC of Swiss Embassy agreed to support our rehabilitation plan. Then I prepared a detailed project proposal and sent to the Hunger Project.

We had identified seventeen Gram Panchayats for evolving a participatory micro reconstruction plan. To carry out the extensive fieldwork I had identified three local NGOs. In the meanwhile I got the support of the District Administration also to take up this exercise. In all the Gram Panchayats, the NGOs had played the role of a facilitator and the communities had worked through the Gram Panchayats for the preparation of the reconstruction plan. Rajiv Gandhi Chair acted as a resource agency to give idea and knowledge input apart from doing the coordination work. All the seventeen Gram Panchayats had evolved a participatory inclusive reconstruction plan and got the approval of the Gram Sabha. Later, it was printed as a document with the signature of the District Collector as Inspector of Panchayati Raj. It was disseminated through a workshop. All the planned activities had been carried out in the respective Panchayats. It was a process-oriented activity and the process was carefully sequenced and recorded as well. What achievements were possible through the planning process, and what setbacks and drawbacks we had to face were recorded and analysed. We prepared process documentation and published the same as a monograph, later on.

Subsequently, I was approached by the action aid international to conduct a study about the role of Panchayats in disaster preparedness and management not only in Tamil Nadu but also in

Andhra Pradesh, Odisha and Gujarat. I accepted the offer and I carried out the study with the support of three local NGOs in the respective states.

Subsequently, after finalizing the draft report I conducted a validation workshop. The report was later published and circulated for wider dissemination. Based on the study the Action Aid International had given another project to conduct an action research on the role of Gram Panchayats in disaster preparedness. We carried out those activities in select Panchayats in Cuddalore, Nagapattinam and Kanyakumari districts of Tamil Nadu. Based on all the above activities we have prepared the process document for dissemination. All the activities were with the sole objective of empowering the local communities and strengthening the Panchayati Raj System in disaster preparedness, disaster relief, rehabilitation and reconstruction work.

Having seen the above activities the Oxfam had inducted me in a team to evaluate their activities in the Tsunami affected areas as an expert in Local Governance. I worked along with Mihir Bhatt in all the evaluation studies. I gained rich experience in the whole process.

The Toolkit foundation of Netherlands approached me for an exercise. I carried out a small work for Netherlands based Toolkit Foundation on the protection of dignity and pride of the communities while receiving relief and involving themselves in reconstruction activities. A national workshop was also conducted for them based on our work in the field. Subsequently, I participated in UN Habit conference in Vancouver, Canada in British Columbia University with the support of the Toolkit Foundation. I made a presentation in the Conference the whole journey was interesting with full of challenges. I got enormous learning.

Details of Panchayat

Sl. No.	*Name of the Panchayat*		*Name of the tsunami affected hamlets under the Panchayat*
1	1.	Prathabaramapuram	Seruthoor Prathabaramapuram (poovathadi) Ramarmadam.
	2.	Viluthanmaavadi keelaiyur union	Thambirankudyiruppu, vadapaathi,Thenpaathi, Manalmedu

(*Contd.*)

Sl. No.	*Name of the Panchayat*		*Name of the tsunami affected hamlets under the Panchayat*
2.	1.	Thirupoondi east Keelaiyur Union	Vairanvankadu, anayath thoppu Vettarkadu fisher colony, Kallarkadu, Thandavamoorthykadu Melakadu Sivankoil Street
	2.	Pudhupalli Keelaiyur Union	Keezpudhupalli, Melapudhupalli
	3 .	Veetaikarraniruppu Keelaiyur Union	Nachiappankadu, Nattankadu, Kaniyankadu, Vadaku Sallikulam, Sadaiyankadu, Soriya Vinayagar Street, Therku Sallukulam
3.	1.	Thennampattinam Sirkali Union	Annappanpettai, Thennampattinam, Konyampattinam, Mathapattinam, Malamoovarkarai, Keelamoovarkarai
	2.	Kaveripoompattinam Sirkali Union	Keelayur, Naidavasal, Pudhukuppam, Poombuhar, Manthakarai
	3.	Perunthottam Sirkali Union	Perunthottam, Agarperunthottam, Periya Perunthottam, Chavadikuppam, Neikarakuppam, Madatukuppam, Kadaikadu

10

Endowment Creation

When I was in Annamalai University as a student, as a research scholar and as a young lecturer, I listened to the lectures of great stalwarts from public life. All these lectures were from different endowments. Those endowment lectures were published later. In the same way, I wanted to arrange spirited public lectures to our students in Gandhigram and for which I wanted to create endowments in our department. In this regard, I approached my old friend who was the Managing Director of a company Janata Chem in Rajapalayam. He readily agreed to create such endowment in our Department with a condition that annually a lecture has to be arranged in honour of Tamil Scholar T.K. Chidambaranatha Mudaliar.

Subsequently, I approached SOCO Trust of Madurai, the Chairman of the SOCO Trust Madurai agreed to create an endowment in honour of Justice V.R. Krishna Iyer. Following the above two I contacted Mr. Paul Bhaskar, Chairman of Peace Trust Dindigul; he agreed to create an endowment in honour of Justice B.N. Bhagawati. Then I went to the Publisher of *Dinamalar* (a Tamil Newspaper) the publisher agreed to create an endowment in honour of its founder T.V. Rama Subbaiyer. Then I approached the management of yet another popular newspaper *Dinathandhi* for creating an Endowment in the name of Ci–Pa Aditanar the founder of *Dinathandhi*. Immediately, the management responded positively and thereby another endowment was created. Yet, another endowment was created in the name of former Chief Minister Late Dr. M.G. Ramachandran with the active support of my friend Dr. R. Thandavan of Madras University. Later I approached the Gandhiniketan Ashram when they celebrated the founder's centenary celebration. They also agreed to create an endowment in the name of its founder G. Venkatachalapathi.

Finally, I approached Catalyst Trust of Chennai after the demise of my beloved friend A.K. Venkata Subramanian, IAS. They also agreed to create an endowment in the name of A.K. Venkata Subramanian.

I can say proudly that the endowment culture has been created in Gandhigram Rural Institute only after we took initiative in our department. Thus we got money from all these agencies signed documents and deposited the amount in a nationalized bank for a longer period. Annually from the interest amount we got from the bank we organized endowment lectures.

Details of the Endowment

Sl. No.	*Name of the Endowment*	*Donar Agencies*
1.	TKC Endowment	P.C. Balarama Raja, Chairman, Janata Chem
2.	T.V. Ramasbaiyer	Dinamalar, Madurai
3.	Justice V.R. Krishna Iyer	SOCO Trust, Madurai
4.	Justice B.N. Bhagwati	Peace Trust, Dindigul
5.	Ci.Pa. Aditanar	Dinathandhi, Chennai
6.	G. Venkatachalapathi	Gandhiniketan Ashram, Kallupatti
7.	M.G. Ramachandran	Dr. R. Thandavan, Madras University
8.	A.K. Venkata Subramanian	Catalyst Trust

Endowments had been created. But, trouble started only when we organized endowment lecture programmes. Because finding suitable persons for endowment lecture was not so easy. With great difficulty I persuaded many legends to deliver endowment lectures. Following eminent persons delivered endowment lectures.

1. Justice V.R. Krishna Iyer
2. Justice E.S. Venkata Ramaiah
3. N. Vittal Former Chief Vigilance Commissioner
4. Dr. George Mathew, Director Institute of Social Science, New Delhi
5. Dr. S.S. Meenakshi Sundaram, Former Secretary, Ministry of Rural Development, Government of India
6. Dr. Suriya Kant Mishra, Minister for Panchayati Raj, Government of West Bengal
7. Mr. Jeyakanthan, a veteran novelist

8. Mr. Vijay Anand, Secretary, Panchayati Raj, Government of Kerala
9. Dr. Vasanthi Devi, Former Vice-Chancellor of Manonmaniam Sundaranar University and an activist
10. Mrs. Soundara Kailasam, well known poet
11. Mr. Krishnaraj Vanavarayar, Chairman, Bharatiya Vidya Bhavan
12. Mr. Badri of Kizhakku Pathipagam
13. Kannan a well known Tamil Literary orator
14. Mr. Venkatesan Sakitya Academy Awardee

With great difficulties I managed to get all these individuals to Gandhigram Rural Institute to deliver endowment lectures. All the eminent persons had delivered excellent lectures on different socially relevant topics. There were other dignitaries who committed to deliver lectures but due to their time constraints they could not make it. If I can name a few of them, they are: Dr. Manmohan Singh, Sri. P. Chidambaram, and Late Ramakrishna Hedge. They had committed but they could not make it.

11

Capacity Building Exercises

My vision for Rajiv Gandhi Chair for Panchayati Raj Studies in Gandhigram was that it should emerge not only as a world class centre for research on decentralized governance but also as an outstanding leadership school. It must take up research, training, and policy advocacy. Hence, steps were taken to prepare tools for training, training ambience and master trainers. First, we identified experts with rich experience in rural local governance. While fixing those resource persons, we made it a point that those experts had proper perspectives on and commitments towards new Panchayati Raj. Quite often in India, we come across knowledgeable people who are insensitive and not willing to come off their pedestal. Ultimately, they end up being uncommitted to the issues of the poor. We are wary of such people, and let them remain asleep.

Once the resource persons are identified, we had to prepare training modules and manuals. We conducted series of workshops to prepare both training modules and manuals inviting different stakeholders. Based on the above exercises we have prepared training modules and manuals. We have developed modules for training rural local governance leaders of all the three tiers. We have specific modules prepared for training women leaders for local governance. Yet another module was prepared to train *dalit* elected representatives. All the modules were published and widely circulated among various training institutions. Most of our publications remain available. Except a few publications brought out by publishers investing their money, we do not hold any copy right because our purpose is dissemination even beyond our reach.

Government training institutions have also prepared such modules for conducting training programmes. We reviewed them to find out if they could be used in our training programmes so that we need not reinvent the wheel. But, we found them very much general or nonspecific. Moreover, we find many of them adopt an instructive-mode which pedagogically we call: *Do's and Don'ts Type*. In other words, they prescribe what to do and what not to do. They tend to focus more on official/bureaucratic rules and procedures, rather than best practices with a developmental perspective. The specific aspects on *dalits,* or women get marginalized in such works. We make a difference by custom-designing our works with sufficient sensitivity for *dalits*, *women*, *and youth* and so on. Organizations which conducted training programme for *dalit* leaders have used our training modules. Organizations which have conducted training programme for women leaders used our training module. All the modules are updated periodically.

After preparing the training modules, manuals have been prepared so as to give them as an operational tool or guide to the leaders who participated in our training programmes. We have prepared comprehensive manual for rural local governance meant for all the three tiers of rural local governance. Apart from the comprehensive manual, specific manuals were also prepared. Manual for Ward members of Gram Panchayat, Manual for Gram Panchayat Presidents, Manual for Block Panchayat Council Members, Block Panchayat Chair Persons, Manual for District Panchayat Chair Persons. Moreover, we have prepared manual for Gram Sabha members and committee members of various sub-committees of the Panchayats. All the manuals have been published through various agencies. Apart from reading the material for semi-literature we have also prepared audio and video material. Video CDs and audio cassettes have been prepared and produced material in large scale for distribution. While preparing such training tools we have involved a whole array of stakeholders. We have involved gender specialist, specialist on marginalized, communication specialist, specialist on administration in all our exercises.

Preparation of all these materials was viewed not merely as an intellectual exercise. It was a soul satisfying experience that we were putting in our efforts, time and intellect for the benefit of empowering the rural community in Tamil Nadu. For preparing and publishing training tools three institutions have supported the Rajiv Gandhi Chair for Panchayati Raj Studies. Rajiv Gandhi Foundation supported for production of comprehensive of training module and manuals for Panchayati Raj Training. The Hunger Project helped us to produce training modules and manuals for training elected women representatives and elected women *dalit* representatives. Population Foundation of India supported us for preparation and production of video and audio training material.

These training materials were used in a series of training programmes we conducted later on. Although our focus was on Gram Panchayat leaders, we have conducted training for leaders and potential leaders of all the three tiers in the Panchayat set-up. This is because we have a perspective that if a transformative leader is shaped for Gram Panchayat, the Gram Panchayat areas can be transformed very easily by the transformative leader. We believe that electing a leader is not in our hands, but shaping a leader can best be done in our hands. Hence preparing transformative leaders for Gram Panchayat was our target.

The Government of Tamil Nadu has developed a perspective that of the three tiers, Gram Panchayat has to be strengthened for effective service delivery at the grassroots level. Hence, powers have been accorded to Gram Panchayat more than the other two tiers. In the party-based political market place, Gram Panchayat was to a considerable extent free from the party-based contest. In this regard working with Gram Panchayat was much easier apart from conducting training programme for Gram Panchayat presidents. We conducted a series of training programmes for the elected representatives of rural local governance, with the financial support of the Ministry of Rural Development and Panchayati Raj, Government of India, the Government of Tamil Nadu, The Hunger Project, and Population Foundation of India.

Over a period of 15 years the Rajiv Gandhi Chair has trained more than 150 master trainers and 18000 elected representatives of rural local governance of all the three tiers. We used the Krishi Vigyan Kendra (KVK) as our training centre to conduct such training over a period of time. The resource persons Mr. Vallinayagam, Mr. N.S. Chidambaram and Mr. S. Subramaniam, Mr. Krishnamurthy have been with us for over fifteen years, now. They are retired Additional Directors of the Department of Rural Development, Government of Tamil Nadu. Apart from conducting the training programmes, we have organized many refresher programmes for the Panchayat leaders of the three tiers. These refresher programmes were organized only for clarifying doubts, and offering practicable suggestions for moving forward in Panchayat activities.

Rajiv Gandhi Chair did not stop with the capacity building exercises of its own. It went to support many of the organizations which conducted capacity building exercise for different stakeholders at Panchayat level.

Percentage of Panchayat Presidents Attended Training

Sl. No.	*Name of the District*	*Total No. Presidents*			*No. Presidents attended the training*			*Percentage of Panchayat Presidents*		
		Men	*Women*	*Total*	*Men*	*Women*	*Total*	*Men*	*Women*	*Total*
1.	Pudukkottai	326	172	428	275	140	415	84	81	83
2.	Dindigul	200	105	305	191	100	291	96	95	95
3.	Thiruchirappalli	275	132	407	255	131	386	93	99	95
4.	Sivagangai	292	153	445	242	112	354	83	73	80
5.	Ramanathapuram	282	147	429	229	116	345	81	79	80
6.	Theni	82	48	130	66	43	109	80	90	84
7.	Karur	109	49	158	91	49	140	83	100	89
8.	Virudhunagar	303	144	447	245	103	348	81	72	78
		1869	**950**	**2819**	**1594**	**794**	**2388**	**85**	**84**	**85**

PANCHAYAT TRAINING PROGRAMME—GRI CONCURRENT EVALUATION

Introduction

The broad particulars about this Report are as below:

Name of the Evaluator	Dr. T.C.A. Srinivasaramanujam
Name of the Project Holder	Gandhigram Rural Institute, Gandhigram
Name of the Project	Capacity Building Exercise for Gram Panchayat Leaders
Reference of Assignment	ORP/TND/14/6/2002 dated 28-5-2003
Dates of Visit	30-31 May 2003

Project

CAPART sanctioned to Gandhigram Rural Institute, Athur Block, Dindigul District, a Project entitled, "Capacity Building Exercise for Gram Panchayat Leaders". The sanction was communicated *vide* ORP/TND/14/6/2002 dated 25-7-2002. The cost sanctioned is Rs. 9,27,500 for a period of two years. The project covers Madurai, Ramnad, Sivagangai, Pudukkottai, Tiruchi, Karur and Dindigul districts, excluding Vadamadurai and Kujiliamparai Blocks. The sanctioning order mentions that there will be training to 35 batches, each batch having 30 participants. Cost is estimated as below:

Item	*Cost (In Rupees)*
Boarding and Lodging @ Rs. 150 per day for 3 days for 30 participants	13,500
Resource Materials @ Rs. 200 for 30 participant Resource Persons	6,000
Hall and Public Address System	1,000
Stationery, Postage and Miscellaneous	3,000
Total for one batch	26,500
Total for 35 batches	9,27,500

In the letter No. OPR/TND/14/6/2002 dated 28-5-2003, Member Convener, CAPART Regional Centre [South Zone] had asked me to make concurrent evaluation of the training programme slated from 31-5-2003 to 2-6-2003. The specific terms of reference for concurrent evaluation are:

1. Quality of the Study Material
2. Quality of the Resource Persons
3. Response, experience and reactions of the participants
4. Involvement of the State Government

Methodology

I followed the following methodology in this study:

1. Study of training schedule
2. Study of course material
3. Participation in training sessions
4. Discussions with participants
5. Discussion with Course Director and Resource Persons
6. Study of the Training Department

Training Schedule

The information given at the Gandhigram Rural Institute was that so for 14 training programmes have been completed as below:

1. Tiruchi—3
2. Pudukkottai—3
3. Sivagangai—3
4. Ramnad—2
5. Dindigul—3

The training under evaluation is 15th in the series. It is the third programme for Ramnad.

CAPART gives grant for training for three days. Gandhigram Rural Institute coordinates with collectors of the districts from which participants come and add two days to cover social development issues. Thus, each training is for a duration of 5 days; CAPART funds the first three days and collectors the last two days.

The training under evaluation was scheduled as below:

Duration (Minutes)	***Subjects***
First Day	
60	Principles of Decentralization, 73rd Constitutional Amendment
60	Tamil Nadu Panchayat Act, 1994
150	Gram Panchayat Administration: Duties, Responsibilities and Powers Discussions; Questions-Answers
30	Gram Sabha and People's Participation
30	Review
Second Day	
120	Multilevel Planning in Gram Panchayat: Discussion
90	Integration of Panchayat Plan and Sectoral Programmes Discussion, Question-Answers
120	Common Property Resource Management Protection of Natural Resources Discussion, Question-Answers
Third Day	
90	Financial Management Finance and Financial Resources Discussion, Question-Answers
120	Maintenance of Accounts and Records and Audit Procedure Discussion, Question-Answers
90	Social Development and Social Justice Discussion, Question–Answers
90	Vision Building Exercise Discussion, Question-Answers
60	Leadership Building
Fourth Day	
90	Status of Indian Women/Rural Women – Social Citizenship – Society and Family related issues faced by women – Problem–solving process – Gender equality role of individuals
120	Total Rural Sanitation
90	Social Development – Listing of issues – Role of Women in Social Development – Role of Panchayat in Social Development
75	Reproductive, Child Health
75	Role of Panchayat in Economic Development
Fifth Day	
240	Computer orientation
120	Exposure visit to Gram Panchayat using Computer

The trainees are divided into three groups of which one is exclusively of women. Sessions are held simultaneously for the three groups. Resource persons rotate between the three groups. The advantage is that the classes are smaller. The disadvantage is that the resource persons have to repeat themselves thrice.

Fourty four participants reported on the first day, 31st May, 2003. Of them 14 were women.

Course Material

All participants are given two printed books in Tamil:

1. Panchayati Raj in Tamil Nadu—Acts, Rules, Schemes
2. Supervision of Panchayats—An Explanatory Manual

The first book is a compendium of 763 pages. The book incorporates all Acts and Rules relating to Panchayati Raj and all Government Schemes implemented at Panchayat level. The second book is a handy manual giving information about rules and procedures applicable to Panchayats.

The course material has great reference value. When the elected Panchayat Presidents go back to their jobs, they will have ready reference to all information relevant to their functions. The elected functionaries need all information in the books to be effective. Most of them are new and inexperienced. The system itself is new and as yet untested. Most functionaries are not fully aware of their powers and methods for exercising them. They are at the mercy of officers and do not always get good guidance. The course material will fill this gap in knowledge.

Training Sessions

I attended the training sessions for all the three groups. Elected Panchayat Presidents were the main participants. Besides, Government officials dealing with Panchayats and Development at the Block Level participated.

Most of the elected functionaries were not aware of the legal framework of Panchayati Raj. Their ideas about their powers, responsibilities and charter were limited. They were also pessimistic about their potentials and overawed by the control of Government officers. For them, the training was an opportunity to know all about their duties and obligations. They expressed surprise to learn that their potential was greater than what they thought. The questions put by them suggested that the information given in the training was an eye-opener to them. Some of them felt that they ought to have been given the training much earlier.

Surprisingly, the Government officers also seemed as unaware of the legal framework as the elected persons. Most of the Acts and Rules are not available in field offices. Even circulars were not within their knowledge. The questions put by them and information given to them in the training sessions revealed that they were not up to date in their knowledge.

The participants were given a questionnaire to assess the training. Their views are sought on the following:

- Course Material
- Each Resource Person
- Their training style
- Class arrangement
- Lodging
- Food
- Cooperation of training institution
- Duration

Except for duration, they were asked to assess on the scale of very good, good and satisfactory. For duration, the scale is sufficient, should be increased and should be reduced.

There are questions to test the grasp of the participants of the broad subjects covered in the training. The questionnaire also seeks to draw the socio-economic profiles of the departments.

The questionnaire gives a good feedback about the training. I saw several reports of previous training programmes and found them informative.

Resource Persons

For conducting the CAPART training programmes, Gandhigram Rural Institute draws on the services of the following four retired Government servants of Rural Development Department:

1. Sri K. Subramanian, retired in 1998 as Additional Director in DRDA office at Chennai.

2. Sri N.S. Chidambaram, retired in 1996 as Principal, Rural Extension Training Centre, Bhavanisagar.
3. Sri K. Vallinayagam, retired in 1992 as Additional Director, Rural Development.
4. Sri S. Krishnamoorthy, retired in 1993 as Assistant Director, Rural Development.

All the four are consultants in State Institute of Rural Development at Maraimalainagar. They have painstakingly collected all latest orders on Panchayati Raj. They have prepared detailed training modules. They have also learnt modern techniques of training pedagogy. Their expression and interactive style are effective.

The institute has many in-house experts to takes sessions on Sanitation, Child Care and Women Development, Leadership Qualities, Vision Building and Computer Orientation. They have considerable research and teaching experience on the subject.

Training Department

Rajiv Gandhi Chair for Panchayati Raj Studies in the Department of Political Science and Development Administration of Gandhigram Rural Institute is the Training Department for this training. As an institution, the Training Department has emerged as a Resource Centre of Excellence in Panchayati Raj. It has conducted many training Programmes for different levels of Panchayat functionaries. It has organized or participated in seminars and conferences relating to Panchayats. It has undertaken studies on the role of Panchayati Raj Institutions in population, health, ecology, gram sabhas, and sanitation, water supply and gender issues. These studies were financed by various agencies. It has published many books, monographs, articles and reports on Panchayati Raj. I was Director General of National Institute of Rural Development, Hyderabad, where there is a Centre for Panchayati Raj Institutions. Its resource base in Panchayati Raj is impressive. What I found in the Rajiv Gandhi Chair for Panchayati Raj Studies is that it is very much stronger than the NIRD centre. The chair is much more actively involved in grassroots study and has direct field exposure. Its database is very strong.

Dr. G. Palanithurai is the head of the Rajiv Gandhi Chair for Panchayati Raj Studies. He is Professor and Head of the Department and Dean. He has completed many projects and published several books and articles on Panchayati Raj. He is guiding all training programmes, which are underway all-round the year. Being Professor of a deemed university, he has research and teaching duties to back-up his training and project work. I found him remarkably well informed on every aspect of Panchayati Raj—legal, administrative, social, political, planning, and developmental. He is an expert and a doyen among the scholars of Panchayati Raj.

The Rajiv Gandhi Chair has other experts also and they have made significant contributions in training and research.

With such resources, the Rajiv Gandhi Chair for Panchayati Raj Studies is a strong Training Department for the CAPART-assisted training programmes.

Conclusion

Based on the above analysis, I make the following evaluation about the Training Programme, Capacity Building Exercise for Gram Panchayat Leaders, held from 31st May to 2nd June, 2003 at Gandhigram Rural Institute:

- The training module is comprehensive.
- The training schedule is well planned.
- It is imaginative to dovetail CAPART funds with grants from collectors and increase the duration by two days to include social development issues.
- The training is well attended.
- Course materials is useful.
- Resource persons are knowledgeable.
- The training is needed for both the elected and government functionaries.
- The Training Department is a Centre of Excellence.
- It has a rich experience in conducting the training.

The project is successful. CAPART can continue to support Gandhigram Rural Institute for future training programmes.

Place: Chennai
Date: 18 July, 2003 **T.C.A. Srinivasaramanujam**

12

Capacity Building with a Difference

Training programmes that are instructive and prescriptive, often, end up as a failure when it comes to getting across the message or in terms of achieving the expected outcome. We have witnessed the arguments of women leaders in many programmes that they did not like some of the training programme organized by Government institutions as they are 'taught' and 'instructed' more on the don'ts. They were more interested in getting insights on how to develop a vision for development; how to achieve their aspirations as a leader; how best they could use the government machinery and schemes in order to make service delivery effective, and so on. But all that they could get was what and what should not be done by the elected representatives; and what and what are punishable offences.

They have attended the training programme with lots of hope and expectations. They could not get ways to achieve their aspirations. Further, the elected representatives could not get insights for making a change. The training banner read: 'leadership training', but what was being instructed was how being submissive can smooth relationships with officers of the government. This was the main orientation, as reported to us. It was precisely orienting the elected leaders to work under/as per the instructions of the government officials, and not as representatives of the people who elected them to power. Many of the elected women representatives felt that that training process disempowered the elected women representatives.

In this context, Rajiv Gandhi Chair for Panchayati Raj Studies took initiatives differently. It focuses its attention to shape transformative leadership through the training programme organized in Rajiv Gandhi Chair for Panchayati Raj Studies. In the training programme organized for elected women representatives with the support of the Hunger Project much focus was given by the Chair on transformation of attitude, behaviour and skill of the elected women representatives. Hence, the training programme explicitly promises that Rajiv Gandhi Chair for Panchayat Raj studies is a support agency and it would continue its activities beyond the training. Further the leadership skill was instilled in them through the training and more specifically by changing the attitude and behaviour. Lots of exercises are given to them in the course of training. The whole training was conducted not in lecture. Lecture was part of it. Attitudinal exercises are given to the leaders by the trainers. Finally, an evaluation was done to find out to what extent the trainees have picked up new skills. When they leave training programmes, they move with hope aspirations, dream plus toolkits for transforming their villages.

Sl. No.	*Title*	*Sponsored Agency*	*Total No. of Leaders Trained*
1.	Empowering Panchayati Raj Institutions on issues of population, Health and Social Development	Population Foundation of India	6834
2.	Capacity building for Gram Panchayat	CAPART	1369
3.	Training of presidents and vice-presidents in Panchayat administration with special reference to water and sanitation	DANIDA	814
4.	Training of women presidents in Gram Panchayat	Social Welfare Board	825
5.	Training of trainers in multi-level planning	State Planning Commission	71
6.	Capacity Building for Weaker Section in New Panchayati Raj System	CAPART	271
7.	Capacity Building exercise for Gram Panchayat Women Leaders	The Hunger Project	390

13

The Hunger Project

I came to know about the Hunger Project through Prof. M.S. Swaminathan. When he was the chairperson of the Hunger Project Council of Tamil Nadu, he had given a project to our Institute and it was handled by my colleague, Prof. N. Narayanasamy. At one of the occasions when Prof. M.S. Swaminathan came to Gandhigram to participate in the programme organized by Prof. S. Narayanasamy I got an invitation too. I attended and gained much information about it. At that point of time, the national head quarter of the Hunger Project was in Bombay. After the creation of New Panchayati Raj System through the 73rd Amendment to the Constitution of India, the thrust area of the Hunger project got changed—to work with Panchayats more. I found it meaningful, but because I was preoccupied with training programmes, I did not think over it seriously.

In the meanwhile, the Hunger Project organized a national workshop at Bangalore and it was presided over by the Global Board Chair John Homes. I was invited to participate in the programme. In the three-day workshop I had an opportunity to interact with Global Board Chair. We had chances to exchange views and interact many times during that meeting. Later I received a mail from the Vice-Chair of the Global Board John Konrad asking about my convenience to have an interaction. A meeting was fixed. The Vice-Chair of the Global Board of the Hunger Project and a newly appointed Country Director Ms. Rita Sarin came to my office in Gandhigram. They had several things to discuss about including the potentials of decentralization in Tamil Nadu, and the possibility for an academic institution like Gandhigram Rural Institute to work with the Hunger Project. The meeting ended there, as if they came for an informal discussion.

Later after taking over charge of the Hunger Project India, Ms. Rita Sarin, organized a workshop in New Delhi. She had invited me to attend that workshop. By that time, she had shifted the office from Mumbai to New Delhi. I attended the workshop and contributed to the discussions. Obviously, I was viewed as a person with strong connections with Panchayats. Subsequently, I received a communication from the Hunger Project stating that I have been nominated as Chairperson of the Hunger Project as Prof. M.S. Swaminathan resigned from the Chairperson position. I met Prof. M.S. Swaminathan at Chennai and informed him about the order. He immediately congratulated, and wished me to take up meaningful activities with the Hunger Project. He gave his ideas to reposition and reorient the Hunger Project in Tamil Nadu.

I sought official permission from GRI, to express my acceptance of that position. The usual academic politics cropped up, and some were of the opinion that this position should be held only by the Vice-Chancellor. The matter was placed in the syndicate meeting of the University. A representative of Human Resource Development Ministry attended the meeting of the syndicate. When local academics raised critical issues on the letter of appointment, the representative of HRD Ministry pointed out that the letter is addressed to Dr. G. Palanithurai by name. Therefore, it is an honour, and that it has to be accepted. On the basis of his argument our University authorities had permitted me to hold the Chairperson position of the Hunger Project in Tamil Nadu. Then I accepted the offer and sent my acceptance letter to the Country Director, New Delhi.

When I took up the responsibility as the Chairperson, Mr. Madhavan was the programme officer of the Hunger Project looking after the programmes in Tamil Nadu. He was knowledgeable, committed, and hundred per cent loyal to the leadership looking for innovative projects in Panchayati Raj. He in fact asked me to take up projects from the Hunger Project. Then I appointed G. Uma as the Coordinator of Hunger Project in Gandhigram. We started the elected women representative leadership projects. We developed training module and based on the module we carried out series of leadership training programmes. Subsequently, I took up the micro plan exercise in select villages in association with select District Administrations. It was fully supported by the Hunger Project. In 74 Gram Panchayats in five districts we helped the Gram Panchayats to evolve a micro-level plan by following the methodology evolved by the State Planning Commission.

In the course of training Gram Panchayat elected women representatives we created a vast pool of resource persons to work in Panchayati Raj. Apart from the training we have created a support structure to help the women leaders and *Dalit* leaders when they are in need while they are in the field. All the good practices and innovations done by the Gram Panchayat leaders were documented for dissemination. Many research articles, monographs, and working papers have been prepared out of data generated from the action research conducted with the support of the Hunger Project.

With the help and support of the Hunger Project we organized several workshops for media men and women. As a result large number of articles have been written and published by both in Tamil and English newspapers on the issues of local governance and more particularly the struggle and success of the women leaders and *Dalit* leaders in Tamil Nadu. Four times prestigious national awards were received by media men and women from the Hunger Project. It is not only the Tamil newspaper but also monthly, fortnightly and weekly magazines have published series of articles on the issue of local governance. To sensitize more number of people to write on local body issues, a series of writers' workshops were conducted and for which the Hunger project extended financial support. It also extended support to publish a supplement on Local Governance in a newspaper for about one year. Further the Hunger project helped to have MoU with All India Radio to broadcast the programme on local governance throughout Tamil Nadu for six months. To document and telecast series of programmes on problems in local governance through local T.V. Channels. Innumerable small and big innovative programmes were conducted in Tamil Nadu on local governance and for which the Hunger Project extended cooperation and support. Yet, another event hosted in Gandhigram by the Hunger Project was the 25th anniversary celebration of the Hunger Project. It was attended by a number of ministers from Tamil Nadu Government along with the higher officials and thousands of local body leaders.

I must make a mention about the role played by this remarkable lady Rita Sarin, Country Director and her Programme Officer Mr. Madhavan. Many innovative programmes were carried out in Tamil Nadu because of the support extended by the Country Director and the Programme Officer. She is extraordinarily a committed person on women leadership. They not only extended financial support but also extended moral and human resource support for all our activities.

14

Federating the Elected Women Representatives

When Dr. N. Markandan was the Vice-Chancellor of Gandhigram Rural Institute, he asked me to contact Dr. L.C. Jain to deliver convocation address in Gandhigram Rural Institute. I contacted him. Later Dr. N. Markandan, Vice-Chancellor also spoke to him officially. He readily agreed to visit Gandhigram Rural Institute and deliver convocation address. While agreeing, he informed that he would come with Ms. Devaki Jain as she is interested to see the Panchayati Raj activities of Rajiv Gandhi Chair. Finally, both of them came. Dr. L.C. Jain delivered the convocation address. On the same day around 10.00 am. both visited our Department and saw the activities and gave constructive suggestions to improve the quality of our activities which were highly valuable. I cherish their visit.

While we were in interaction I informed Ms. Devaki about a question raised by many of our elected women representatives in the training programme. The question was: "Is there any organization or institution to support the elected women representatives when they are facing problem in the field?" They need more of handholding support and facilitation rather than mere information provision. Sri L.C. Jain intervened and asked us why you think of a support facility outside. I asked back, wouldn't it be better if an organization took responsibility in this regard. Then Ms. Devaki Jain informed me that she would call me later for a programme. A few days later I got a call from New Delhi and it was from Devaki Jain. She told me that the Ford Foundation found the idea credible and has agreed to help me in such an initiative. But, she also told me that such initiative should not be restricted to a State alone. It should be an exercise in a few

States. Further, she asked me to take up the task of coordinating such initiative in South India. I was entrusted with the responsibility of search for like-minded organization for collaboration.

Later, upon her invitation, I went to Bangalore to discuss about that proposal. I attended the programme along with Alleamma Vijayan of Saki, Dr. Chos Chanthankulam of CRM of Kottayam and a few representatives of Loksatta of Hyderabad. We had a meeting in Bangalore and developed a joint-proposal within the framework given by the representative from the Ford Foundation. I took responsibility of organizing federation and federation activities in Tamil Nadu; Saki took responsibility of coordinating the whole exercise, in Kerala; and Lok Satta took responsibility of organizing such federation in Andhra Pradesh. Ms. Devaki Jain took the responsibility of organizing the federation activities in Karnataka. The proposal was approved by the Ford Foundation. It was the first initiative in the whole country in federating elected women representatives. We chalked out a guiding principles and framework under which all the four institutions worked for federating the elected women representatives. For about six years we carried out the elected women representatives' federation activities with the support of the Ford Foundation and with the guidance of Devaki Jain. Six years of federation activities have been documented and it came out in the form of a book too.

Annual State Level Convention of Women Panchayat Presidents

Date	*Year*	*Annual meet*	*Venue*	*Sponsored by*
5th August	2001	Annual Convention of Elected Women Representatives in local bodies	Gandhigram	Singamma Srinivasan Foundation, Bangalore
3rd May	2002	Annual Convention of Elected Women Representatives in local bodies	Gandhigram	Singamma Srinivasan Foundation, Bangalore
15th May	2005	Annual convention of elected Women Representatives in local bodies	Gandhigram	Singamma Srinivasan Foundation, Bangalore

(*Contd.*)

Regional-Levels Meet on Associating Women Representatives in Local Bodies

Date	*Year*	*Regional meet*	*Venue*	*Sponsored by*
21st Dec.	2000	South Zone	Madurai	Singamma Srinivasan Foundation, Bangalore
21st Mar.	2001	Central Zone	Karur	Singamma Srinivasan Foundation, Bangalore
16th Feb.	2001	North Zone	Chengalpattu	Singamma Srinivasan Foundation, Bangalore
2nd Feb.	2001	Second Regional Meet	Tiruvarur	Singamma Srinivasan Foundation, Bangalore
6th Jan.	2002	Network Meeting	Tiruvarur	Singamma Srinivasan Foundation, Bangalore
2nd Feb.	2002	Women Panchayat Leaders special meet, Hon'ble Mr. Venkaiah Naidu, Rural Development Minister, Government of India	Gandhigram	Singamma Srinivasan Foundation, Bangalore
28th Aug.	2000	State level Consultation Meet on Feminist Perspective	Gandhigram	Singamma Srinivasan Foundation, Bangalore
23rd Oct.	2000	State Level Ngos Meet	Gandhigram	Singamma Srinivasan Foundation, Bangalore
8th May	2002	Network Meeting with Ford Foundation Programme Officer	Gandhigram	Singamma Srinivasan Foundation, Bangalore

15

Micro Plan Preparation

Government of Tamil Nadu has developed a perspective towards New Panchayati Raj System. As per the perspective Panchayats should be made as only an implementing agency. It was reluctant to enact a confirmative legislation. Even after enacting the confirmative legislation it was reluctant to conduct election. In Tamil Nadu politics both political parties (the DMK and the AIADMK) never have similar views on any issue, though they have similar ideologies. But, they concur on one issue, namely the Panchayati Raj. Both want only two tier Panchayati Raj System. Secondly, both do not want District Panchayat and District Planning Committee. Both want a strong Gram Panchayat to implement the programmes of the state government. In this context we wanted to develop a planning culture at the bottom. When we were discussing about this idea both Mr. Naresh Gupta then Member Secretary, State Planning Commission and Dr. K. Palanithurai, then Member State Planning Commission suggested that planning exercise could be done at the Gram Panchayat level as the Government of Tamil Nadu is interested in strengthening the Gram Panchayat. State Planning Commission had already evolved a planning manual and it could be used for preparing the Micro Plan for Gram Panchayat. First, it could be started as pilots in select Panchayats. It was the suggestion of some of the Panchayat leaders also.

To take up this exercise I initiated a discussion with the Hunger Project. Ms. Rita Sarin the Country Director of the Hunger Project immediately agreed to help the select Panchayats to evolve a participatory development plan. Based on the discussion I initiated a dialogue with some of the District Collectors. First, I started this exercise in Pudukkottai district when Mr. Hitesh Kumar Makwana was the district collector. I extended the same exercise in Sivagangai district and later to Tuticorin and in Dindigul districts. Nearly 74 Gram Panchayats were selected and the District Administration of the respective districts extended all cooperation to evolve a development plan. With a view to making this exercise take off without much hurdles, the district administration had selected the Gram Panchayats based on two criteria, namely the integrity and commitment of the Panchayat leader and conflict free Panchayats. Finally, plan document was prepared and approved by the Gram Sabha signed by the district collector as inspector of Panchayats and the coordinating officer of all the departments of the State Government. It was a path breaking exercise done by Rajiv Gandhi Chair. For one district the Centre for Rural Management, Kottayam Kerala helped us to prepare the plan based on Kerala's experience. For other districts we helped the Gram Panchayats. Based on the experience the whole process was documented and it was published in the form of a book.

Details of the Gram Panchayats while planning Exercise was done

Sivaganga District

Sl. No.	*Name of Village*	*Block*
1.	Manalur	S. Pudhur
2.	Urathuapatti	S. Pudhur
3.	Kizhavayal	S. Pudhur
4.	Kozhikudipatti	Singampunari
5.	Vadavanpatti	Singampunari
6.	Sevalpatti	Singampunari
7.	Kalipuli	Kallal
8.	Veppankulam	Kallal
9.	P. Netpugapatti	Kallal
10.	Velangudi	Thirupathur

Pudukkottai District

Sl. No.	*Name of Village*	*Block*
1.	Parambur	Annavasal
2.	Melapudhuvayal	Gunnandarkoil
3.	Neunjikudi	Ponnamaravathi
4.	Mookkampatti	Pudukkottai

(Contd.)

Sl. No.	*Name of Village*	*Block*
5.	Veerasilai	Thirumayam
6.	Meenaveli	Viralimalai
7.	Merpanaikadu	Aranthangi
8.	Poovalur	Avudaiyarkoil
9.	Pudhukulam	Kandarvakootai
10.	Izhakadividuthi	Karambakudi
11.	Idayathimangalam	Manamelkudi
12.	Melathur	Thiruvarankulam
13.	K. Rayavaram	Arimalam

Tuticorin District

Sl. No.	*Name of Village*	*Block*
1.	Ottanatham	Ottapidaram
2.	*Puthia*mputhur	Ottapidaram
3.	Kodiyankulam	Ottapidaram
4.	Pattinamaruthur	Ottapidaram
5.	Tharuvaikulam	Ottapidaram
6.	Sriparangusanallur	Srivaikundam
7.	Siruthondanallur	Srivaikundam
8.	Thirupani Chettikulam	Srivaikundam
9.	Parakiramapandi	Srivaikundam
10.	Mukkani	Srivaikundam
11.	Mettilpatti	Puthur
12.	Mathalapuram	Puthur
13.	Kadalkudi	Puthur
14.	Thappathy	Puthur
15.	Iyanrajapatti	Puthur

Dindigul District

Sl. No.	*Name of Village*	*Block*
1.	Sithargalnatham	Nilakkottai
2.	Kodanginaickenpatti	Nilakkottai
3.	Noothulapuram	Nilakkottai
4.	Karisalpatti	Reddiarchtram
5.	Pannaipatti	Reddiarchtram
6.	Kamatchipuram	Reddiarchtram
7.	Silvarpatti	Reddiarchtram

(*Contd.*)

Sl. No.	*Name of Village*	*Block*
8.	Athoor	Athoor
9.	N. Panjampatty	Athoor
10.	Thevarappanpatty	Athoor
11.	Kallikkampatty	Athoor
12.	Anaipatty	Dindigul
13.	M.M. Koviloor	Dindigul
14.	Balakrishnapuram	Dindigul
15.	Mullipadi	Dindigul
16.	Thottanoothu	Dindigul

16

Our Adjunct Professors

In Gandhigram Rural Institute, Department of Political Science and Development Administration is the only department has this unique programme of having Adjunct Professors. We have made an empanelment of select specialists in varied fields of development, who can transfer rich knowledge input to students from their experience. Since, I am the coordinator of the UGC Innovative programme M.A. Governance and Development and the coordinator of UGC-SAP, I found resources in the budget of both projects to invite resource persons. This resource has been used to invite the adjunct professors.

I took initiative to contact Dr. S.S. Meenakshisundaram a very knowledgeable, well experienced civil servant having very rich experience in Panchayati Raj and Rural Development. He worked in Karnataka during Ramakrishna Hedge for the introduction of New Panchayati Raj. Later, he worked in Prime Minister's Office while 73rd Amendment was drafted. Subsequently, he was the Secretary for Rural Development, Government of India with rich experience he could contribute substantially to the students. Against this background, I contacted him he agreed to be with us. Further I contacted yet another civil servant whom I rate as extraordinarily a brilliant officer, people friendly, and critical of the functioning of government. He worked with Mr. Mani Sankar Aiyar when he was the minister for Panchayati Raj, Government of India as Joint Secretary. After he joined back in Karnataka, he could not find suitable climate for working in the administration. He is the most sought after man in the civil society to give input on the functioning of local governance. His deep insights in local governance attracted me towards him. Hence, I contacted him. He also agreed to serve us as adjunct professor.

Later yet another superstar among civil servants I contacted was Mr. S. Swaminathan. He was the Chairman of the State Administrative Reform Commission of Tamil Nadu. His knowledge on State Administration is vast. He also accepted graciously to serve as adjunct professor. He has written several books also. He served as Finance Secretary in the Government of Tamil Nadu. Subsequently I have asked Dr. S.N. Sangita of Institute for Socio-Economic Change (ISEC), Bangalore to become an adjunct professor. Since he is specializing on Governance and Development Politics, I thought he would be a source of great input. He also readily agreed to serve as adjunct professor. Finally, I wanted to bring one resource person form the discipline of Economics. Prof. R. Elango, Dean Faculty of Humanitics came to my mind as I know from 1980s. He was a strong believer of building a knowledge pool in the country by orienting and shaping young research scholars for quality research in social sciences. Though he was a professor in Economics his activities were always in all the disciplines of Social Sciences. His research acumen was of high value and it always benefited the young scholars. I know him personally from my student days. Hence, I requested him, he was extremely happy to be with us in this man making process. Thus, I got their consent and sent the same to office for approval. Gandhigram Rural Institute office took nearly about six months to give approval.

Every year all these adjunct professors used to visit Gandhigram Rural Institute and delivered series of lectures. When Adjunct professors come, we make the class into sessions. We provide modest accommodation and UGC approved honorarium to them. Their contributions are unfathomable. They come with elaborate preparations and they share it with students. It was a new experience for the students. These resource persons have given a lot of areas for research in Development Management. When our university prepared for reaccreditation of NAAC, our administration requested us to put a board in the Department about the new practice of keeping adjunct professors. We took photographs of all the resource persons and gave it to Estate Office; they brought and fixed a very big board at the entrance of our Department. It was not only appreciated by the NAAC team, but also by the UGC team which visited our University for evaluation of Tenth Five Year Plan activities.

17

Our Resource Persons

For any activity quality human power is the most essential, and a basic requirement. We have capacity building exercises, action research, foundational research, policy advocacy, media sensitization, awareness creation programmes and a few others in Rajiv Gandhi Chair. All tasks can be taken simultaneously. It needs a variety of resource persons. Our major task and mandate is capacity building. Even in capacity building, we have to conduct different types of capacity building. For Gram Panchayat Presidents, Elected Gram Panchayat women Presidents, Elected Gram Panchayat Dalit leaders, Ward Members, Officials, NGO representatives, media representatives and a few other segments involved in Panchayat Raj Activities. For all, quality training has to be imparted. For this task we have incorporated a list of retired officials who are thorough on Panchayat administration. Not only they are knowledgeable; they are sensitive and committed too. More importantly they are honest and sincere. They have full faith in Panchayati Raj. They are Mr. M. Vallinayagam, Mr. N.S. Chidambaram and Mr. S. Subramaniam. They worked in Government of Tamil Nadu in the Department of Rural Development and Panchayati Raj for about thirty five years. They are thorough in their knowledge from the fundamentals to philosophy of Panchayati Raj. They give their input to our awareness creation activities, capacity building exercises and research activities. Often, the whole training sessions are handled by them. I used to discuss with participants a global overview, context and the current wave of decentralization, the implications of decentralization and expectations after the training. Panchayat Administration has been taught as per the provisions of the Tamil Nadu Panchayat Act. This is the major part of the training.

These aspects had been covered by the three resource persons, namely M. Vallinayagam, N.S. Chidambaram and S. Subramaniam.

Gender is yet another component which was handled by Dr. G. Uma she was thoroughly trained by Mrs. Bimla Chandrasekar. Mrs. Bimla Chandrasekar was a source of strength for our team to handle the subject 'gender'. Mrs. Bimala Chandrasekar is the Director of EKTA, a Madurai based NGO, working for Women Empowerment. Dr. V. Ragupathy handled subjects like natural resource management and use of social capital for Panchayat Administration. Dr. M.A. Thirunavukkarasu handled the subjects on mobilization of people for development discourse and development participation. He also handled subjects like micro planning and social development. We have drawn resource persons from different organizations periodically. One important individual who worked with us substantially in the training programmes not only in taking classes for the Panchayat leaders but also bringing lot of government orders to clarify doubts of the elected Panchayat leaders. Hence he has been affectionately called: G.O. Krishnamoorthy. He keeps all the government records in his house for ready reference. Many Panchayat leaders contact him to get information on rules and procedures of dealing issues.

18

Panchayat Manual

For every elected representative Rajiv Gandhi Chair for Panchayati Raj Studies has given one important reference document, namely Panchayat Manual compiled by Prof. G. Palanithurai. The manual has Panchayat Act, Panchayat Rules and Government Orders relating to Panchayat Administration. Along with the above government schemes and programmes (both centre and state) were also the part of the manual. A letter written by the Prime Minister to the Panchayat leaders and the charter of Panchayats are integral part of the manual. It is a reference document. But to read the document, guidance is necessary. Hence in the training programme, Mr. N.S. Chidambaram used to take one hour to explain how to use the Panchayat manual. That manual went five editions. This exercise was done meticulously in the second day of training. Many Panchayat leaders have used it as a reference material and they kept it in Panchayat for public reference. This manual was published by South Vision, Chennai. Apart from the above manual, a separate set of manuals have been prepared for Gram Sabha member, Gram Panchayat ward members, Gram Panchayat Presidents, Gram Panchayat Vice-Presidents, Gram Panchayat Committee members, Block Panchayat ward members, Block Panchayat Presidents, Block Panchayat Vice-Presidents, Block Panchayat Committee members, District Panchayat ward members, District Panchayat Presidents, District Panchayat Vice-Presidents, District Panchayat Committee members. The responsibilities, roles and powers given to each one in the total Panchayati Raj System of Tamil Nadu have been explained in the respective manual.

There is yet another manual prepared in English jointly by Prof. G. Palanithurai, Mr. M. Vallinayagam, Mr. N.S. Chidambaram and Mr. S. Subramaniam. It was published by the Concept Publishing Company, New Delhi. It is meant for officials.

19

Narratives of Achievements at Grassroots

Tamil Nadu (Sivagangai District): Gandhigram training makes a *dalit* woman realize her worth as a trained Panchayat leader. A rural *dalit* woman (Ms Chinnamma) narrated her story, and the story goes like this: "I was only a masonry helper in construction activities in Orathupatti in Sivagangai district. I worked for daily wage and helped my family. Once the seat of Gram Panchayat president post was reserved for *dalit* women, some of the community leaders asked me to file a nomination. In Sivagangai district the community system was strong. Without knowing what the post was and the responsibilities of the position, I agreed to do so, as I had to obey the community. I became Gram Panchayat President. I was drawn towards Gandhigram for training. I attended the training programme organized by Rajiv Gandhi Chair for Panchayat Raj Studies, Gandhigram. It was a unique programme where I realized my worth. In my house I had no toilet. In one of the sessions, I learnt personal hygiene, and environmental sanitation. The trainer taught how to use toilets; how to sit in a chair in public places; how to make conversation with others and more particularly with officials. Now, I am working with people on environmental sanitation. I started cleaning my surroundings. Simple things like personal hygiene, avoiding open-defecation, and hand-washing practice by children could help avoid a lot of diseases, besides earning dignity as civilized human beings." Mrs. Chinnamma, Gram Panchayat President in a tiny Sivaganga village works on sanitation issues with all zeal. That's her take-away, which remained in her mind. Among the several possibilities that the training exposed to, she took a message home that was on sanitation. This narration was recorded in a National Workshop organized for experience sharing organized by Rajiv Gandhi Chair. Her narration was an eye opener to us that we must capture such stories and disseminate for motivating other leaders. I started visiting Gram Panchayats and wrote stories about success, struggles, incidents, and innovations by the Gram Panchayats. All these monographs have been titled as Leadership Matters in grassroots governance." All the interesting stories were published by the Rajiv Gandhi Chair with the support of the Hunger Project.

20

Training Environment

It is a mandate of Rajiv Gandhi Chair that human dignity and self-respect are not negotiable matters. Hence everyone involved in the training programme has to conduct themselves in a dignified way to respect the dignity of the trainees as they are drawn from different socio-economic strata. They are from Dalit section and they are from other marginalized segments and more particularly women. When they come for training they should feel totally a friendly and connected atmosphere. They should feel that they have a place where they wanted to be. In such a way training ambience has been created in Rajiv Gandhi Chair for Panchayat Raj Studies. Providing hostel accommodation, food, training material and treating them in the class rooms and hostels, they should be treated with utmost care before the formal training, and a get together is arranged in a training hall just like a festivity to know each other and to connect each other. Finally, when they give their feedback out after the training, all the resource persons cell phone numbers have been given for contact in future. Apart from the classroom interaction, exposure visits had been arranged to model Panchayats.

21

Preparation of District Human Development Report

The State Planning Commission (SPC) of Government of Tamil Nadu, decided to take up the task of preparing District Human Development Reports (DHDRs) for select districts. The SPC approached some institutions to carry out the task, of them Rajiv Gandhi Chair for Panchayati Raj Studies is one. I received a call from the Member Secretary, SPC. He asked me to participate in a workshop organized by the SPC. I went to Chennai and participated in the programme, where the Member Secretary and his staff along with experts from the UNDP Office, New Delhi briefed about the assignments. It sounded an interesting and a useful assignment. For many it was not attractive especially because they felt that the fund made available was too meagre to carry out the exercise meaningfully. To me, it was attractive as I thought a team of us could gain enormous knowledge in the preparation process. Moreover, my interest was to find out how Panchayati Raj could involve in this process, of achieving human development. I agreed to undertake this exercise.

I took up two districts for preparation of HDRs, viz. Dindigul and Nagapattinam. Dindigul—because GRI is located in Dindigul district; and Nagapattinam—because of our familiarity with the district since our post-Tsunami reconstruction works. Several rounds of discussions were held with respective district administration. District officials were trained and oriented to look at the district and their operational role from the human development perspective. It was a stupendous task. Of the two district administrations, Dindigul was active in helping us in providing the data needed to write up the report. One District Collector was to be mentioned here as he evinced keen interest and he was sincere in his support. Mr. Murgaiah was enthusiastic and hence, he openly appealed to the officials to give reliable data. We found that district officials had the practice of presenting only the progress of any government scheme. Beyond that they have no perspective to look at the reality of the society. For this purpose we have to collect data from the Gram Panchayat level, Block Panchayat level too. Down below the level of district, there is no data base at all. First time, we started the process of collecting massive data from the village Panchayats. Periodically, I conducted review meetings. Later I attended many workshops organized by the UNDP in this regard. I got rich experience and knowledge on this subject. I have sent a few research staff to the workshops organized by the State Planning Commission. It took nearly two years to complete the process. In the meanwhile change of government took place, and as a result initial enthusiasm started fading. Member Secretary, SPC was also transferred. Later it became a routine work. But successfully the exercise was completed and reports were published. When the documents were published it was a low key affair as the ruling party could not claim any political advantage out of it. Further conditions of the district were not good as per the human development indicators.

Here in this exercise we have gained lot of advantages. Capacity building took place for my project staff. We have evolved a course for our M.A. Programme. I personally gained a lot of insights on human development. To some extent, some of the government staff picked up this approach started working on it on their own. One of my Ph.D. students started her work on elected women representatives and human development.

I visualized the potentials of Panchayati Raj in working on the MDG through this process. I have given a number of exercises to my students in the lines of HDI. I have written a number of research articles and published.

22

Persons Who Influenced Me

It was a day in 1991, first and foremost late V. Padmanabhan, Managing Trustee of Gandhigram Trust discussed with me about the activities to be done in Gandhigram Rural Institute. He had made it a regular practice to invite me to participate in the activities of the Gandhigram Trust. On many occasions, he invited me to deliver lectures in Gandhigram Trust. In all my conversations he used to discuss with me the perspective of Gandhigram Institutions. He also advised me to look at the issues from Gandhian perspective. During those periods, meeting him for a longer period was not possible. But, he invited me for discussion many times and he took longer times to clarify some of the critical questions. He patiently answered all my questions to my satisfaction. At times, I have raised questions that shake the very foundation of the Gandhian institutions and he fairly indicated the deviations have caused our own institutions to drift away from the basic objectives. But, his response was always analytical and scientific. He never pointed fingers at individuals who were responsible for such deviations, if at all there were some. When he gave answers to my questions he made it very clear to me that I have to work well within the framework of Gandhian institutions.

He told me plainly that Gandhigram Rural Institute needs no Vice-Chancellors but it needs only leaders with Gandhian perspective. Further he explained that Gandhigram Rural Institute staff needs a thorough orientation in Gandhian values. Further Gandhigram Rural Institute is not a university in general terms. It is a unique institute experimenting Gandhian perspective of education. This has to be kept in mind by everyone of the staff of Gandhigram Rural Institute. He informed me that I have to contextualize the Department in terms of academic programme, research initiatives and outreach activities.

He gave a clue that I have to work in Panchayati Raj Activities. It is still very fresh in my memory, he told me one day: "*Dr. Palanithurai, you are from conventional university, observe the way Gandhigram Rural Institute is working; analyze its strength and weakness; and you work on the side of its strength. You have a space and you will find that space expand as you start working with a mission. Remember you will be known throughout because of your activities.*" This observation made me to work deeply in decentralization. When I met many times, I did not realize that he was orienting me.

For field visits, we go for long journey. During our travel he asked me to sit by his side and in the travel process he used to discuss many issues relating to Gandhian Constructive Works which made me to work on these ideals. But now I realize he passed on such information and insight very consciously to orient me in Gandhian lines. He has also given input for preparation of papers for presentation outside Gandhigram. He reminded me very often that in all my presentations Gandhian perspective should be reflected. In my academic career he made an everlasting impact through his interactions and inputs. I took a conscious decision that I have to work in Gandhigram Rural Institute with Gandhian Perspective. That decision was not merely out of his persuasive talks, but out of my conscious evaluation and conviction by reading Gandhi. I strongly believe in Gandhi and I visualize that Gandhi is the future of the world if at all this world should sustain for generations. I never used Khadi before I came to Gandhigram. He only taught me the value of Khadi and hence I started wearing Khadi. Now I enjoy wearing Khadi. Thus, late V. Padmanabhan has had a profound influence in the way I think and work, and he turned my academic activities towards Panchayati Raj.

Dr. M. Aram

I was about to leave the institution because of the internal politics of the institute. Dr. M. Aram former Vice-Chancellor met me in Chennai in a programme. He took me after the programme to Sakthi Guest House for lunch. He requested me not to leave the Institute. He told me that Gandhigram is a small institute but a very significant one. He further told me that Gandhigram needs individuals to take forward the Institute and to contextualize the same. By doing so, naturally your name will also go round along with the name of Gandhigram.

He persuaded me to remain in Gandhigram. When I organized my first Panchayat programme in Madurai (I organized that programme in Madurai as my institute has not permitted me to organize it in the campus due to internal politics). He came and inaugurated the programme as a member of Rajya Sabha. He many times appreciated me for my Panchayati Raj activities. I never worked under him when he was the Vice-Chancellor of Gandhigram Rural Institute. But, I maintained vibrant academic relations with him and his organization Shanti Ashram in Coimbatore. He personally invited me for many of his programmes. Till his demise I maintained a good intellectual relationship with him.

23

AKV: A New Guide

A.K. Venkatasubramanian, retired IAS officer with a difference, he was affectionately called 'AKV'. We knew each other for over fifteen years. We often interacted and shared views over phone, and whenever we meet in meetings. He was a purebred IAS officer. He had rare ability to comprehend issues, analyze them and communicate to larger audience. I was deeply impressed and influenced by his way of doing things. When he was in service he used to tell me that we have to work for building good citizens in this country to rejuvenate Indian democracy. The moment he retired he started working with a civil society origination. After his retirement he came through Catalyst Trust for reaching out the society for citizenship building. On many occasions he gave clarity to the issues of governance and administration. Whenever I sought his help for our programmes and village activities he readily agreed and provided needed help. He participated many of our activities in Gandhigram Rural Institute and other places. Basically his specialization was mathematics, but his clarity on theoretical issues of governance and administration were admirable. Further he was deeply influenced by Mahatma Gandhi. In the same way he was influenced by Thiruvalluvar. He has unequivocally made his mission clear to everyone that he would work for creating better citizens for better governance. He, in fact, created citizens' centres in many places to provide needed information to the citizens. I closely worked with him in his mission by training the citizen centres organizers. Later, I helped him to make Panchayat as citizen's centre. Continuously, I have conducted training programmes for them. He left an indelible mark in the minds of everyone who worked with him. His sudden demise created a void in the civil society space as he provided needed input to make every civil society organization to become a right-based and citizen centric one. In memory of him I have created an endowment in our Department.

24

A New Friend in Decentralization

Mr. R. Ragunathan is yet another interesting person who influenced me a lot in Panchayati Raj activities for about one decade. I came to know much about him whenever I interact with Panchayat leaders of Karnataka and the academics more particularly the researchers of institute for social and economic change, Bangalore. At that point of time I developed an inclination to meet and interact with him. Within a short span of time I met him in Delhi when Mani Shankar Aiyar became a Cabinet Minister for the Ministry of Panchayati Raj, Government of India in the first UPA regime. He was the Joint Secretary to the Ministry. From the day of the first meeting to the present we are working together on Panchayati Raj. Whenever I visited New Delhi, I made it a point to meet him. We discussed whole range of issues in decentralization. I met many intellectuals who are specializing in decentralization. Of all the specialist whom I interact with, Mr. Ragunathan is one who has deep understanding of the subject and equally he has deep commitment on the issue. He has shown much affection towards me and he used to appreciate me. He openly tells everyone that how I work with Panchayat in the negative climate for decentralization of powers in Tamil Nadu. He provided enormous amount of literature he got from various agencies abroad on decentralization. All the materials are very valuable for my research and teaching. Now he took voluntary retirement and act independently as consultant. One day I went to him in Samrat Hotel office in a holiday. We had a long discussion on the current stage of decentralization and later we went to a hotel for our lunch. After finishing our lunch we went to Rajghat to take oath that we have to work for Gram Swaraj. That pledge makes us to work in Panchayati Raj till today.

25

Role in World Bank Project

For poverty reduction and empowerment of the poor, a project was conceived by the Department of Social Welfare, Government of Tamil Nadu. It was submitted to the World Bank. The project proposal had completely ignored the Panchayati Raj Institution. I wrote a letter to the World Bank, New Delhi and a letter to the Secretary, Panchayati Raj and Rural Development. When the World Bank team came for a preliminary visit I was asked to meet them in Chennai. I went and briefed them as to how incorporating Panchayats could enhance the programme effectiveness. In the second draft the role of Panchayats was incorporated. When a team from the World Bank visited Dindigul district, I was asked to lead the team. The District Collector, Dindigul asked me to organize a preliminary workshop in Gandhigram. We organized a preliminary workshop in Gandhigram and took the team to the field. At the point of time the programme was known as: "Puthu Vazhvu Project". Later it has been changed to "Vazhnthu Kattuvom Project".

The project was sanctioned and it was almost handed over to the Panchayati Raj and Rural Development Department. In this process, unexpectedly, I earned the displeasure of some of the I.A.S officers. The project had taken shape in such a way to completely go under the Panchayati Raj Department. The project was originally designed by Social Welfare Department with the aim of empowering self-help groups in the state. During the implementation process, I was asked to make a presentation in a workshop about the training of project staff. I went to Chennai and I made a small presentation. In this presentation I had incorporated a concept "Emotionalization" in the training programme designed by me to train the project managers. Dr Ruth Alsop came from Washington D.C. of the World Bank asked me to explain the concept. I elaborated the concept and she appreciated.

Later the Government of Tamil Nadu advertised in the newspapers for resource agency to train the project managers. I came across the advertisement calling for bids. But, I did not apply because I felt that I might face administrative obstacles at the University. Being a university employee prevented me from participating in bidding. Later, I was asked by our Vice-Chancellor to send a proposal as per the request from the officials of the project of Government of Tamil Nadu. Hence, I have submitted a project proposal. It was approved by the Government and I conducted the training programme along with two other agencies. I found carrying out this World Bank capacity building programme was very cumbersome with a lot of formalities, and related delays. The procedures were elaborate. It was not new to me, since I am working in a centrally funded academic institution; query and delays are the routine process in the name of accountability. It was very difficult and challenging to adhere to their procedures and schedules.

Since this project was unique compared to other projects of poverty reduction, it was necessary to prepare the project staff for a totally different responsibility. We had to abide by a given target while giving equal importance to the process. Since the project was empowerment and poverty reduction, no other external agency had to work for alleviating poverty of the poor. It was the responsibility of the poor to lift themselves out of poverty. It was not wholly about poverty reduction as such, their empowerment was more important than poverty. The philosophy was poverty reduction could be achieved meaningfully only through empowerment.

In Indian context, so far we have developed a culture that we alleviate the poverty of others. In this context how to prepare the project staff is the major question. The project staff has to work as facilitator but with the sense of emotional attachment with the impoverished to empower them. Beyond the role of a facilitator they should not go to reach out the target. There is no target in the project. The target of the project is only the process. For that task we prepared the district project managers. We conducted the training programmes for batches of trainees at various levels for about two years. It was an excellent opportunity to learn for ourselves a great deal about methodologies in fieldwork, and strategies for poverty reduction. I felt a positive impact even in my capacity to deal with rural development problems after conducting a series of a training programme for the project managers.

26

Rajiv Gandhi Chair Building

All the time I found difficulties in securing space for the projects of Rajiv Gandhi Chair for Panchayati Raj Studies. At one point of time we had twenty four project staff. We have publications and to store published materials we required space. We have to conduct training programmes and for which we needed space. Seminars, workshops and training progrmmes are the regular activities of the chair. Periodically Panchayat leaders used to come for consultation and discussions. Delegation of local body leaders used to visit our Chair from different states and different countries. For all those activities we had to make temporary arrangements in classrooms, or some makeshift arrangements. We have enormous amount of training materials for dissemination they were to be stored. We were in 12 × 12 rooms until 1991, but in 2000 we were occupying a two stored building with fifteen rooms in 6000 square feet. It was enough only to house the department, staffrooms, and classrooms. So, even after getting a big building we demanded more space for the department.

Authorities were gracious enough to concede our demand by seeing the progress of the department but at the displeasure of other Departments. Seeing the displeasure I found out a way for constructing a separate building for Rajiv Gandhi Chair for Panchayat Raj Studies. When I shared this idea with my colleagues they had nothing more than a smile to offer. How to get several lakhs for this infrastructure building, and who would contribute five million rupees for this project was the major question. I approached Mr. G.K. Vasan, Rajya Sabha M.P. and a central minister. He readily agreed to offer Rs. 10 lakh. Subsequently, I met our local Member of Parliament Mr. N.S.V. Chithan. He also gave an equal amount for this building. Later, I approached Prof. M.S. Swaminathan, who gave Rs. 10 lakh.

Dr. Sundarshana Nachiappan donated Rs. 10 lakh for library of Rajiv Gandhi Chair. All these dignitaries gave financial support for Rajiv Gandhi Chair for Panchayati Raj Studies. Our work plus the support of well-wishers like the eminent persons mentioned above now we have a big building with training halls in the name of M.S. Swaminathan and G.K. Moopanar. We have a resource centre to store resource material for researchers and Panchayat leaders. We have a computing hall for offering training to Panchayat leaders in IT. We have seminar hall in the same building.

27

Collaboration with a Newspaper

Rajiv Gandhi Chair for Panchayati Raj Studies works with the mission of building a movement for grassroots governance and development. To achieve this mission we have to reach out to the masses. Primarily the potentials of the new Panchayati Raj System have to be taken to the people and particularly to the rural poor, women and *dalits*. They are the main stakeholders and they should get maximum benefit out of it. Apart from doing research, policy advocacy and training we wanted to reach out to the masses for creating awareness about the new system and to sensitize them on the issues of development and governance by providing needed information. It could be possible only through mass media. Tamil Nadu is fairly a literate state hence we thought that the newspaper is the best instrument. We were on the lookout for publishing a supplement in any one of the daily newspaper (vernacular) in Tamil Nadu. Buying space in a newspaper involves money. It is not so easy to get space in newspaper.

We approached many newspapers in this regard. We convinced successfully Mr. Lakshmipathy, publisher of a newspaper *Dinamalar*. It has got wider circulation in Tamil Nadu. When I approached the publisher of *Dinamalar*, I took the Programme Officer from the Hunger Project, New Delhi. Mr. Madhavan said that if *Dinamalar* agreed to publish it regularly, it would be a pioneering programme. Publisher of *Dinamalar* Mr. Lakshmipathy agreed to publish a full page supplement under the title **"Panchyat Malar"** every Monday. For all other practical purposes co-ordination has been done by Mr. Paul Raj in *Dinamalar*. He further made it clear that the material published in the special supplement every week Monday will have a disclaimer. He asked me to take responsibility for the material published in that page. I agreed to it. My address was printed in the supplement citing that materials published in that page wre the contributions of not the paper but the Rajiv Gandhi Chair. The layout of the supplement was fed into my computer through which we have created the supplement. It was also decided the newspaper will allot one page for it and the content has to be prepared by the Rajiv Gandhi Chair for Panchayati Raj Studies. Hence we required a research associate, a computer operator and a lawyer to make sure it went with no errors especially in legal sense of the term.

The content consisted of substantial issues of Panchayati Raj, question and answers, development issues, rules and regulations, welfare scheme details and Government order pertinent to Panchayati Raj. Further success stories and struggles were covered based on the field investigations. Every Friday the whole page supplement had to be made ready in the format of the Newspaper with suitable photos, data and other diagrams, if any. Friday evening the whole matter reached the Madurai office of the Newspaper *Dinamalar* in the form of CD. Any clarification from the newspaper office was done on Saturday. Thus, every Monday the supplement was published. We got questions from officials, Panchayat leaders, Citizens, NGOs and they were responded every week. We handled thousands of questions through this supplement. A team was involved in the whole process of preparing the supplement. For the entire exercise the Hunger Project, New Delhi supported financially. This publication lasted for one year. The Hunger Project also gave a national award for the publisher Mr. Laskshmipathi. In the whole of India no newspaper had taken such initiative. It was historic and a high impact making exercise.

Every Monday many people read the *Panchayat Malar* and kept all the issues in file. They used to write letters to government officials citing the references quoted in the *Panchayat Malar*. *Panchayat Malar* was a source of reference to many. In the beginning we wrote much about the roles and responsibility of each one elected to the rural local governance system. From Gram Sabha member to District Panchayat Presidents what were the roles to be performed by everyone in the governance arrangement of the rural local governance system. Those who read the write up used to send questions and for all the questions we gave replies in the subsequent issues. After one year a stakeholders workshop was organized large number of readers of *Panchayat Malar* attended and made useful suggestions to improve *Panchayat Malar*. It was a path breaking exercise done in Tamil Nadu. The Hunger Project tried to replicate the same in other states in India.

28

Collaborations with All India Radio

While I was in the thick of the "*Panchayat Malar*" activities large number of people asked me to reach out even beyond the newspaper-reading literates in the villages. For the semi-literates, radio is the best medium by which one can reach out to the unreached. In this context, I initiated a discussion with the Hunger Project Country Director Rita Sarin. She informed that if All India Radio (AIR) agreed to give space it can be done. I contacted the All India Radio, Madurai. The Director of the station readily agreed to the proposal positively. But, when we demanded our programme be broadcast at prime time, they took a second thought if it was possible. We had to wait for a month as all other regional stations have to agree to this proposal. The coverage of the programme planned was for the whole region of Tamil Nadu. Finally, it was agreed that on every Monday between 7.00 to 7.30 pm it would be broadcast all over the Tamil Nadu. But the AIR demanded we pay a nominal amount, especially because we occupy the prime time. The Hunger Project agreed to pay for it, and thus it was made as the Hunger Project sponsored programme.

Once it was agreed and MOU was signed, the programme was launched. Weekly recording was taking place. It was a new experience for me, as it required a music troop to play signature tunes, theme music, background music etc. Further an anchor was needed to coordinate the programme for every episode. Anchor had to have a good voice. Experts were needed to make a brief talk about the subject and give reply to the questions. To cover the success stories and stories of struggles we had to identify such Panchayat leaders, and we had to bring such people to recording theatre. They were to be recorded properly by interviewing those people. For this task also we needed experts. Finally, all the events were to be arranged in a sequence as designed by the experts in All India Radio. For exactly thirty minutes we had to record programme for the every week. Every Friday, the cassette had to be handed over to All India Radio Madurai. They checked it on Saturday. If there was any problem we had to attend to it immediately so that it could be broadcasted on Monday. As an academician I felt it much complicated, and very methodical and disciplined at the same time.

But, we did it with much enthusiasm. We sought the help of a retired professor from Gandhigram Rural Institute. Late Prof. V. Rengarajan helped me in writing script and poems for jingles on Panchayati Raj. Angu music troop from Dindigul helped me in producing needed music. All the project staff identified the model Panchayat leaders and they were brought to studio for recording. For question and answer, Mr. Vallinayagm—a retired Additional Director for Rural Development helped by visiting Gandhigram every week. The whole programme was carried out for six months. It was one of the important programmes of Rajiv Gandhi Chair for Panchayati Raj Studies with the financial support of the Hunger Project.

29

One Semester Germany Experience

Cologne University of Germany invited me to teach some courses to the students, who are interested in Indian studies for one semester starting from April first to 30th September, 2011. Though I was informed well in advance offer letter came only in the month of February from Cologne University. As per original schedule I agreed to go over to Germany to take up this assignment in 2012. All of a sudden I was requested by Prof. Niclas Ulrikas to take up this assignment in 2011. Since, I fixed marriage for my only daughter on 21st of March, 2011 my friends helped me in organizing the marriage and they relieved me from all the responsibilities in Gandhigram. I reached Cologne on 1st April, 2011 at 8.30 am. On 4th evening we had a meeting with a large number of students in the seminar hall of the Indology Department of Cologne University. I was introduced to the students by Prof. Nicolas Ulrikas of Indology Department and the courses I was to offer to the students in the whole semester. Even before my arrival in Cologne my name was put up in the university website as Guest Professor visiting the University for one semester. Since my name was in the website of the University, the students who were interested in Indian Studies could go through my profile by browsing through the Rajiv Gandhi Chair Website. They were fully aware of my specialization and hence they asked me about the courses I was to offer. I explained to them the courses I was planning to offer. There was a discussion on the contents of the courses. I put them across and clarified. They also indicated what they were more interested in. Finally, I agreed to give the following three courses:

(a) Indian Society,
(b) Rural Local Governance, and

(c) Critical Issues of development in India.

The third one critical issues of development was given as colloquium. Once the courses were decided, yet another discussion started on the timing of the courses. Students had already registered for other courses also. They did not want any clash in timings of courses. I did not expect it, but it took several rounds of discussions to come to a consensus on timings. All the above courses had to be given in Indology Department. It was to be mentioned here that some of the students could not be accommodated as their timings were not suitable to timings fixed by majority who participated in the discussions. Seventeen students had registered for the course on Indian society; eleven students had been registered for Rural Local Governance in India. For the colloquium, depending on the topic the students could choose. They needed no registration.

Once everything was finalized in Indology Department Prof. Niclas Ulrikas, Vice-Director of the DAAD project associated with Centre for Modern Indian Studies informed me that I had to take one more course to the Centre for Modern Indian Studies. Then I contacted Prof. Dr. Malhias Pilz, Director of Modern Indian Studies. He briefed that a course was announced to the master students from the Centre for Modern Indian Studies. I had to organize only bloc seminar. It was for the whole day from 10.00 am to 4.30 pm. I agreed to give the bloc seminar titled "Education and Business in India". It had to be conducted as a workshop. This bloc seminar had to be conducted in a hall at the Centre for Modern Indian Studies. Prof. Mathew Pilz enabled me by providing Teacher Assistants to conduct the bloc seminar. The classrooms in Indology and seminar hall in Centre for Modern Indian Studies were fully equipped electronically to conduct the classes' more effectively. Computer was provided to me. I kept it for six months. A new official email id was created for official transaction (gpalanit@mi.kolen.de). Students used to contact me only through that e-mail. I had handled the classes from 4th April to 15th July, 2011. Five students joined the "Education and Business in India". For all the courses, I had given references with full details. It was one hour thirty minutes duration. One hour fifteen minutes I used to take and fifteen minutes I had given to the students for questions.

In the bloc seminar I used to make presentations, which was followed by discussions. During my presentations I had to show the different websites for references. Students had registered for their courses through a centralized process for using the programme given by the University. It was centralized management, but each programme was decentralized. Students had wide choices to finalize the courses, but all within the established framework. The whole educational programme was carried out through electronic mode. Without having adequate skill in operating computer it was very difficult to run a course effectively. We could use dust-free chalk pieces, over head projector, and white board; and yet computer PowerPoint slides served as the powerful instrument. Hence, I put computer to the maximum use in my class room interactions. What I learnt in the whole process of one semester teaching in Cologne University could be narrated as follows.

Students were very serious in attending the classes. They were alert, active, committed, serious, sensitive, attentive, and communicative and future oriented. Since they select the courses, they were keen in attending the classes, taking notes, raising questions, asking for references. Because the classroom was active and students were attentive, teachers found enormous interest in conducting classes. Totally I was absorbed in the classroom lectures. Teaching such students was always enjoyable. Students were punctual to the class. When they had a point of view of clarification, they put their hands up, indicating that they have something to get clarified. After discussion and clarification lecture continued. Students asked for established references for many of our arguments, and ask for data to support an argument. In such a way they develop their skill, capacity and capability.

Generally, during arguments in India, the non-seriousness of Indian students was associated with tuition-fee waiver (or they need not pay any tuition fees). But, in Germany also students were not paying tuition fees and yet they were serious in studies. One big difference I observed was: In Germany for the sake of showing a big number in the enrolment of students in higher education, students were not given admission. The rigorous process they have does not allow non-serious students to get admitted in higher education. In the secondary school system filtration takes place very effectively and students are allowed to go for higher education only through passing the examination called Abitur. Hence the students coming to higher education institution feel that it is their fortunate they got through and they are going to be in higher place in the society because of their higher education background. When they go for higher education, they need not pay the tuition fees and moreover they get lot of concessions from the government. I could see complete seriousness of the students in their studies.

When they come for classes they come with preparation since they got references well in advance from the teacher. They make presentations on the topics they have chosen. Their presentation is made in the allotted time and they are submitted in the form of CDs to the course teacher.

One day there was a heavy rain in Köln. I doubted if the students could make it to the class, and thought that the attendance might be very thin. After reaching the Department, before the class started, I went to the classroom to check how many students had arrived. To my surprise I found that all the students were present. As usual I completed my class. After the class was over I asked the students how they reached the class in the heavy rain. One student (Mr. Hans, I quite remember his name) said that Germans have to work in hard weather conditions. The way they dress and their energy level enabled them to carry out their day-to-day tasks without any problems, effectively and efficiently. He showed me his bag. He had leather jacket, a pull over, a sweater, an umbrella, a light banyan, a cake, a cold drink, writing note book, pen, pencil, marker and a small bough having different types of cards. Intra-day variation in weather conditions is very unpredictable in Germany, and so everyone carry all protective clothes. Depending on the change in weather they wear dresses, for which Indians are not exposed to. Whether it is winter or spring or summer, people have to use the suitable cloth and they have to carry out their works. All the time I could observe seriousness in the students of Higher Education in Germany.

I never had the experience of conducting a bloc seminar in India in Gandhigram. It was a new experience for me. But, it was thrilling and enjoyable experience. Morning 10.00 am I had to start my presentations on the theme chosen for the day. Once my presentation was over students have to raise questions on the presentation, for which I had to be prepare to answer/clarify. Subsequently, I gave some exercise to the students on the presentation and discussion.

Once they completed that exercise I had to make my second presentation. After the presentation, again it is followed by questions and discussions and subsequently I gave exercises to the students, which goes for almost one hour. Then I had to continue the seminar till evening 4.30. Finally, I gave an assignment of documenting the whole seminar of the day and the report had to be prepared by every student. In the report every student had to write important points they learnt in the presentation plus discussion. Further, they have to indicate what they expect from the teacher for the next

(*Contd.*)

bloc seminar. In such a way the bloc seminar was conducted. The reports were prepared by the students individually for every bloc seminar.

It was part of the evaluation methodology that every student would be evaluated in the bloc seminar based on a paper submitted by the students. Every student selected a problem and a paper had to be prepared. To prepare a paper general guideline is given. The paper has to be prepared based on the guidelines.

In all these bloc seminars, one exercise that does not fade from my memory is this. I mentioned earlier in this book that all the discussions and presentations were on the issue of development in India. Whenever I put across serious of problems and crisis of the Indian society, the students identified opportunities for business. They identified more than 60 business ventures out of the development crisis faced by Indian society. It revealed their mental-orientation. It brought forth their optimism. It made open their problem-solving mind-set. It was a remarkable exercise. All the students submitted their reports as per schedule. Once the reports were submitted; they have computer software that identifies the originality of the paper. Once it is confirmed that they have not lifted the material, the documents get passed on to the course teacher for evaluation. In such a way the bloc seminar was organized. It was an interesting exercise I was involved in.

30

UGC Innovative Programme

The University Grants Commission (UGC) had given an advertisement calling for proposals to design innovative academic programmes. I saw that advertisement and held a discussion with my colleagues. I found the idea interesting because we strongly felt that our 5-year Integrated M.A. Programme in Development Administration was indeed an innovation, and successful. Almost all the departments especially in social sciences and more particularly the political science are not able to hold up the lure of the engineering. No matter whether you become practical engineer by mind-set or an engineer in a paper certificate, the reality is both parents and students are after engineering programmes. And so, social sciences do not get adequate students. The paradox is our department has got more than hundred students in M.A. Development Administration.

Ten years ago, I could sense a tilt taking place towards more skilled courses or job oriented courses. I felt that social science courses would face severe setback in the years to come. Hence, I mooted a proposal to the then Vice-Chancellor that I wanted to launch a new programme not for the sake of taking students in a new nomenclature but to provide an academic programme which would provide job opportunities to them in the development sector. He asked me to write a small note on the objective of the programme and the expected job market. I wrote a small note and he called me for a discussion. We had nearly two hours discussion and finally, he asked me to constitute the Board of Studies. With the help of my colleagues I prepared a detailed syllabus for M.A. 5-year integrated programme on Development Administration. We prepared the programme in such a way that the students could go in three streams. First, for writing competitive examination to go for civil services; secondly, orient them to go as middle level managers in development organizations; and thirdly, they could go for higher studies for academic positions. We have taken best modules from the best institutions of the world for the programme.

Exceptionally and unconventionally we reconstituted the Board of Studies by incorporating not routine academics from other university but more resourceful persons from the civil society and civil service to critically review our proposal. The Board of Studies consisted of retired civil servants, representatives of civil society and academics from leading research institutes like Institute for Socio-Economic Change (ISEC), Bangalore. The Board thoroughly and critically examined the courses and modules from the perspective of prevailing development trends, the context, market and the objectives of GRI. The programme was thrashed out, and lots of modifications were done. It was finalized. Then I placed it before the Academic Council. For about one hour Academic Council reviewed and discussed the programme. Their finding was there was no such precedence in social science to have five year integrated programme in the nearby universities, so we had better stop it. But, then the Vice-Chancellor strongly opined that the Department of Political Science came out with an innovative proposal and that it was to be appreciated. Since, it was innovative, we should not view it with the conventional norms of approving a programme. He wanted it be considered seriously off-the-beaten track and approved. The programme got approved.

The programme is going successfully till date. The in-take is 20. Every year twenty students pass out, and of them at least fifteen students find employment opportunity either in the development organizations or in research organizations. Based on the success of the M.A. Five-year Integrated Programme on Development Administration, I prepared a proposal to start yet another M.A. Programme in Governance and Development. This programme was designed with an objective of meeting the market needs in international NGOs. For the increasing need of man power requirement in large number of development organizations, research institutions, we designed this programme. I submitted the proposal to UGC and I was asked to make a presentation. I made a presentation and I got the sanction.

31

UGC Special Assistance Programme

First the time I submitted a proposal for Special Assistance Programme (SAP) to UGC from GRI. When my proposal reached the Registrar Office for onward transmission, the then Registrar Dr. M. Kanniappan gave my copy to the Mathematics Department and asked the then Head of the Department to prepare a proposal for Special Assistance Programme. When I contacted our office, they informed me that the department of mathematics is also preparing proposal for the same they demanded a model copy and hence the office has given our copy to them. Finally, the two proposals had been sent to the UGC by our office. I went to the UGC to make a presentation. I made a presentation. It was appreciated as I have replied to all their queries to their satisfaction. But somehow it was approved that time.

Once when I was in New Delhi, I met the Joint Secretary to the UGC who was responsible for it. I asked him why our proposal was not sanctioned. I found honesty in his response, and at the end of the brief discussion, he asked me to apply again. With a learning perspective, I started asking some probing questions on why the proposal was turned down, and what drawbacks they found in it. He told me openly that politics in academic institutions are much worse than the real politics that politician's are involved in. His symbolic reply was: 'Don't ask me the reasons, but I insist you apply again'. Then I applied again. When I made presentation in the UGC, there was no academic from Tamil Nadu in the expert panel and I found one professor from Jawaharlal Nehru University (JNU), New Delhi. This JNU person asked me a series of questions. I replied all the questions. It was like competing with the Department of Political Science in many Central Universities. But the good news was that I got it the next time. It was also for local governance because I covered substantial grounding through my action research projects.

Here I want to make it clear that I did not work for elevating the status of the Department or to elevate my position. But, I worked hard for the fifteen years in local governance with an intension and objective of transforming the rustic folk through local governance. In this process the Department has emerged as a strong unit of specialization in rural local governance.

32

Infrastructure Development from Projects

Normally, for infrastructure and for basic facilities Academics look for help from the UGC. I found out that a Department can get all the basic facilitates, equipments, infrastructure even without the support of the University Administration and the UGC. All the time I used to tell my friends that excepting the building all the facilities in the Department of Political Science were obtained through the projects. In our Department we have more than forty computers, five printers, copier machines, Wi-Fi system, Generator set, separate library developed from the projects. The air-conditioned seminar hall has five hundred chairs, desks, executive tables, executive chairs have been purchased from the projects. One computing room with twenty personal computers with two air-conditioning machines. They have been created exclusively for the use of the students, faculty and project staff. A seminar hall with a capacity of 50 seats with AC had been created in the Department. Even for stationery, we rarely rely on the provision from the central office. Since in every project we have an item of stationery in the budget we utilize the provision to procure stationery. We lend our seminar hall to other Department for conducting small meetings, seminar or workshop. We have LCD and laptops for each teacher and each researcher.

When I joined in 1991 the Department was functioning in 12 × 12 room. There was no Attender and there was no clerk. Now every teacher is sitting in a single room with one Personal Computer (PC) and one laptop. Every teacher is provided with one bureau and small book rack to keep their books and records. Their PCs are connected with internet. Research scholars have separate rooms with adequate furniture. From the provisions available in the SAP budget I have created smart classrooms also in the Department. We have two main buildings now. One is the department in the old building, and other is Rajiv Gandhi Chair for Panchayati Raj Studies building, which is newly constructed. The one I mentioned constructed out of the funds Rs. 40 lakh given by four Members of Parliament. Now we have class rooms for all the students with adequate facilities, project rooms, smart classrooms, seminar hall, computing room, and research scholar's room, department library, training halls, project office, department office, and stock room. All the facilities have been developed through projects. Compared to what we have created, the amount of money we get in every five year plan for the improvement of our department was miniscule. Since, it is a small university, we got only relatively less money from the UGC, and within the amount all the departments have to be developed. Seeing the improvements of the department, our University authorities allocate even less for our department, perhaps on the assumption that can build on our own. Take a look at the pictures below for the facilities we have developed in a single department.

33

The Ford Foundation Project

My association with the Ford Foundation is one and half decades old. Working with the Ford Foundation is always a creative and enjoyable experience. Since it is context-specific and creative, it was always challenging as well. I must mention that GRI's association with the Ford Foundation is six decades old. Ford Foundation works like a partner in your development/research endeavour and never as a donor who have provided financial assistance to a recipient. It is memorable, enjoyable and eventful relationship as it works on ideas. We may succeed or fail in our attempts and activities but we gain rich experience. They Ford Foundation had the mandate to work with the excluded, marginalized and the deprived. But it is always supportive, facilitative and enabling. If at all we faced any problem in executing project activities, they have never been due to the Foundation, but due to the poor handling of the same at our end in our university. But the Foundation looks for response from the person who is holding the project not on the Institute. From project formulation to account settlement the Foundation closely worked with the project staffs.

I started the project work with the Ford Foundation during the period of Mr. Mark Robinson, who was the programme officer for a division. I met him in different meetings in New Delhi and other places and I had long conversation with him three times. Finally, when Ms. Devaki Jain discussed with him about the proposal of federating the elected women representatives based on her visit to Gandhigram and discussion with me, he has agreed to discuss the concept further. Later in Singamma Srinivasan Foundation, Bangalore we met and discussed the proposal and he gave his suggestions. Later a well developed proposal was sent to the Ford Foundation, New Delhi. The Foundation gave sanction to the project. As a partner I associated myself with the Ford Foundation project coordinated by Devaki Jain. We carried out the activities for about three years in Tamil Nadu with our own partners. The whole journey was innovative, creative, challenging, and joyful. And it was facilitated by the Ford Foundation. The first phase was evaluated by an external agency from the London School of Economics. She submitted a report and based on the report the project was extended for one more term. Another three years we continued our activities. In the meanwhile Mark Robinson had gone back to his country, England. Another Programme Officer joined in the Ford Foundation. Dr. Bishnu Mohapatra joined and extended his support to all the activities. I documented all the activities carried out in Tamil Nadu and I analyzed the process also. Totally for six years we actively facilitated the elected women representative's federations. In the meanwhile several agencies started supporting such initiatives not only in Tamil Nadu but also in other states.

The Ford Foundation changed its priority of activities and it wanted to concentrate on governance and accountability issues. Hence, after completing the six years project I have submitted yet another project on "Globalization and Decentralization" to the Ford Foundation. I was asked to make a presentation before the Global team in New Delhi. I made a presentation for about ten minutes. There itself they have approved the concept note. Then I have prepared the detailed proposal. It is an action project. The idea of the project was to study the impact of globalization at the grassroots without having any predetermined notion. The crux was to find out if globalization processes brought forth any significant advantage, and if it had brought out, how those advantages could be harnessed through the decentralization of powers. In the same way, if we find any threat or negative impact out of globalization, how the threat could be effectively tackled through decentralization of powers.

Accordingly seven rural development sectors, namely livelihood of the poor, water supply, sanitation, fishing, crafts and skills, agriculture, plantation sector and so on have been selected for analysis. All the reports have been presented in a validation workshop. The experts who were invited for the workshop commented on the reports. Based on the comments reports were published. Based on the experience of the first phase second phase of the project was sanctioned. It was really a challenging task and I continued the studies in another set of issues and reports were published after the validation workshop. On the whole process, several articles and monographs were written.

Based on the experience local body leaders were federated to tackle the issues arising out of globalization. In order to help the local body leaders, NGOs were federated. Subsequently, the local body leaders and NGO representatives were periodically invited for training and refresher programmes. In order to disseminate the research findings a news letter was published periodically and distributed among the media representatives local body leaders, NGO representatives and academic institutions. All our activities were supported and facilitated by the Ford Foundation.

34

Publication of Books and Monographs

It is always my habit to connect myself with the academic world through publications of books and articles in research journals. Apart from books I write thematic monographs. Books are published through reputed publishers from New Delhi. Monographs are published with the support of funding agencies. Apart from research articles and books I write popular articles and they are being published by Tamil magazines and newspapers. I compile all the popular articles which are already published in newspaper and magazines, and publish them in the form of books. They are being published by the publications of the left-oriented groups as the articles are relating to development issues and governance.

35

Role in *Paadam* (A Tamil Monthly Journal)

I teach Development Administration to the students at master's level. I have a firm belief that unless we have development politics we cannot expect development administration deliver public goods effectively and efficiently. I have been discussing this concept with many public figures whoever I happened to hold a discussion with. My friend Mr. Narayanan, a committed social worker came to Gandhigram for a programme. During that time we had a discussion on publishing a Tamil magazine on Development Politics. He immediately responded that he wanted to take up this assignment. He laid out two conditions. One, I should be a member in the editorial team and secondly, I should agree to contribute one article on governance and development politics for each issue without demanding remuneration. I responded positively. Till date I have been contributing one article for each issue of *Paadam*. *Paadam* is a Tamil word meaning 'lesson'.

Primarily *Paadam* was intended to create awareness among the well meaning citizens on development crisis in India and development alternative. The articles in *Paadam* are not mere essays or perceptions. They are all well-researched articles with data, analysis and with evidences. It is not intended to criticise policies, programmes and schemes of the government but to critique policies and suggest ways and means to improve them. The intension is not to bring problems alone for discussion, but to be part of solutions. Mr. Narayanan being the editor always looked for articles with substance on critical issues of development. He is always looking for credible people to write for *Paadam*. *Paadam* normally invited articles from select individuals. Sometimes he paid for articles. There are certain individuals who are continuously struggling with people to secure entitlement of the poor. Such individuals are invited to write article for *Paadam* and for them he pays. All the articles I have contributed are in my CV appended in this volume as part II. *Paadam* publishes articles on health, education, science, technology, youth, children, women, labourers, agriculture, governance, administration, marginalized, dalits and social evils.

36

Global and Local: A News Letter

"Global and Local" is a news letter, we have published periodically with the support of the Ford Foundation. We have undertaken series of research on several issues which affected the rustic folk in the rural areas. We have undertaken sectoral studies. The primary concern is to disseminate the research findings with various stakeholders. To reach out to the policy makers, NGO representatives, media representatives, opinion makers, Panchayat leaders news letter has been periodically prepared and published. Every news letter, one thematic research finding will be presented. While discussing the issues based on field research, solutions and actionable points will also be given. For each and every issue, grassroots reactions have been captured and presented. One Guest most probably an eminent person and an expert, will be asked to contribute for a column. Views and Counter-views on the same theme will also be collected from different stakeholders and the same are being published stories both success and struggles are captured and published. Policy review been done with the help of an expert and they are also published. Moreover occasional papers and monographs have been prepared based on the data collected extensively from the field.

37

Broader Connections

My basic desire is to make everything simple. We are living in the world of complexities. I have a crude notion that people are marginalized in development and governance because both have been mystified and complicated. In order to enable the excluded to be included in the process of governance and development, both have to be simplified and demystified. When I go to any place for delivery of lecture, I go with full preparation. My speech would be in the form of power point presentation. All academic presentations are well prepared on serious issues of governance, decentralization and development. The prepared presentations are kept in my resource centre. They can be used by any student, researcher, or teacher at anytime. All such presentations are kept in a rewritable CD and they are in the resource room. Many such presentations are with animation background.

38

Seminars, Workshops and Conferences

From 1991 onwards I have been organising conferences, seminars, and workshops on themes related to decentralized governance and administration. It is always my design to invite people who are relevant there and those who can contribute substantially on the theme of the event. I invite representatives from civil society, media, and representative of the people, retired officials and academics who are active in the chosen filed. We always do our work in a focused way to generate ideas for policy advocacy. We conduct workshops for preparation of training modules and curriculum for specific courses and programmes. All our seminars and workshop documents have been either printed with the funds available with us or published through reputed publishers.

39

SARVAM: A Rural Transformation Unit

SARVAM is Sri Aurobindo Rural and Village Action Movement working in two villages in Villupuram district of Tamil Nadu. Its primary role is to facilitate the community to take responsibility of their life and destiny. It has to help the entire village community to take charge of their own destiny and future. It has to work for the empowerment of the community. In the villages a transformative experiment was underway for more than five years. I was asked to make an analysis of the whole experiment. Further, the Sri Aurobindo Society asked me to be in their board to guide the rural development activities. Our University has given consent and after I associated myself with SARVAM activities, I visited many times the field and guided the people who worked in the project as Coordinators. In this process, I have learnt as much as what I have given to the project. After a thorough analysis of the outcomes of all the rural development activities done by SARVAM I distilled the basic principles that worked in the process of transformation of the village community. I made this presentation to the Cadbury officials (who actually contributed resources to SARVAM for rural development activities under Corporate Social Responsibility) and a World Bank team. In fact, both advised me to use it as a tool for policy advocacy to change the rural development policy and approach. SARVAM experiments are exciting experiments which have emerged as an alternative paradigm for rural development. They further asked me to take it to both Centre and State Planning Commissions to influence them for policy corrections. Before moving further they asked me to make a story that is documenting the whole experiment for dissemination. I am doing it now which will be published soon. In order to disseminate the principles of rural transformation a new institute has been created. It is called International Institute for Rural Transformation. The main objective and purpose of this institute is to create transformative leaders for rural development. To perform the above, a training programme has to be designed. Further this institute has to disseminate the basic principles of transformation based on the experiments conducted here and elsewhere. It should act as a policy advocacy unit. To activate the whole process, the Sri Aurobindo Society requested me to take up the responsibility. I asked them to contact our institute authorities. They contacted our university authorities. They have requested the authorities of the university to depute me to the newly created institute. They have agreed to the conditions stipulated by our Institute. They have sent the order directly to our Vice-Chancellor.

Still, I am doing the work assigned to me by SARVAM with the old arrangement.

40

Media Role in Our Activities

The Department of Political Science and Development Administration at Gandhigram Rural Institute is performing the three dimensional activities, namely Academic, Research and Outreach professionally. Whether it is academic programme, or research programmes, or outreach programmes, they are being carried out professionally with a sense of commitment and sincerity. The focus will be on outcome not on output. From 1991 onwards our programmes came in print and electronic media. In our entire programme one would find the presence of hard core academics, activities from the civil society and people from government. In such a way we maintained seriousness in our programmes. We conducted programme not for the sake of programme.

Whenever we organise programmes and events we used to invite the media for coverage. Promptly media attended all our programmes and they are covered. All the press clippings had been collected and they come to seven volumes. Special interviews have conducted with author published in newspapers and magazines.

41

Cambodian Team Visits

Whenever any team comes either from others states of India or from other countries people at the helm of affairs advised them to visit Gandhigram for the simple reason that they get needed reading material and they will be engaged meaningfully through a scientific process. When Members of Parliament in Cambodia demanded reservation of seats for women, the Government of Cambodia constituted a committee with Members of Parliament to visit India to get know what is the impact of one-third reservation of seats for women in local bodies. They were brought to Gandhigram for an interaction.

We invited experts, civil society representatives, officials, elected members representatives for interaction. The team visited Gandhigram Rural Institute and participate in our programme. We prepared needed reading material and supplied the same to them.

42

Popular Article Writings

For along I have not written any popular article to newspapers and magazines for popular or public consumption. Many of my friends asked me to write popular articles on governance, politics, administration and development. Yet, I was not convinced and apart from the conviction I never thought that it is my duty and responsibility to connect directly with the community. I realised when I joined in Gandhigram Rural Institute. Since a teacher has to discharge three responsibilities, namely teaching, research and outreach, the third activity outreach, has to be done effectively through writing popular articles in Tamil newspapers and magazines. I started writing popular articles after joining Gandhigram Rural Institute. I started writing articles for *Dinamani* Tamil newspaper. After started publishing articles in *Dinamani* I was contacted many for writing such articles in small magazines. Later I was asked to write article for *Tamil Ozai* another Tamil newspaper. By following the *Dinamani* and *Tamil Ozai* I have started writing articles for *Janasakthi*. I have published major articles as central page in *Dinamani* or *Tamil Ozai* or *Janasakthi*. I used to get telephone call at least not less than fifty appreciating, commenting, criticising the articles. In my opinion I am known to a section of readers in Tamil Nadu only through these articles. *Dinamani* is published by express group of companies; *Tamil Ozai* is being published by Pattali Makkal Katchi supporters and *Janasakthi* a newspaper of the Communist party of India.

Following the newspapers I have been asked to write article for Tamil magazines, namely *Om Sakthi*, *India Today*, *Puthia Thalaimurai*, *Junior Vikatan* occasionally. Apart from the articles I have written, articles by others in magazines have quoted me statements and observations. Apart from the above I gave interview to newspapers, magazines and electronic media.

43

Outreach Activities

Outreach activities generally mean reaching out to the society by moving out from the classroom and laboratory exercises. Teachers in higher learning institutions have teaching and research activities confined to the institutions. Moving beyond teaching and research to reaching out to the stakeholders is outreach. But, it is not practiced in over conventional higher learning institutions. Academic and research institutions are in vacuum and they are in the society and it is the responsibility of the higher learning institutions to involve themselves in the affairs of the communities and society by extending an idea, or knowledge, or technology or any service or contribution directly.

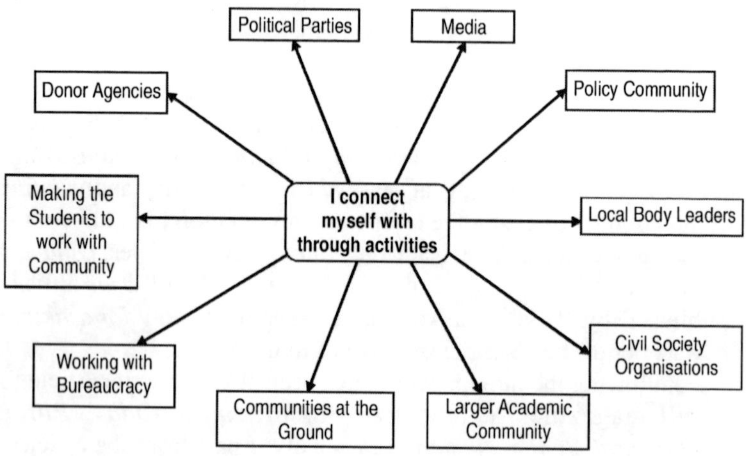

I conduct extension activities in different forms. It may be awareness creation in the villages, conducting capacity building exercises for the local body leaders, providing expert opinion to the members of legislative assembly or members of parliament, serving in committees of the government for policy advocacy, providing needed information input to the political parties.

Apart from the above I putt students in the villages, institutions and organizations to learn the existing culture in the villages, institutions and organizations. While learning from the places, they do some services in the villages and organizations. Village stays are minimum number of days but maximum number of days they stay in organizations and institutions.

While students are involved in outreach activities, their concern for poor, marginalized will be increased. Along with that their sensitivity in increased. Staying in a remote village with several difficulties increases the coping up skill among the students. Their leadership, commitment passion, concern, ability to connect and other inmate talents are exhibited. Outreach programmes not only making the students to serve the communities but also to learn from the communities.

44

Translated the Speeches of VIPs

First time in my life I got an opportunity to translate the speeches of Prime Minister of India when he came to Madurai. My Vice-Chancellor informed me that he was invited to translate the speech of the Prime Minister when he came to launch the Sethusamudram Project in Madurai. He asked me to go along with him. I went with him to get the details and adopt formalities. Next day morning I got a telephone call from the chairman of the Sethusamundram Project and he informed me that the speeches of the Prime Minister and Sonia Gandhi have to be translated by you and not your Vice-Chancellor. I told him that he has already agreed to perform the task and now you are changing the decision. He clarified that we got the written order from our authority that the speech has to be translated by Prof. G. Palanithurai. Yet another call came from the office of the Vice-Chancellor. I took up the receiver and our Vice-Chancellor was in the line. He asked me to translate the speech of the Prime Minister. Initially hesitated, later I was forced to accept this role. I had many occasions in the past to translate the speeches of Gandhians who visited Gandhigram from the north India and abroad. I went to Madurai and met the Chairman of the project. He briefed me that he would get the tentative speech around 2 O'clock in the afternoon for the 4 O'clock function. It was only tentative. I was taken to the control room around 1 O'clock. I got the speech. I started reading many ministers came inside and asked for the text. I have not shown and I kept quiet. Later they went out from the room. I reached the venue of the programme. I was kept behind the podium. When Prime Minister reached the stage I was instructed to meet the Prime Minister. I met him in the same stage. He briefed the methodology to be followed in the translation. Even before he came to dais I was briefed by the Minister in charge of the Ministry T.R. Balu that I should not translate sentence by sentence but I have to translate the essence of the speech. Since time available for the meeting was limited. I did job and I saw a news item in the next day newspaper that I have deliberately oriented the name which was mentioned by the Prime Minister in his speech. It became a controversy. I contacted the chairman of the project and asked him about the news item about the controversy. He told me that the translation was excellent to the satisfaction of the organizers and the Prime Minister office. Every one appreciated the translation and the controversy is due to the remarks made by both the minister and a party leader in the meeting and incidentally your name was dragged and you need not bother. This was his reply. Later the same controversy appeared in a magazine also.

Later when Prime Minister came to inaugurate the four lane roads, I got invitation from the surface Transport Ministry. The programme held very near to Dindigul and I did the same translation for the Prime Minister. That was my second translation for the Prime Minister. It was appreciated by everyone. There was no controversy during that time.

In yet another occasion I got invitation to translate the speech of the Vice-President of India Dr. Hammid Ansari in Mayiladuthurai. During that I was in a field conducting fieldwork for my project. I was aked to go over to Mayiladuthurai to attend the programme. I went to the programme venue and met the local MLA who was in charge of the programme. He told me that Mr. Manisankar Aiyar asked you to translate the speech of the Vice-President of India. He further informed me that he has fixed a few college teachers to translate the speeches of other VIPs. I translated the speeches of the Vice-President of India. Mr. Manisankar Aiyar appreciated me for the work done by me.

After a long gap, I received a phone call from Mr. G.K. Vasan and he asked me to translate the speeches of the Prime Minister who was visiting Chennai. I have agreed to do so. But I informed him that it was the political meeting. Later I received a telephone call from him and he told me that since it was a political party election campaign meet, any party functionary would perform the task. Someone did the translation during that meeting and it was not to the level of expectation and in the middle of the meeting the person who translated the speech has been changed.

It was my fortune that I got the opportunity to translate the speeches of our Prime Minister and Vice-President of India. Whenever our Chancellor came to Gandhigram, I used to translate the speech of our chancellor for the Tamil audience.

45

Meeting Rahul Gandhi

I met the Vice president (Currently President) of Indian National Congress Rahul Gandhi three times. Two times our discussions were brief. Third time it was for one and half hours in his office at Delhi. What I found in him is seeking truth and honestly discussing with others with a learning spirit. I met many politicians and interacted with them many times. I find rare qualities in him. In our political culture our political leaders try to give an image that they are knowledgeable and they use to talk more and they will make others to listen. Whereas in the case of Rahul Gandhi, he was open, simple, eager to listen open to advice and ready for interaction. His approach of keeping others to his level and speaking plainly will attract everyone. Normally whenever I met politicians I keep myself respect intact. In all the three meetings I found in rahul Gandhi is his indomitable energy to rejuvenate his party. Normally party leaders that too at a higher level refuse accept the reality and will not face criticism. But he is of a different type. He accepts reality, and openly admits the lapses in his party. He makes everyone whom he meets to feel that they have to work with him and in such a way he treats everyone. In all my interactions and his responses I found in him the democratic leadership respecting people and believing people. At one point of time I said that public relation activities of the opposition are very effective and at the Congress camp is not effective. His reply really touched me. He said people cannot be delivered and truth cannot be covered. Congress has to work with the people for them and earn the heart of the people. For goods advertisement will work and to in the hearts, one has to work on the truth. This was the reply which attracted me very much.

First time when I met in Vingna Bhawan I also shared dais with him along with Mr. Manisankar Aiyar. In front of him I spoke and my speech was on empowerment. I said "in our country we have His/ Her Excellency President of India, Honourable Prime Minister, Honourable Ministers, most respected Members of Parliament, His/ Her Excellency Governor of a State, Honourable Chief Minister, Honourable Ministers, most respected Members of Legislature Assembly, respected officials, where is our citizens? Are they honourable? The reality is they are mere beneficiaries and petitioners and rarely they are voters and never they be the honourable citizens." In the same meeting he took reference from my speech and he said that the need of the hour is to empower our people. In all his speech he maintained that to transform this country we have to work with people. Never had he said that I will transform the country. What I found in him is remarkable insight into the transformative process of the society. He may not be an aggressive politician with an appetite for power; but he will be a matured politician with respect for contribution, history, people and concern for poor. Hence, I feel that I had a fortune of meeting him thrice personally and I spoke in a dais along with him. I met many intellectuals who met Rahul Gandhi and asked their opinion. None told me that he is not a Prime Ministerial material.

Against the background, when I was asked by a Tamil magazine to write about Rahul Gandhi that too why Rahul Gandhi should become the Prime Minister of India.

My Upward and Downward Connectivity

On decentralization process, it was our intension, aim, and goal to make our Department as a modal centre for policy consolation and action congltataion. Constantully, I connect myself with policy community at the top and community at the ground. Having work in this area and created a track record. Government of India and Government of Tamil Nadu put me as nameless of many committees. State Planning Commission, State Finance Commission, High Power Committee for Devolution, Training Committee assigned tasks to me periodically and they put me in committees. All those committees I have performed my roles.

Part–II

CURRICULUM VITAE OF PROF. G. PALANITHURAI

1. Executive C.V. of Prof. G. Palanithurai

Prof. G. Palanithurai is an academic activist working in the Department of Political Science and Development Administration, Gandhigram Rural Institute—Deemed University, fully funded by the Government of India. He specializes in Grassroots Democracy, Decentralized Governance and Development Management. He has 3-4 Years of experience in teaching, research and outreach programmes. He has designed and introduced two innovative M.A. Programmes, Development Administration (5 year integrated) and Governance and Development. He was a member of the Board of Studies in nine Central and State Universities during different periods. He has held several administrative positions such as Dean, Faculty of Social Sciences, Dean, Students Welfare, Member, Executive Council, Member Senate, Member, Finance Committee and Chairperson of many Committees of the Institute. He managed the University in the absence of the Vice-Chancellor as Chairman, Interim Administrative Committee. He has successfully supervised eighteen Ph.D. theses. At present eight scholars are pursuing research leading to the Ph.D. degree under his supervision. He was the Chairman, Research Advisory Committee for six years. He was a Visiting (Guest) Professor in Cologne University, Germany for six months from April to September 2011. Currently he is the General Secretary of the Indian Association for Vocational Education and Training Studies. He is the member of Executive Council of Indian Academy of Social Sciences. He has authored 61 and edited 22 books, 130 articles in refereed journals and 42 chapters in edited volumes, 95 monographs, and 339 popular articles in popular dailies and magazines in his area of specialization. He has prepared 42 reports based on research for National, International agencies including Government of India, Government of Tamil Nadu, Government of Kerala and State Planning Commission of Tamil Nadu. 21 books have been reviewed for different journals in social sciences. He has organized two International Programmes, (Conferences and Workshops), 25 National Programmes and 69 Regional Programmes with the financial support of various agencies. He has made presentations in 46 International Conferences, 240 National Programmes and 119 Regional Seminars and Conferences. Ten Endowment Lectures have been delivered in different Universities. Under his leadership the Department has been inducted into the Special Assistance Programme (SAP) of the UGC. He is the Coordinator of the UGC SAP of the Department of Political Science and Development Administration. He is the Coordinator of the UGC Innovative Master's Programme—Governance and Development. He was the Coordinator for preparation of Self Study Report for the accreditation of the Institute by the NAAC. He coordinated for the visit of the peer team of NAAC and during that period the Institute got 'Five' star status. He was also the Coordinator for the preparation of Tenth Five Year Plan Proposal for the Institute. He was the Warden of the Men's Hostel for a period of three years. He was a member of the Project Monitoring Committee of the University. He has availed himself of fellowships from Shastri Indo-Canadian Institute twice, World Academy of Art and Science, USA, Toolkit Foundation, and Netherlands, to visit abroad and to conduct studies and to write books. He has visited the US, Canada, Malaysia, Singapore, Sri Lanka, Senegal and Germany on academic assignments. He is the Chairperson of the Tamil Nadu Council for Sustainable Development, succeeding Dr. M.S. Swaminathan. He carried out both pure and action research projects with the support of various funding agencies to the tune of Rs. 5.47 crores. He carried out recently three action projects, namely 'Global Local' for the Ford Foundation, "preparing District Human Development Report" for the UNDP and "Panchayats and Disaster Management" for ActionAid International. He is a member of many committees of both the state and the federal governments on Decentralization and Rural Development. His action research activities are supported by the Ford Foundation, Swiss Development and Cooperation, the Hunger Project, Rajiv Gandhi Foundation, Population Foundation of India, DANIDA, Action Aid International, Ministry of Panchayati Raj, Ministry of Rural Development, Government of India, Toolkit Foundation, Netherlands, UNDP, UNICEF, State Planning Commission, World Bank and other agencies in India and abroad. He has carried out 58 projects both pure and action research to the tune of Rs. 5.47 crore. He has evolved innovative training modules to train Panchayat leaders as transformative leaders. His training modules specifically for social development, gender justice, social justice, disaster preparedness and management, globalization and decentralization have been published and widely used. He has trained nearly 8000 Gram Panchayat leaders, and of them 5000 are women and Dalit Presidents, with the support of various agencies. He has developed a leadership school in the Rajiv Gandhi Chair for Panchayati Raj Studies. He has created a support structure for the Elected Women Representatives. He has facilitated for formation of "Federation of Elected Women Representatives, Elected Dalit Women Representatives, and 'Federation of Elected Dalit Representatives". He was a Member of High Level Committee headed by the Minister for Local Bodies Government of Tamil Nadu for Devolution of Powers. He is a member of the Special Committee headed by the Minister for Local Bodies, Government of Tamil Nadu to devolve adequate resources to village panchayats.

To support the activities of the Panchayat leaders, he has created a forum named "Tamil Nadu Campaign for Panchayati Raj" with the support of NGOs. He has worked for the preparation of the Tenth and the Eleventh Five Year Plan for Tamil Nadu through the State Planning Commission. He worked for the 1st, 2nd, and 3rd State Finance Commissions and for which he conducted a number of studies related to panchayat finance. In collaboration with a popular Tamil daily *Dinamalar* (with 5 lakh circulation) he published a special supplement for one full page on Grassroots democracy entitled '*Panchayat Malar*' for one year. In collaboration with All India Radio, he broadcasted a programme on "Good Governance through Local Governance" every Monday between 7.30 and 8.00 pm throughout Tamil Nadu. He is the editor of a Newsletter "Global and Local" published with the support of the Ford Foundation. He has created eight endowments with the help of several agencies and donors. He helped seventy four Gram Panchayats to prepare micro plans. He has been involved in tsunami relief work and helped seventeen Gram Panchayats to evolve reconstruction micro plans with the support of the Hunger Project. He prepared two District Human Development Reports for Dindigul and Nagapattnam districts with the support of UNDP and Tamil Nadu State Planning Commission. He took initiative to sign MoU with University of Hannover and Cologne University. He has mobilized resources to the tune of Rs. 46 lakh from four Members of Parliament to construct a building for Rajiv Gandhi Chair for Panchayati Raj Studies. He was the adviser to Tata Institute of Social Sciences team for the preparation of Devolution Report

2014-15 for the Ministry of Panchayati Raj, Government of India. He is a co-lead with TISS to evaluate a major educational programme in nine states in India. He is working with IRMA, Anand team to evaluate the impact of MGNREGA in nine states. He is a mentor for Prof. Ulrich Alfred a Fulbright Scholar working on Sri Aurobindo and Gandhi. He undertakes internship activities for the students of IIT, Mumbai and students of Tata Institute of Social Sciences, Mumbai. He served as a member in search committee to select Director for KILA, Kerala. He is an adviser to SARVAM, the rural transformation unit of Sri Aurobindo Society, Pondicherry. He is a member of the executive board of the social science research wing of the Sri Aurobindo Society.

2. Mailing Address

Department of Political Science and Development Administration
The Gandhigram Rural Institute—Deemed University
Gandhigram–624 302, Dindigul District
Tamil Nadu, South India.

Phone	: 0451–2452371 (O), 0451–2451063 (R)
Fax	: 0451-2454466, Mobile : 09159099809
E-mail	: gpalanithurai@gmail.com
Website	: http://rajivgandhichairgri.org

3. Education

1984	: **Ph.D.,** Annamalai University, Political Science/ Legislative Behaviour.
Dissertation	: **“The Role of Political Parties in Tamil Nadu Legislature”**.
1981	: **M.A.,** Political Science, Sri Venkateswara University, Tirupati, Andhra Pradesh, India.
1978	: **M.A.,** History, Annamalai University, Tamil Nadu, India.
1976	: **B.A.,** History, University of Madras, Tamil Nadu, India.

4. Teaching Experience

July 1999 to Present : Professor, Department of Political Science and Development Administration.

September 1996 to	:	Rajiv Gandhi Research Professor,
July 1999	:	Rajiv Gandhi Chair for Panchayati Raj Studies.
April 1991 to September 1996	:	Reader, Department of Political Science and Development Administration, Gandhigram Rural Institute.
October 1984 to March 1991	:	Lecturer in Political Science, Annamalai University.

5. Administrative Experience

Head of the Department	:	From 1991 to 2009
Dean Faculty of Social Science	:	From 2003 to 2005
Member, Syndicate	:	From 2003 to 2005
Member, Finance Committee	:	From 2003 to 2005
Chairmen Research Advisory Committee	:	From 2008 to 2013
Member, Senate	:	From 2003 to 2005
Warden, Men's hostel	:	From 1996 to 1999
Member, Planning and Monitoring Board	:	From 2013 to 2016

Chairmen Interring Administrative Committee
(In the absence of Vice-Chancellor)
Member, Project Monitoring Committee for three years
Chairmen Board of Studies of the Department of Political Science from 1991 to 2006

Courses taught: Modern Political Analysis, Indian Government and Politics, Government and Politics of Tamil Nadu, Political Sociology, Development Administration, Philosophy and Process of Development, New Panchayati Raj System, Decentralized Governance, Social Development and People's Participation,

Governance and Development, Governance and Delivery of services, Globalization and Decentralization and Development Theory.

Courses offered in Cologne University: Indian Society, Governance at Grassroots, Critical issues in Development, and Rural Management to the Students at Masters Level.

Role in Different Activities and Organizations

Coordinator	UGC SAP DRS I and II
Coordinator	UGC Innovative PG Programme
Chairperson	Research Committee of Political Science Discipline in XXXIX Social Science Congress 2015
Coordinator	Rajiv Gandhi Chair for Panchayati Raj Studies
Coordinator	for the preparation Self-Study Report for the first NAAC evaluation
Member	in peer team to visit other universities for NAAC evaluation
Member	IQAC Jayaraj Annapackiam College for Women in Periakulam for three years
Coordinator	for International Students Activities of Gandhigram Rural Institute
Member	in Board of Studies of nine Central and State Universities in different periods
Member	Planning Board of Tamil Nadu Open University for three years
Member	Planning Board of Gandhigram Rural Institute
Member	in Working Group of State and Central Planning Commission during Ninth, Tenth and Eleventh Five Year Plan periods.
Consultant	For Ist, IInd and IVth State Finance Commissions of Tamil Nadu
Member	Core Committee constituted by the Ministry of Panchayati Raj Government of India to apprise the power devolution in Tamil Nadu and Pondicherry
Chairman	of the Core Committee to implement panchayat Yuva Sakthi Abhiyan in Tamil Nadu constituted by the Ministry of Youth Affairs, Government of India.

Expert Member High Level Committee under the Chairmanship of the Local Body Minister Goverment of Tamil Nadu to devolve further powers to local bodies.

Member, National Level Committee, Goverment of India to draft a Model Panchayat Manual.

Member in the State Level Committee constituted by the Goverment of India to celebrate 50th Year of Indian Republic.

Translated the speech of the Prime Minister Dr. Manmohan Singh at Madurai on Sethu Samudram Project Inauguration on 2nd July, 2005.

Translated the speech of the Prime Minister Dr. Manmohan Singh at Dindigul during the inauguration of Four Lane National Highway Road Works on 4th February, 2006.

Translated the Inaugural speech of Vice-President of India Dr. Abdul Hamid Ansari during his visit to Mayiladuthurai on 21st September, 2008.

Member, Research Advisory Committee, **Indira Gandhi National Open University**, New Delhi.

Member, Advisory Committee of the Centre Dr. B.R. Ambedkar Studies, **PSGR Krishnammal College for Women**, Coimbatore.

Member, Advisory Committee of the Centre for Research and Development, **Sree Sawaswathi Thyagaraja College**, Coimbatore.

Mobilized resources (Rs. 40 lakh) from four members of Parliament for the construction of Seminar and Training Halls for Rajiv Gandhi Chair.

Chief Editor of a Bi-Annual **Journal of Grassroots Governance** published by Academy of Grassroots Studies and Research, India for three years.

Member in the Editorial Board of the (ICFAI) **Journal of Public Administration** for three years.

Member, Editorial Board of **Paadam**, a monthly Journal of Development Politics in Tamil.

Chief Editor of a Bi-monthly "**Global and Local**" News Letter published with the support of The Ford Foundation.

Nominated as the Chairman of the State Council of The Hunger Project in Tamil Nadu.

The Hunger Project is a voluntary agency working in 80 countries to end Hunger. Its Head Office is in New York and country office is in New Delhi. Previously it was headed by Dr. M.S. Swaminathan.

Member, Governing Council of State Resource Centre for a period of three years.

Part of the Social Watch Coalition for the Preparation of **Citizens' Report**.

To strengthen Panchayati Raj System in Tamil Nadu, he took initiative to form a network of NGOs and CBOs. The name of the network is "**Tamil Nadu Campaign for Panchayati Raj**".

"Good Governance through Local Governance", a 30 minutes programme every Monday from 7.30 p.m. to 8.00 p.m. throughout Tamil Nadu over All India Radio was conducted for six months as a sponsored programme by The Hunger Project.

Prepared 12 weekly episodes on the major achievements of Elected Women Representatives in Panchayats for Doordarshan telecast under "Makkal Mantram Programme". Specific programmes were executed for Sun TV, Jaya TV and Star Vijay TV on Panchayat related issues.

As a consultant, created a **Federation for Elected Women Representatives** and facilitated its effective functioning. Tamil Nadu Elected Women Representatives Federation is a model for women leaders of other states.

In the same way, helped Dalit women leaders to form their own Federation to highlight their problems for redressal.

Enabled the Panchayat leaders to form a forum to mitigate ill effects of Globalization.

For speedy and effective dissemination of information related to grassroots democracy a weekly supplement entitled "**Panchayat Malar**" in partnership with a popular daily *Dinamalar* (four lakh circulation) was published for one year. The supplement was published every Monday.

Conducted Seven Media Workshops to Sensitize the Media Persons on the Importance of Decentralization and implications of Globalization.

Member in Indian Government Delegation to Pakistan 30th June to 4th July, 2007 through the Ministry of Panchayati Raj.

Member in Indian Government Delegation to Norway during 2008 through the Ministry of Panchayati Raj.

Nominated as visiting faculty to the Chhattisgarh Academy of Administration, Chhattisgarh.

Fifteen Scholars Guided by him were awarded Ph.D. Degrees.

Seven Scholars Guided by him were awarded M.Phil. Degrees.

Eight Scholars are pursuing Ph.D. Programmes under his supervision.

Created eight endowments on eminent personalities with the support of donor agencies.

Also enabled the NGOs to form a network to work with Panchayats which are affected by Globalization.

Member in the Editorial Advisory Board of the Madhya Pradesh Journal of Social Science.

Member in the Advisory Board of the South Asian Journal of Politics.

Member of the IQAC of PSG Krishnammal College for Women in Coimbatore for a period of two years from 2014 to 2015.

Reviewer for the manuscripts related to decentralized democracy for publication in two popular foreign publishing houses.

Coordinator for the preparation of Tenth Five Year Plan Proposal for Gandhigram Rural Institute.

Adviser to Rural Development Unit of Sri Aurobindo Society.

Member in Sri Aurobindo Institute of Research in Social Science.

7. Research Fellowship and Awards

Received the **Dr. Ram Reddy All India Political Science Association's National Award** for the distinct research and outreach work done for rural transformation for the year 2016.

Shastri Indo-Canadian Institute's Faculty Enrichment Fellowship (2007) to visit Canada under Canadian studies programme to evolve a course on **Comparative Local Governance in India and Canada**. He was in Leth Bridge University with Prof. Trevor Harrison.

Shastri Indo-Canadian Institute's Faculty Research Fellowship (1989-90) to visit Canada under Canadian Studies programme to write a book on **Ethnic Conflict Management in Canada**

and India—A Comparative Study, (1989)—worked with Prof. Dale C. Thomson in McGill University, Montreal, Canada.

Fellowship of World Academy of Art and Science (USA) from 1996 to December 1998—visited Canada to participate in the World meet of the Academy held in British Columbia University, Vancouver, during November 1998.

Republic Day Award for the best contribution made in the field of Rural Development and Panchayati Raj. It was given on 26th January, 2005.

Best Service Award given by the District Administration for the services rendered to Panchayats in the year 2006.

Seven Generations Award in recognition of the initiatives taken for the uplift of the less fortunate in India by the Rural Development Mission of the US, 2007.

8. Pure Research and Action Research Projects

Carried out projects, both Pure Research and Action Research, to the tune of Rs. 5,60,60,824 funded by The Hunger Project, Action Aid, Swiss Development Agency for Cooperation, Ministry of Panchayati Raj, Government of India, Ministry of Rural Development, Government of India, The Ford Foundation, UGC, DANIDA, ICSSR, UNICEF, UNDP, Population Foundation of India, PRIA, CAPART, Rajiv Gandhi Foundation, State Finance Commission and State Planning Commission.

9. Adviser to Tiss Projects

For the preparation of Devolution Report 2015-16 for the Ministry of Panchayati Raj, Government of India acted as adviser to the project.

For the preparation of Training Module to train Elected Women Representatives sponsored by the National Commission for Women.

To evaluate a major educational programme in nine states in India.

10. Adviser to Rural Development University

Member in the advisory committee of the Karnataka State Rural Development and Panchayati Raj University.

11. Consultancy

Undertaken major consultancy for Oxfam International to evaluate the tsunami relief and rehabilitation works carried out by the partners of Oxfam affiliates.

Undertaken a consultancy to NCAER, New Delhi to write policy note on the report prepared by NCAER on Decentralization in India.

12. Role in Search Committee

Member, Search Committee to select Director for Kerala Institute of Local Administration (KILA), Kerala constituted by Government of Kerala.

13. Training Tools Preparation

Twelve training manuals and modules have been prepared and published to train and build the capacity of Local Body leaders and officials who are in Local Bodies.

14. Building the Capacity of the Leaders

Capacity Building exercise was carried out with the support of several funding agencies for 8000 leaders of Gram Panchayats of Tamil Nadu and 5000 of them are women and Dalits over a period of 15 years.

Served as a resource person in a team which conducted training programmes for the MLA's of some regional political parties and left parties in Tamil Nadu.

15. Major Initiative for Micro Level Planning

With the cooperation of the District Administration a major initiative was made for preparing a perspective plan for development at the Gram Panchayat level in 74 Gram Panchayats in Tamil Nadu on a pilot basis to study the process of micro level planning. Government of Tamil Nadu has scaled up this exercise to the whole of the State through a major scheme called "Namathu Gramam".

16. Role in National Institute of Rural Development and PR (NIRD & PR)

Master Assessor to Accredit Resource Persons to conduct Training Programme for Panchayati Raj Leaders in the training institutions throughout the country with the support of Ministry of Panchayati Raj, Government of India.

17. Major Work Initiated in Tsunami Affected Areas

Actively participated in reconstruction work in tsunami affected areas by developing micro level plan with the active participation of the communities to reconstruct the villages in 17 Gram Panchayats with the support of SDC and The Hunger Project, New Delhi.

18. Projects Undertaken

Sl. No.	*Title of the Project*	*Funding Agency*	*Fund*	*Remarks*
1.	Impact of MGNREGA at Household Decision Making	IRMA Anand	1200000	Ongoing
2.	UGC SAP, DRS-II	UGC	3200000	Ongoing
3.	Evaluating Rural Infrastructure	State Planning Commission	470000	Completed
4.	Writing Policy Note for the Study conducted by NCAER,	NCAER and IDRC	500000	Completed
5.	Impact of MGNRGA in Kerala	SIRD	1080000	Completed
6.	Critical Mass to Critical Action	ICSSR	345025	Completed
7.	UGC SAP, DRS-I	UGC	3900000	Completed
8.	M.A. Innovative Programme	UGC	4100000	Completed
9.	Globalization and Decentralization	Ford Foundation	5530000	Completed

(*Contd.*)

Sl. No.	*Title of the Project*	*Funding Agency*	*Fund*	*Remarks*
10.	Role of Youth in Micro Level Planning	Common Wealth Youth Programme	115860	Completed
11.	Disaster Management and Micro Planning for Reconstruction in 17 Gram Panchayat	SDC and the Hunger Project	1500000	Completed
12.	Role of Panchayats in Disaster Preparedness and Management in the States of Gujarat, Orissa, Andhrapradesh, Tamil Nadu and Kerala	ActionAid India	1603581	Completed
13.	Poverty Reduction and Empowerment	The World Bank	5600000	Completed
14.	Preparing District Human Development Report	UNDP	300000	Completed
15.	Globalization and Decentralization: Phase I	Ford Foundation	5800000	Completed
16.	Empowering Panchayats for Managing Disasters	Disaster Mitigation Institute	130000	Completed
17.	Women Leadership, Media Sensitization and Micro Level Planning	The Hunger Project	2500000	Completed
18.	Regional Workshop for Women Panchayat Presidents in Tamil Nadu	SIRD	300000	Completed
19.	Training Programme for the Tribal Women Panchayat Leaders	SIRD	35000	Completed

(*Contd.*)

Sl. No.	*Title of the Project*	*Funding Agency*	*Fund*	*Remarks*
20.	Training Module Preparation	Rajiv Gandhi Foundation	80000	Completed
21.	Federating Elected Women Representatives	Ford Foundation	1500000	Completed
22.	Leadership Training	The Hunger Project	3400000	Completed
23.	Process of Women Empowerment: an Analysis	District Administration	76000	Completed
24.	Preparing Administrative Manual for Local Bodies	PRIA	60000	Completed
25.	Leadership Training	The Hunger Project	700000	Completed
26.	Micro Level Planning	The Hunger Project	3800000	Completed
27.	Conscientizing the Panchayat Leaders on Social Development	District Administration, Tuticorin	336000	Completed
28.	Conscientizing the Panchayat Leaders on Social Development	District Administration, Pudukkottai	50000	Completed
29.	Conscientizing the Panchayat Leaders on Social Development	District Administration, Karur	74140	Completed
30.	Conscientizing the Panchayat Leaders on Social Development	District Administration, Theni	64900	Completed
31.	Conscientizing the Panchayat Leaders on Social Development	District Administration, Ramanathapuram	181170	Completed
32.	Conscientizing the Panchayat Leaders on Social Development	District Administration, Sivaganga	154660	Completed
33.	Conscientizing the Panchayat Leaders on Social Development	District Administration, Trichy	134000	Completed

(*Contd.*)

Sl. No.	*Title of the Project*	*Funding Agency*	*Fund*	*Remarks*
34.	Conscientizing the Panchayat Leaders on Social Development	District Administration, Pudukkottai	113000	Completed
35.	Capacity Building Exercise for Local Body Leaders	CAPART	927500	Completed
36.	Implementation of Village Based Management System in Panchayats in Cuddalore and Villupuram Districts	DANIDA	3508260	Completed
37.	Evolving training modules for Panchayati Raj Leaders and Functionaries in Tamil Nadu	Rajiv Gandhi Foundation	50000	Completed
38.	Women Empowerment through Panchayati Raj to end Hunger	The Hunger Project	3244213	Completed
39.	Pre-Election Voters Awareness Campaign in Tamil Nadu	PRIA	360000	Completed
40.	Panchayati Raj and Primary Education in Tamil Nadu	PRIA	100000	Completed
41.	Interface between panchayat leaders and SHG leaders in Tamil Nadu	UNICEF	110000	Completed
42.	Documenting Successful Panchayati Leaders of Tamil Nadu	UNICEF	279000	Completed
43.	Training the SHG leaders in Panchayati Raj Administration	District Administration, Villupuram	120000	Completed

(*Contd.*)

Sl. No.	*Title of the Project*	*Funding Agency*	*Fund*	*Remarks*
44.	Evaluating Performance of Women and Dalit Panchayat Leaders	PRIA	82500	Completed
45.	Evaluating Functional Efficiency of Gram Sabha	II State finance Commission	90200	Completed
46.	Training SHG Leaders in Panchayati Raj Administration	District Administration, Cuddalor	140000	Completed
47.	Training Panchayati Leaders Sanitation	District Administration, Cuddalor	64790	Completed
48.	Impact study of Anna Marumalarchi Scheme in Dindigul District	District Administration, Dindigul	25300	Completed
49.	Federating Elected Women Representa-tives Phase I	Ford Foundation	990000	Completed
50.	Training the project Officers of District Rural Development Agency in Multi Level Planning	State Planning Commission	130000	Completed
51.	Training Gram Panchayati Leaders on Water Supply in Cuddalore and Villupuram	DANIDA	344000	Completed
52.	Capacity Building Exclusion for Dalit and Women Leaders of Local Bodies	CAPART	249600	Completed
53.	Training Panchayati Raj in Micro Level Planning	CAPART	374000	Completed
54.	Community Action for Social Development	Population Foundation of India	383000	Completed

(*Contd.*)

Sl. No.	*Title of the Project*	*Funding Agency*	*Fund*	*Remarks*
55.	Training Panchayati Leaders on Social Development Issues	Population Foundation of India	516750	Completed
56.	Ethnic Identity and National Loyalty of an Ethnic Group	ICSSR	76000	Completed
57.	Political Culture and Political Behaviour of a Rural Community	GRI	20000	Completed
58.	Role Perception of Legislators: A Case Study of Tamil Nadu	ICSSR	36000	Completed
		Grand Total	**54704449**	

Publications

19. Books (Total: Books 61)

2017 : **Rural Development through Gandhian Model Transformation** (Tamil) Madurai: Gandhi Smarak Nidhi, 2017.

2017 : **Looking Back the Efforts in Decentralization in India**, New Delhi: Concept Publishing Company, 2017.

2017 : **Critical Issues in Higher Learning Intuitions in India**, New Delhi: Concept Publishing Company, 2017.

2016 : **Peoples Politics for Better Democracy** (Tamil): Madurai Gandhi Smarak Nidhi, 2016.

2015 : **Critical Mass for Critical Action,** New Delhi: Gyan Publishing Company, 2015.

2015 : **Integral Rural Development,** New Delhi: Concept Publishing Company, 2015.

2014 : **An Analysis of Two Lok Sabha Elections in Tamil Nadu**, New Delhi: Concept Publishing Company, 2014.

2014 : **Village Placement Programme: An Experiment in Learning**, New Delhi: Concept Publishing Company, 2014.

2012 : **Status of Dalits and Elected Dalit Representatives in Rural Local Bodies,** New Delhi: Concept Publishing Company, 2012.

2012 : **A Comparative Analysis of Grassroots Governance in Germany and India**, New Delhi: Concept Publishing Company, 2012.

2012 : **A Comparative Analysis of Grassroots Governance in China and India**, New Delhi: Concept Publishing Company, 2012.

2012 : **Elected women Representatives and Empowerment,** New Delhi: Concept Publishing Company, 2012.

2012 : **Governance Issues in India: From Grassroots Perspective,** New Delhi: Concept Publishing Company, 2012.

2012 : **Social Relevance of Higher Education,** New Delhi: Concept Publishing Company, 2012.

2012 : **Rural Local Body's Finance in Tamil Nadu,** New Delhi: Concept Publishing Company, 2012.

2011 : **Tamil Nadu Rural Local Bodies: Responsibilities and Powers (Tamil) Manual for Local Body Leaders,** Chennai: Barathi Puthakalayam, 2011.

2011 : **Globalization and Rural Development,** New Delhi: Concept Publishing Company, 2011.

2011 : **Remembering G.K. Moopanar**, New Delhi: Concept Publishing Company, 2011.

2010 : **Rajiv Gandhi's Vision on Local Governance,** New Delhi: Concept Publishing Company, 2010.

2009 : **Youth Voluntarism and Development**, New Delhi: Concept Publishing Company 2009.

2009 : **Where our Society is proceeding? Critical Essays on Governance and Society** Vol. II (Tamil) Chennai: New Century Book House, 2009.

2008 : **Critical Issues in Decentralization of Powers in India,** New Delhi: Concept Publishing Company, 2008.

2008 : **Networking of Elected Women Representatives,** New Delhi: Concept Publishing Company, 2008.

2008 : **Panchayats in Disaster Preparedness and Management,** New Delhi: Concept Publishing Company, 2008.

2008 : **Rural Reconstruction through New Panchayati Raj System (Tamil),** Chennai: New Century Book House, 2008.

2007 : **Communities, Panchayats and Governance at Grassroots,** New Delhi: Concept Publishing Company, 2007.

2007 : **Globalization and Decentralization**, New Delhi: Concept Publishing Company, 2007.

2007 : **Planning at Grassroots: Government's Participation in People's Plan—An Experiment,** New Delhi: Concept Publishing Company, 2007.

2007 : **Third General Election to Local Governments in Tamil Nadu: Expectations and Shocking Realities**, New Delhi: Concept Publishing Company, 2007.

2007 : **Evolving Grassroots Democracy,** New Delhi: Concept Publishing Company, 2007.

2007 : **Change Makers at Grassroots Democracy,** New Delhi: Concept Publishing Company, 2007.

2006 : **Handbook of Tamil Nadu Panchayat Administration,** New Delhi: Concept Publishing Company, 2006.

2006 : **Empowering Women: Building Capability of Rural Women,** New Delhi: Concept Publishing Company, 2006.

2006 : **Electorate Expectation and Reasoning of Voters Participation,** New Delhi: Concept Publishing Company, 2006.

2006 : **An Introduction to Legislature (in Tamil),** Chennai: New Century Book House, 2006.

2006 : **Where We Are Proceeding? Critical Essays of Governance and Development, Vol. I (in Tamil),** Chennai: New Century Book House, 2006.

2005 : **Emerging Dimensions of Decentralization in India**, New Delhi: Concept Publishing Company, 2005.

2005 : **Ethnic Identity and National Loyalty of an Ethnic Group**, New Delhi: Concept Publishing Company, 2005.

2005 : **Evaluation of Process and Performance of Women and Dalit Leaders in Gram Panchayats**, New Delhi: Concept Publishing Company, 2005.

2005 : **Experience of Training and Capacity Building of Local Body Leaders**, New Delhi: Concept Publishing Company, 2005.

2005 : **Functional Efficiency of Gram Sabha: Problems in Direct Democracy**, New Delhi: Concept Publishing Company, 2005.

2005 : **New Public Management in Action: A Study in Pudukkottai District Administration**, New Delhi: Concept Publishing Company, 2005.

2004 : **Three Tier Panchayati Raj System in Tamil Nadu: Act, Rules, Government Orders and Rural Development Schemes (in Tamil)**, Chennai: South Vision, 2004.

2003 : **Dynamics of Social Transformation and Entitlement of People**, New Delhi: Concept Publishing Company, 2003.

2003 : **Tamil Nadu Panchayati Raj System with Act in Original**, New Delhi: Concept Publishing Company, 2003.

2002 : **Panchayati Raj in Tamil Nadu: Act, Rules and Schemes (in Tamil),** Chennai: South Vision Publications, 2002.

2001 : **Capacity Building Exercise for Local Body Leaders**, New Delhi: Concept Publishing Company, 2001.

2000 : **Grassroots Democracy in Indian Society**, New Delhi: Concept Publishing Company, 2000.

2000 : **New Panchayati Raj System at Work: An Evaluation**, New Delhi: Concept Publishing Company, 2000.

2000 : **New Panchayati Raj System in Tamil Nadu (in Tamil)**, Chennai: South Vision Publication, 2000 (II Edition 2002, III Edition 2004).

1999 : **Contemporary Issues in Development Dynamics**, New Delhi: Kanishka Publishers and Distributors, 1999.

1998 : **Perception of Grassroots Democracy and Evaluation of Political Performance**, New Delhi: MD Publications, 1998.

1996 : **Participation in the Development Process: Grassroots Level Experiences**, New Delhi: Kanishka Publishing House, 1996.

1996 : **Poly Ethnicity in Canada and India: A Comparative Analysis**, New Delhi: MD Publishing House, 1996.

1995 : **Pathway to Endless Opportunities.** New Delhi: Kanishka Publishing House, 1995.

1994 : **People's Perception of Politics**: **An Indian Perspective.** New Delhi: Kanishka Publishing House, 1994.

1993 : **Dynamics of Tamil Nadu Polity in Sri Lankan Ethnicity,** New Delhi: Northern Book Centre, 1993.

1993 : **Indian Polity—Myth and Reality**. New Delhi: Kanishka Publishing House, 1993.

1993 : **Management of Ethnic Conflict in India and Canada: A Comparative Analysis.** New Delhi: Kanishka Publishing House, 1993.

1991 : **Role Perception of Legislators: A Case Study of Tamil Nadu,** New Delhi: Konark Publications, 1991.

1989 : **Reaction and Response in Legislature,** Annamalai Nagar: Annamalai University Publication, 1989.

20. Edited Books (Total: 22)

2015 : **Deliberative Democracy,** New Delhi: MJP Publishers, 2015.

2014 : **Critical Mass to Critical Action**, New Delhi: Concept Publishing Company, 2014.

2014 : **Experience of Decentralization in South Indian States**, Chennai: MJP Publications, 2014.

2013 : **Federating Elected Women Representatives in India,** New Delhi: Concept Publishing Company, 2013.

2008 : **Perspectives of Rajiv Gandhi: Memorable Quotes from Rajiv Gandhi,** New Delhi: Concept Publishing Company, 2008.

2008 : (Ed) **Dynamics of New Panchayati Raj System: Panchayat Finance Vol. VII,** New Delhi: Concept Publishing Company, 2008.

2007 : **Standpoints on Globalization and Decentralization**, New Delhi: Concept Publishing Company, 2007.

2007 : (Ed) **Dynamics of New Panchayati Raj System: Capacity Building Experience**, Vol. VI, New Delhi: Concept Publishing Company, 2007.

2005 : (Ed) **Dynamics of New Panchayati Raj System in India: Experience of Micro Level Planning**, Vol. V, New Delhi: Concept Publishing Company, 2005.

2004 : (Ed) **Dynamics of New Panchayati Raj System in India: Empowerment of Women,** Vol. IV, New Delhi: Concept Publishing Company, 2004.

2004 : (Ed) **Dynamics of New Panchayati Raj System in India in Select States,** Vol. III, New Delhi: Concept Publishing Company, 2004.

2002 : (Ed) **Dynamics of New Panchayati Raj System in India in Select States**, Vol. II, New Delhi: Concept Publishing Company, 2002.

2002 : (Ed) **Dynamics of New Panchayati Raj System in India in Select States**, Vol. I, New Delhi: Concept Publishing Company, 2002.

1999 : **Ethnic Movement in Transition**, New Delhi: Kanishka Publishers and Distributors, 1999.

1997 : **Dimensions of New Panchayati Raj System (in Tamil)**, Gandhigram: Rajiv Gandhi Chair for Panchayati Raj Studies, 1997.

1997 : (Ed) **Major Issues in New Panchayati Raj System**, New Delhi: Kanishka Publishers, 1997.

1996 : (Ed) **Empowering People: Issues and Solutions**, New Delhi: Kanishka Publishing House, 1996.

1995 : (Ed) **New Panchayati Raj System: Status and Prospects,** New Delhi: Kanishka Publishing House, 1995.

1994 : **Empowering People for Prosperity: A Study in New Panchayati Raj System**, New Delhi: Kanishka Publishing House, 1994.

1993 : (Ed) **Ethnic Movement in India: Theory and Practice**. New Delhi: Kanishka Publishing House, 1993.

1993 : (Ed) **Caste Politics and Society in Tamil Nadu,** New Delhi: Kanishka Publishing House, 1993.

1992 : (Ed) **Perspectives on Indian Regionalism,** New Delhi: Kanishka Publishing House, 1992.

21. Chapter in Books (Total: 45)

2015 : "An Analysis of Pro-Poor Scheme in Tamil Nadu" in M.R. Biju (ed.), **Local Governance and Rural Empowerment** New Delhi: Concept Publishing Company, 2015.

2017: "Two Decades of Decentralization in Tamil Nadu" in Yatindra Singh Sisodia, Ashish Bhat and Tapas Kumar Dalapati (Ed) **"Two Decades of Panchayatairj in India: Experience, Issues Challenges and Opportunities**. Jaipur: Rawat Publication, 2017.

2017 : "Theoretical Nuances of Democratic Decentralization in India" in **Two Decades of Panchayati Raj in India: Experiences, Issues, Challenges and Opportunities** (Eds) Yatindra Singh Sisodia, Ashish Bhatt, Tapas Kumar Dalapati, New Delhi: Rawat Publication, 2018.

2017 : "Impact of Globalization in the life and livelihood of the poor", in Scaria Pannackal SVD and Vasundhara Mohan and (Eds) **Globalization and Religion: Interaction and Divergencies**, Concept Publishing Company, New Delhi, 2017.

2016 : "Decentralized Governance and Development: A view from the Grassroots of Society" in A.V. Satish Chandra from **Centralized Government to Decentralized Governance,** New Delhi: Viva Books, 2017.

2016 : "Panchayati Raj System in Tamil Nadu" in K. Raman Pillai, K. Sureshkumar and K. Sukumaran Nair (eds) **Panchayati Raj Experience in India**. New Delhi: Kalpaz Publications, 2015.

2016 : "Other Official/Governmental Programmes: Government Initiatives for Preparing Youth for World of Work" in Matthias Pilz (ed), **India: Preparation for the World of Work Education System and School to Work Transition** Wiesbaden: Springer US, 2016.

2015 : "Role of an Industrialist in Tamil Nadu Legislature" in **Contribution of Arulselvar in Literature** (eds) M.P. Gurusamy and S. Jayaraj Madurai: Gandhi Museum, 2015.

2014 : "Status of Decentralization in Tamil Nadu" in George Mathew (ed) **Status of Panchayati Raj in the States and Union Territories of India,** New Delhi: Concept Publishing Company, 2014.

2013 : "Human Development Scenario in Rural Areas: An Analysis of Human Dignity Index" in Yatintra Singh Sisudia (ed), **Human Development Experience in India,** New Delhi: Rawat Publications, 2013.

2012 : "Role of Panchayats in Establishing Communal Harmony through the Process of Governance and Development" in **Secularism and Pluralistic Democracy in India** (Eds) V. Ragupathy and Vasundra Mohan. New Delhi: Concept Publishing Company, 2012.

2012 : "Role of ICT in Scientific Decision Making at Grassroots" in M.R. Biju (ed), **Rural Development Under Decentralized Governance,** New Delhi: Concept Publishing Company, 2012.

2011 : "R.V. the Visionary Leader President", **R. Venkataraman Centenary Celebration Commemorative Volume**, Gandhigram: Centenary Committee, 2011.

2009 : "Governance for Development at Grassroots" in M. Moni and Suresh Misra (eds) **Rural India: Achieving Millennium Development Goals and Grassroots Development.** New Delhi: Concept Publishing Company, 2009.

2009 : "Status of Dalits and Dalit Gram Panchayat Leaders in Tamil Nadu" in Rakesls Hooja and Sunil Dutt (Eds) **Fifty Years of Panchayati Raj and Decentralised Development.** New Delhi: Indian Institute of Public Administration, 2009.

2009 : "Role of State: Self Governing Institutions" in **Voluntary Sector: Still Relevant in a Changing Development Scenario (eds)** Saraswathi G. Rao and Saju C. Mannarath. New Delhi: Welfare Hunger Life, 2009.

2009 : "Governance and Development: Initiatives from Below" in Yatindra Singh Sisodia (ed) **India's Development Scenario: Challenges and Prospects,** New Delhi: Rawat Publications, 2009.

2009 : "Panchayats; Relevance, Potentials and Demonstration" in Yatindra Singh Sisodia (ed) **India's Development Scenario: Challenges and Prospects,** New Delhi: Rawat Publications, 2009.

2009 : Restructuring Local Governance in the Era of Globalization" in (Ed.) Sudha Menon, **Decentralised Local Governance Perspectives and Experience,** Hyderabad: The ICFAI University Press, 2009.

2009 : "Planning Human Development at Grassroots in Tamil Nadu" in (Eds.) S. Bhaskaran and B. Sumathi **Human Development in India Initiatives and Experiences**. Hyderabad: The ICFAI University Press, 2009.

2009 : "Where is Neo Gandhism? In **Gandhi Today** (Ed) S.V. Prabhath, New Delhi: Serials Publications, 2009.

2008 : "Micro Level Planning Experience from Tamil Nadu" in Mahipal (Ed), **Decentralized Planning and Development in India,** New Delhi: Mittal Publications, 2008.

2008 : "Role of Panchayats in Sustainable Social Development" in M.R. Biju (ed) **Panchayati Raj System: Towards Sustainable Rural Livelihood and Development**, New Delhi: Kanishka Publishers Distributors, 2008.

2008 : "Public-Public and Public-Private Partnership in Maintenance of Drinking Water" in B.K. Thapliyal, S.S.P. Sharma, P. Shiv Ram and U. Hemant Kumar (Eds), **Democratization of Water,** New Delhi: Serials Publications, 2008.

2007 : "Potentials for Social and Economic Transformation through Decentralized Governance" in D. Sundar Ram (Ed), **Panchayati Raj and Empowering People: A New Agenda for Rural India,** New Delhi: Kanishka Publishers and Distributors, 2007.

2007 : "Role of Caste Groups in New Panchayati Raj System: A Case Analysis of Tamil Nadu" in D. Sundar Ram (Ed), **Dynamics of Grassroots Governance in India: Dreams and Realities,** New Delhi: Kanishka Publishers and Distributors, 2007.

2007 : "Rajiv Gandhi's Framework for Devolution of Powers for Democracy and Development in India" in D. Sundar Ram (Ed), **Rajiv Gandhi: A Visionary of Modern India,** New Delhi: Kanishka Publishers and Distributors, 2007.

2007 : "Panchayats: Relevance and Potentials" in T.M. Joseph (Ed) **Local Governance in India: Ideas, Challenges and Strategies**, New Delhi: Concept Publishing Company, New Delhi, 2007.

2007 : "New Panchayati Raj System in Tamil Nadu" in M.R. Biju (ed) **Decentralization: An Indian Experience,** New Delhi: National Publishing House, 2007.

2006 : "Ambedkar's Vision on Dalit Leadership at Grassroots Institutions in Tamil Nadu" in S. Ramachandran (ed), **Dr. Ambedkar's Versatile Contributions,** Chennai: University of Madras, 2006.

2006 : "Panchayati Raj System in Tamil Nadu", **The State of the Panchayats: A Mid Term Review and Appraisal,** New Delhi, Ministry of Panchayati Raj, Government of India, 2006.

2005 : "Building the Capacity of Grassroots Leaders" in Y. Sisodia (ed) **Panchayati Raj Functioning in India,** Jaipur: Rawat Publications, 2005.

2005 : "Development Roles Reversed: People's Initiative and Government's Participation" in L.C. Jain (Ed), **Decentralization and Local Governance**, New Delhi: Orient Longman, 2005.

2002 : "Issues of Development and Governance at Grassroots" in M.L. Sondhi (ed), **Towards a New Era: Economic Social and Political Reforms,** New Delhi: Haranand Publications, 2002.

2001 : "The Paradox of an Ethnic Movement" in **Politics, Policy and Reconstruction: India Since Independence** (Ed) Rev. Sebastian Alapattukunnel, Jaipur: Aalekh Publishers, 2001.

2001 : "Synergization of Institutional Arrangements for Development and Social Justice at the Grassroots—A Case Analysis" in **Emerging Institutions for Decentralized Rural Development**, Vol. II (Ed) by S.P. Jain, Hyderabad: National Institute of Rural Development, 2001.

2001 : "The Paradox of an Ethnic Movement" in **The Dravidian Movement**, (ed) R. Thandavan, Chennai: The Academy of Public Affairs, 2001.

2000 : "Corruption at Micro Level and ways to contain it" in **Corruption at the Grassroots: The Shades and Shadows** (Eds) N. Narayanasamy, M.P. Boraian and M.A. Jeyaraju, New Delhi: Concept Publishing Company, 2000.

2000 : "Panchayati Raj in Tamil Nadu", **Status of Panchayati Raj in the States and Union Territories of India 2000**, (Ed) George Mathew, New Delhi: Concept Publishing Company, 2000.

1999 : "Parliamentary Reform in India" in **Parliamentary Institutions in India: Development or Decay** (Ed), D. Sundarram, New Delhi: National Publishing House, 1999.

1999 : "A Report of Gram Sabha Functioning in Tamil Nadu" in **Strengthening Village Democracy**, (Eds.) R.C. Choudhury and S.P. Jain, Hyderabad: National Institute of Rural Development, 1999.

1999 : "Gandhian Framework of Development in 21st Century" in **Gandhism after Gandhi**, (Ed) Anil Dutta Mishra, New Delhi: Mittal Publications, 1999.

1999 : "Crises of Governance and Coalition Government in India" in **Coalition Politics in India: Search for Political Stability,** (Ed) D. Sundar Ram, Jaipur: National Publishing House, 2000.

1996 : "Value Crisis and Mahatma Gandhi: A New Credo for Humanism" in A.D. Mishra (Ed) **Gandhian Approach to Contemporary Problems**, New Delhi: Mittal Publications, 1996.

1992 : "Ethnicity and Development: A Study in Reformulation" in G. Palanithurai and R. Thandavan (Eds.) **Perspective on Indian Regionalism,** New Delhi: Kanishka Publishing House, 1992.

1985 : "Role of Legislature in Development: A Case Study of Tamil Nadu" in R.B. Jain (ed.), **Legislative Process and Development,** New Delhi: Gitanjali Publishing Company, 1985.

22. Monographs and Working Papers (Total: 71)

2010 : **Rural Development Scenario: A Qualitative Assessment for Action in Tamil Nadu,** Gandhigram, Rajiv Gandhi Chair for Panchayati Raj Studies, 2010.

2010 : **Decentralization of Powers: Acceleration or Deceleration,**

Gandhigram, Rajiv Gandhi Chair for Panchayati Raj Studies, 2010.

2010 : **Rural Development in the New Economic Order** (*Tamil*), Gandhigram, Rajiv Gandhi Chair for Panchayati Raj Studies, 2010.

2009 : **How Some Panchayats becomes a model? Actionable Agenda to become a Model**, Gandhigram: Rajiv Gandhi Chair for Panchayati Raj Studies, 2009.

2009 : **Sand Mining in Tamil Nadu Procedures and Practices: A Guide for Panchayat Leaders**, Gandhigram: Rajiv Gandhi Chair for Panchayati Raj Studies, 2009.

2009 : **Gram Sabha Mobilization for Empowerment of the Marginalized** (*Tamil*), Madurai: Peoples Watch, 2009.

2009 : **Citizenship Building through Citizen's Centres,** Gandhigram: Rajiv Gandhi Chair for Panchayati Raj Studies, 2008.

2008 : **Managing Globalization: Role of Local Self Government,** Gandhigram: Rajiv Gandhi Chair for Panchayati Raj Studies, 2008.

2008 : **Managing Globalization: A Guide to Local Body Leaders** (*Tamil*), Gandhigram: Rajiv Gandhi Chair for Panchayati Raj Studies, 2008.

2008 : **Special Economic Zone: How to Handle it?: A Guide to Local Body Leaders,** Gandhigram: Rajiv Gandhi Chair for Panchayati Raj Studies, 2008.

2008 : **National Rehabilitation and Resettlement Policy 2007: A Guide to Local Body Leaders,** Gandhigram: Rajiv Gandhi Chair for Panchayati Raj Studies, 2008.

2008 : **Globalization: Concerns at the Grassroots,** Gandhigram: Rajiv Gandhi Chair for Panchayati Raj Studies, 2008.

2007 : **Inspector of Panchayats: Role and Responsibilities,** Gandhigram: Rajiv Gandhi Chair for Panchayati Raj Studies, 2007.

2006 : **Administration of Gram Panchayats in Tamil Nadu (*Tamil*)**, Chennai: Bharati Puthakalayam, 2006.

2006 : **Bases of Decentralization of Powers (*Tamil*)**, Chennai: New Century Book House Pvt. Ltd., 2006.

2006 : **Gram Sabha: Role and Responsibilities (*Tamil*)**, Chennai: New Century Book House Pvt. Ltd., 2006.

2006 : **Gram Panchayat Management (*Tamil*)**, Chennai: New Century Book House Pvt. Ltd, 2006.

2006 : **Block Panchayat Management (*Tamil*),** Chennai: New Century Book House Pvt. Ltd., 2006.

2006 : **District Panchayat Management (*Tamil*),** Chennai: New Century Book House Pvt. Ltd, 2006.

2006 : **Role and Responsibilities of Ward Members of Gram Panchayat and Block Panchayat (*Tamil*),** Chennai: New Century Book House, 2006.

2006 : **Manual for Village Level Planning (*Tamil*),** Chennai: New Century Book House Pvt. Ltd, 2006.

2006 : **Statutory Committees in Gram Panchayat** (*Tamil*), Chennai: New Century Book House Pvt. Ltd., 2006.

2005 : **Second Generation Reform in Decentralization**, Gandhigram: Rajiv Gandhi Chair for Panchayati Raj Studies, 2005.

2005 : **Are They Withdrawing from Public Space?,** Gandhigram: Rajiv Gandhi Chair for Panchayati Raj Studies, 2005.

2005 : **New Panchayati Raj System in Tamil Nadu**, Gandhigram: Rajiv Gandhi Chair for Panchayati Raj Studies, 2005.

2005 : **Elected Women Representatives and Emerging Alternative Governance,** Gandhigram: Rajiv Gandhi Chair for Panchayati Raj Studies, 2005.

2005 : **Good Governance at Grassroots**, Gandhigram: Rajiv Gandhi Chair for Panchayati Raj Studies, 2005.

2005 : **Planning for Development at Grassroots in Tamil Nadu**, Gandhigram: Rajiv Gandhi Chair for Panchayati Raj Studies, 2005.

2004 : **A Framework for Devolution of Powers for Democracy and Development**, Gandhigram: Rajiv Gandhi Chair for Panchayati Raj Studies, 2004.

2004 : **Governance: From the Perspective of Elected Women Representatives (EWRs)**, Gandhigram: Rajiv Gandhi Chair for Panchayati Raj Studies, 2004.

2004 : **Capacity Building of Grassroots Leaders,** Gandhigram: Rajiv Gandhi Chair for Panchayati Raj Studies, 2004.

2004 : **Women in Governance at Grassroots**, Gandhigram: Rajiv Gandhi Chair for Panchayati Raj Studies, 2004.

2004 : **Status of Financial Devolution to Panchayats in Tamil Nadu**, Gandhigram: Rajiv Gandhi Chair for Panchayati Raj Studies, 2004.

2004 : **Media and Grassroots Governance**, Gandhigram: Rajiv Gandhi Chair for Panchayati Raj Studies, 2004.

2003 : **Gram Sabha: An Instrument for Empowerment of People**, Madurai: RCPED, 2003.

2003 : **Dalit Leadership in Panchayats**, Gandhigram: Rajiv Gandhi Chair for Panchayati Raj Studies, 2003.

2003 : **Panchayats, Communities and Social Development,** Gandhigram: Rajiv Gandhi Chair for Panchayati Raj Studies, 2003.

2003 : **Synergization of Traditional Panchayats with Formal Panchayati Raj System in Managing Community Affairs**, Gandhigram: Rajiv Gandhi Chair for Panchayati Raj Studies, 2003.

2003 : **Development Roles Reversed: People Initiative and Governments Participation,** Gandhigram: Rajiv Gandhi Chair for Panchayati Raj Studies, 2003.

2003 : **Building Alliances and Capabilities among the Elected Women Representatives of Grassroots,** Gandhigram: Rajiv Gandhi Chair for Panchayati Raj Studies, 2003.

2003 : **Tamil Nadu Panchayati Raj System: An Annotated Bibliography,** Gandhigram: Rajiv Gandhi Chair for Panchayati Raj Studies, 2003.

2001 : **Recommendations for Effecting Functioning of Panchayati Raj System in Tamil Nadu,** Gandhigram: Rajiv Gandhi Chair for Panchayati Raj Studies, 2001.

2001 : **Good Governance at the Grassroots,** Gandhigram: Rajiv Gandhi Chair for Panchayati Raj Studies, 2001.

2001 : **Towards Decentralization of Powers**, Gandhigram: Rajiv Gandhi Chair for Panchayati Raj Studies, 2001.

2001 : **Empowerment of Women: Problems Faced by the Elected Women Representatives, Experience from Tamil Nadu,** Gandhigram: Rajiv Gandhi Chair for Panchayati Raj Studies, 2001.

2000 : **The Genre of Women Leaders in Local Bodies: Experience from Tamil Nadu**, Gandhigram: Department of Political Science and Development Administration, 2000.

1999 : **Researchable Issues and Problems in the Area of New Panchayati Raj System,** Gandhigram: Rajiv Gandhi Chair for Panchayati Raj Studies, 1999.

1999 : **Understanding Indian Politics from the Perspective of Tamil Polity**, Gandhigram: Department of Political Science and Development Administration, 1999.

1998 : **Election, Issues and Options**, Gandhigram: Rajiv Gandhi Chair for Panchayati Raj Studies, 1998.

1998 : **Election is an Expression of Feelings of the People**, Gandhigram: Rajiv Gandhi Chair for Panchayati Raj Studies, 1998.

1998 : **New Panchayati Raj System in Tamil Nadu: Changes and Challenges**, Gandhigram: Rajiv Gandhi Chair for Panchayati Raj Studies, 1998.

1998 : **Sustaining Parliamentary Democracy**, Gandhigram: Rajiv Gandhi Chair for Panchayati Raj Studies, 1998.

1998 : **Grassroots Democracy is the Challenge of the Indian Civil Society**, Gandhigram: Rajiv Gandhi Chair for Panchayati Raj Studies, 1998.

1998 : **Rural Reconstruction and Public Participation**, Gandhigram: Rajiv Gandhi Chair for Panchayati Raj Studies, 1998.

1998 : **Containing Corruption: A Micro Experiment**, Gandhigram: Rajiv Gandhi Chair for Panchayati Raj Studies, 1998.

1998 : **Participatory Governance: A Reality**, Gandhigram: Rajiv Gandhi Chair for Panchayati Raj Studies, 1998.

1997 : **New Panchayati Raj System: Are hopes belied?: Views from the presidents of Gram Panchayats.** Gandhigram: Rajiv Gandhi Chair for Panchayati Raj Studies, 1997.

1995 : **Women in New Panchayati Raj System**: Gandhigram: Department of Political Science and Development Administration, 1995.

1995 : **Central Governments Intensive Rural Development Programmes** (*in Tamil*), Gandhigram: Rajiv Gandhi Chair for Panchayati Raj Studies, 1995.

1994 : **People in New Panchayati Raj System** (*in Tamil*), Vadamadurai: CHERU, 1993

1994 : **Politics and Economics in New Direction** (*in Tamil*) Dindigul: PMK Trust, 1994.

1994 : **How should the New Panchayati Raj System take shape** (*in Tamil*), Vadamadurai: CHERU, 1994.

1994 : **New Panchayati Raj System in Tamil Nadu** (*in Tamil*), Gandhigram: Department of Politics and Public Administration, 1994.

1994 : **New Panchayati Raj System: Questions and Answers** (*in Tamil*), Vadamadurai: CHERU, 1994.

1993 : **New Panchayati Raj System** (*in Tamil*), Gandhigram: Department of Politics and Public Administration, 1993

1992 : **Reasoning of Political Participation,** Gandhigram: Department of Politics and Public Administration, 1992.

1991 : **10th General Election, Logic Behind Voting: A Synoptic View,** Gandhigram: Department of Politics and Public Administration, 1991.

1989 : **Political Communication and Political Mobilization: A Study in Dravidian Movement.** Annamalai Nagar: Department of Political Science, 1989.

1988 : **Ethnic Political Parties and Electoral Behaviour in Tamil Nadu,** Annamalai Nagar: Department of Political Science, 1988.

1988 : **Changing Contours of an Ethnic Movement: A Study in Dravidian Movement.** Annamalai Nagar: Department of Political Science, 1988.

1988 : **Ethnic Organizations in Tamil Nadu** (*in Tamil*), Madurai: Tamil Development Institute, 1988.

23. Pathfinders Series (Total: 24)

2006 : **Leadership Matters in Grassroots Governance**: Pathfinders Series—XXIV-Tsunami, Gandhigram: Rajiv Gandhi Chair for Panchayati Raj Studies, 2006.

2006 : **Leadership Matters in Grassroots Governance**: Pathfinders Series—XXIII-Athangaraipatti, Gandhigram: Rajiv Gandhi Chair for Panchayati Raj Studies, 2006.

2006 : **Leadership Matters in Grassroots Governance**: Pathfinders Series—XXII-Noothulapuram, Gandhigram: Rajiv Gandhi Chair for Panchayati Raj Studies, 2006.

2006 : **Leadership Matters in Grassroots Governance**: Pathfinders Series—XXI-Kanyakumari, Gandhigram: Rajiv Gandhi Chair for Panchayati Raj Studies, 2006.

2005 : **Leadership Matters in Grassroots Governance**: Pathfinders Series—XX-Melachinthalacherry, Gandhigram: Rajiv Gandhi Chair for Panchayati Raj Studies, 2005.

2005 : **Leadership Matters in Grassroots Governance**: Pathfinders Series—XIX-K. Keeranur, Gandhigram: Rajiv Gandhi Chair for Panchayati Raj Studies, 2005.

2005 : **Leadership Matters in Grassroots Governance**:

Pathfinders Series—XVIII-Michalepattinam, Gandhigram: Rajiv Gandhi Chair for Panchayati Raj Studies, 2005.

2005 : **Leadership Matters in Grassroots Governance**: Pathfinders Series—XVII-Veerapandianpattinam, Gandhigram: Rajiv Gandhi Chair for Panchayati Raj Studies, 2005.

2005 : **Leadership Matters in Grassroots Governance**: Pathfinders Series—XVI-Grandline, Gandhigram: Rajiv Gandhi Chair for Panchayati Raj Studies, 2005.

2005 : **Leadership Matters in Grassroots Governance**: Pathfinders Series—XV-Thamaraikulam, Gandhigram: Rajiv Gandhi Chair for Panchayati Raj Studies, 2005.

2005 : **Leadership Matters in Grassroots Governance**: Pathfinders Series—XIV-Anaikuppam, Gandhigram: Rajiv Gandhi Chair for Panchayati Raj Studies, 2005.

2005 : **Leadership Matters in Grassroots Governance**: Pathfinders Series—XIII-Maravamangalam, Gandhigram: Rajiv Gandhi Chair for Panchayati Raj Studies, 2005.

2005 : **Leadership Matters in Grassroots Governance**: Pathfinders Series—XII-Konamoolai, Gandhigram: Rajiv Gandhi Chair for Panchayati Raj Studies, 2005.

2005 : **Leadership Matters in Grassroots Governance**: Pathfinders Series—XI-Koonavelampatti, Gandhigram: Rajiv Gandhi Chair for Panchayati Raj Studies, 2005.

2005 : **Leadership Matters in Grassroots Governance**: Pathfinders Series—X-Keerapalayam, Gandhigram: Rajiv Gandhi Chair for Panchayati Raj Studies, 2005.

2005 : **Leadership Matters in Grassroots Governance**: Pathfinders Series—IX-Appipalayam, Vanduvancheri, Thiruvasi, Gandhigram: Rajiv Gandhi Chair for Panchayati Raj Studies, 2005.

2004 : **Leadership Matters in Grassroots Governance**: Pathfinders Series—VIII-Odanthurai, Gandhigram: Rajiv Gandhi Chair for Panchayati Raj Studies, 2004.

2004 : **Leadership Matters in Grassroots Governance**: Pathfinders Series—VII-Rajendrapuram, Gandhigram: Rajiv Gandhi Chair for Panchayati Raj Studies, 2004.

2004 : **Leadership Matters in Grassroots Governance**: Pathfinders Series—VI-Nallukottai, Gandhigram: Rajiv Gandhi Chair for Panchayati Raj Studies, 2004.

2004 : **Leadership Matters in Grassroots Governance**:

Pathfinders Series—V-Kuthambakkam, Gandhigram: Rajiv Gandhi Chair for Panchayati Raj Studies, 2004.

2004 : **Leadership Matters in Grassroots Governance**: Pathfinders Series—IV-K. Rayavaram, Gandhigram: Rajiv Gandhi Chair for Panchayati Raj Studies, 2004.

2004 : **Leadership Matters in Grassroots Governance**: Pathfinders Series—III-Sakkarakottai, Gandhigram: Rajiv Gandhi Chair for Panchayati Raj Studies, 2004.

2004 : **Leadership Matters in Grassroots Governance**: Pathfinders Series—II-Devipattinam, Gandhigram: Rajiv Gandhi Chair for Panchayati Raj Studies, 2004.

2004 : **Leadership Matters in Grassroots Governance**: Pathfinders Series—I-Semmipalayam, Gandhigram: Rajiv Gandhi Chair for Panchayati Raj Studies, 2004.

24. Research Articles (Total: 128)

2018 : "Research on Skill Education: A Wakeup call for Indian Universities", **University News**, Vol. 56: No. 09, 26th February-04th March, 2018.

2018 : "Informal Learning among Handloom Weavers: A Case Analysis of Chinnalapatti, Tamil Nadu, India" **TVET@Asia**. Issue No. 10, January, 2018, ISSN: 2196 839X.

2017 : "New Narratology of Women Domestic Workers in Tamil Nadu: A Micro Analysis", **South Asian Journal of Socio-Political Studies.** Vol. XVIII: No. 1, July-December, 2017.

2017 : Mismatch in Teaching Learning Process in Higher Learning Institutions", **University News**, Vol. 55: No. 38, September 18-24, 2017.

2017 : "Nehru's Framework of Panchayati Raj and Rural Development", **Madhya Pradesh Journal of Social Science**, Vol. 21: No. 1, June 2017.

2017 : "Decentralization in India: An Unfinished Agenda", **Loyola Journal of Social Sciences**, Vol. 31: No. 1, January-June, 2017.

2017 : "Fourteenth Finance Commission: A Game Changer for Gram Panchayats in India", **Local Government Quarterly**, Vol. LXXXVIII: No. 1, January-March, 2017.

2017 : "Implementation of Manual Scavengers Act, 2013 in Tamil Nadu: A Micro Analysis", **Politics and Journal of Governance**, Vol. 6: No. 1, March, 2017.

2017 : "Need of the hour is Value Education not in Thought but in Action" **University News**, Vol. 55: No. 11, 13-19, March 2017.

2017 : "An Evaluation of the scheme meant for Excluded rural habitations", **South Asia Journal of Socio-Political Studies**, Vol. XVII: No. 2, January-June 2017.

2017 : "Need People Centric Research", **University News**, Vol. 55: No. 1, January 2-8, 2017.

2016 : "Decentralization and Neo Social Development", **KILA Journal of Local Governance**, Vol. 3: No. 2, July-December 2016.

2016 : "Focus is missing in the Document for the creation of World Class Institutions", **University News**, Vol. 54: No. 48, 28 November to 4th December, 2016.

2016 "Democracy Promotion through Decentralization of Powers in India", **Local Government Quarterly**, July-September 2016, Vol. LXXXVI: No. 3.

2016 : "Decentralization: Unfinished Agenda" **Gandhi Marg,** Vol. 38: No. 1, April-June 2016.

2016 : "Higher Education for Rural Transformation", **University News**, Vol. 54: No. 5, February 1-7, 2016.

2016 : "Student Engagement is the Need of the Hour", **University News**, Vol. 54: No. 1, 4th January, 2016.

2015: "Occupational Shifts and Social Change in Tamil Nadu: A Study on a Silent Agrarian Revolution in the Making", **Journal of Rural Development**", Vol. 34: No. 4, October-December, 2015.

2015 : "Quality Enhancement in Higher Learning Intuitions in India", **University News**, Vol. 53: No. 46, November 2015.

2015 : "Pressure Groups for strengthening Grassroots Democracy, **The Indian Journal of Public Administration,** Vol LXI: No. 3, July-September 2015.

2015 : "Where are we on Decentralization?', **Local Government Quarterly,** Vol. LXXXV: No. 3, July–September, 2015.

2015 : "New Paradigm of Social Science Research in the Era of Globalization", **University News**, Vol. 53: No. 37, September 14-20, 2015.

2015 : "Democracy and Decentralization-Strategy to tackle the issues of Exclusion", **KILA Journal of Local Governance,** Vol. II, No. 1, January-June 2015.

2015 : "Interface between Academia and Policy Community", **University News**, Vol. 53. No. 24, June 15-21, 2015.

2015 : "Academic Freedom in Higher Learning Institutions: A Narrative from Personal Experience", **University News,** Vol. 53: No. 3, January 19-25, 2015.

2014 : "Lok Sabha Elections 2014 in Tamil Nadu", **Madhya Pradesh Journal of Social Science**. Vol. 19: No. 2, December 2014.

2014 : How does Development take place? A Case Study of a Social Transformation Experiment by Sri Aurobindo Society Pondicherry, **Journal of Development Management and Communication**, Vol. No. 4, October 2014-2015.

2014 : "Accountability in Higher Learning Institutions in India", **University News**, Vol. 52: No. 49, December 8-14, 2014.

2014 : "Democracy and Decentralization: A tool and a strategy to tackle the issues of exclusion", **The Grassroots Governance Journal,** Vol. XII: No. 2. July-December 2014.

2014 : "Development Scheme or Vote Catcher: An Analysis of a Scheme in Tamil Nadu", **South Asian Journal of Socio-Political Studies**, Vol. XV: No. 1, July-December 2014.

2014 : Role of Support Agency for Elected Women Representatives: A Narration of Two Decades Experience in Women Empowerment, **The Indian Journal of Public Administration,** Vol. X: No. 3, July-September 2014.

2014 : "Organizing People Politics in India", **Social Science,** Vol. 11: No. 42, January-March 2014.

2014 : "Skill Development in Higher Learning Institutions: A Micro Analysis", **The Indian Journal of Industrial Relations,** Vol. 49: No. 3, January 2014.

2013 : "Decentralization: Acceleration or Deceleration", **The Grassroots Governance Journal**, Vol. XI: No. 2, July-December 2013.

2013 : "Direct Benefit Transfer: Perspective of Stakeholders, **South Asian Journal of Socio-Political Studies**, Vol. XIV: No. 1, July-December 2013.

2013 : "Non-Seriousness in Learning and Teaching in Social Science: A Micro Analysis", **University News**, Vol. 51: No. 42, October, 21st–27th, 2013.

2013 : "Ethical Governance and Society: Concerns at Grassroots", **Indian Journal of Public Administration**, Vol. LIX: No. 3, July-September 2013.

2013 : "Village Placement Programme: An Enabler to Learn about

Communities", **University News,** Vol. 51: No. 27, 8th–14th July, 2013.

2013 : "Democratization through Decentralization", **Madhya Pradesh Journal of Social Science,** Vol. 17: No. 1, June 2013.

2013 : "Substantiating Democratic Decentralization through Free Fair Elections: Case of Local Bodies Election in Tamil Nadu", **The Indian Journal of Public Administration,** Vol. LIX: No. 2, April-June 2013.

2012 : "Agenda Setting for Social Science Research in India", **Social Glance,** Vol. 1, October-December, 2012.

2012 : "Rural Development Scenario: A Qualitative Assessment for Action in Tamil Nadu", **Journal of Parliament Studies**, Vol. 4, No. 2, July-December, 2012.

2012 : "Right to Information Act in India: A Note on Praxis", **Social Action,** Vol. 62, No. 3, July-September 2012.

2012 : "New Tasks for the New Vice-Chancellor", **University News,** Vol. 50: No. 21, May 21-27, 2012.

2012 : "Relevance of the Rural Institute in India", **South Asia Politics,** Vol. II: No. 1, May 2012.

2012 : "A Model Social Business to Eradicate Needless Blindness", **Jharkhand Journal of Development and Management Studies,** Vol. 10: No. 1, January–March, 2012.

2011 : "Rural Transformation and Rural Governance", **Social Science** (*Tamil*), Vol. 33, October-December 2011.

2011 : "Governance from the Perspective of Gandhi", **World Focus**, Special Issue, Vol. XXXII: No. 8, August 2011.

2011 : "Reduction of Corruption at Grassroots", **The Indian Journal of Public Administration**, Vol. No. 3, July-September 2011.

2011 : "Where We Lead in Higher Education in India", **University News**, Vol. 49: No. 39, September 26th to 2nd October 2011.

2011 : "A Place to Convert Noise to Voice", **Yojana**, Vol. 55, February, 2011.

2010 : "New Panchayati Raj System in Tamil Nadu", **Social Science in Perspective**, Vol. 2: Nos. 2 and 4, July-September and Octember–December 2010.

2010 : "Problems in Realizing the potentials of Decentralization in India", **South Asia Politics**, Vol. 9: No. 7, November 2010.

2010 : "Higher Education in Lower Order", **The Indian Journal of Public Administration**, Vol. LVI: No. 3, July-September 2010.

2010 : "Ensuring Accountability and Transparency in Development Activities at Grassroots", **The IUP Journal of Governance and Public Policy**, Vol. 5, No. 3, September 2010.

2010 : "Higher Education in India: Where are we Leading", **University News**, Vol. 48, No. 28, July 12-18, 2010.

2010 : "Accountability and Transparency at Grassroots", **The Indian Journal of Public Administration**, Vol. LVI: No. 1, January–March, 2010.

2010 : "Role of ICT in Scientific Data Generation and Management", **South Asian Journal of Socio-Political Studies**, Vol. X: No. 2 January-June 2010.

2010 : "Gandhian Framework of Development", **World Focus**, No. 366, June, 2010.

2010 : "An Analysis of 15th Lok Sabha Elections in Tamil Nadu", **Madhya Pradesh Journal of Social Science**, Vol. 14, No. 2 December 2009.

2009 : "Problems and Scope in Handling RTI from Grassroots Perspective", **The Indian Journal of Public Administration**, Vol. LV, No. 3, July-September 2009.

2009 : "Democracy, Development and Conflict at Grassroots", **Local Government Quarterly**, Vol. LXXXIX: No. 3 July-September 2009.

2009 : Local Governance as a Factor in Centre-State Relations in India", **ICFAI University Journal of Public Administration,** Vol. V, No. 2, April–June 2009.

2009 : "Rural Universities in the Era of Globalization", **University News**, Vol. 47: No. 33, August 17-23, 2009.

2009 : "Larger Role of Academics in Rural Human Life", **University News**, Vol. 47: No. 16, April 20-26, 2009.

2009 : "Hind Swaraj: A Contextual Review for Grassroots Action", **Jarkhand Journal of Development and Management,** Vol. 7: No. 1 January-March 2009.

2008 : "Politics of Exclusion and Inclusion", **Social Science** (*Tamil*) Vol. 6: No. 21.

2008 : "Governance and Administration: Reforms at Grassroots", **The ICFAI University Journal of Public Administration,** Vol. 4: No. 4, October 2008.

2008 : "Local Bodies in Partnership with Private Agencies for Delivery of Services", **The Indian Journal of Public Administration**, Vol. LIV: No. 3, July-September 2008.

2008 : "Reforming Governance and Administration for a New Social Order", **Journal of Extension and Research**, Vol. X, Nos. 1 and 2, January 2008.

2008 : "Gram Sabha: Conception, perception and practices", **The Grassroots Governance Journal**, Vol. VI, No. 1, June 2008.

2008 : "Democratizing Society and Governance", **Gandhi Marg,** Vol. 30: No. 1, April-June 2008.

2008 : "Critical Interventions on the Critical Issues by the Civil Societies", **South Asia Politics,** Vol. 7, No. 3, August 2008.

2008 : "Politics of Panchayati Raj" (*In Tamil*), **Social Science,** Vol. 5:No. 19, March-May 2008.

2008 : "Restructuring Local Governance in the Era of Globalization", **The ICFAI Journal of Governance and Public Policy**, Vol. 3: No. 1, March, 2008, 23-34.

2008 : "Constitutional Laws Vs Community Laws in India: Conflict and Synergy", **The Grassroots Governance Journal,** Vol. V: No. 1, December, 2007.

2008 : "Synergy between the Potentials of the New Panchayati Raj System and the Youth in India", **Endeavour: Journal of Youth Development,** Vol. 1: No. 2, July-December 2007.

2008 : "We can also do it," **University News** (A Weekly Journal of Higher Education), Vol. 46: No. 5, February 4 to 10, 2008.

2007 : "Role of Panchayats in Service Delivery: A Case Study", **Punjab Journal of Politics,** Vol. 31, 2007.

2007 : "Administrative Reform at Grassroots", **Indian Journal of Public Administration**, Special Number Vol. LIII: No. 3, July-September, 2007.

2007 : "Crisis in Governance, Politics and Administration", **South Asia Politics,** Vol. 6: No. 6, October 2007.

2007 : "Critical Issues in Democratic Decentralization of Powers in India", **South Asia Politics**, Vol. 6: No. 1, May 2007.

2007 : "Role of Panchayats in Social Development", **South Asian Journal of Socio-Political Studies**, Vol. 7: No. 2, January-June, 2007.

2007 : "Planning for Development at Grassroots in Tamil Nadu", **The ICFAI Journal of Public Administration**, Vol. III: No. 2, April 2007.

2007 : "Participatory Governance in Indian Politics", **The Indian Journal of Political Science**, Vol. XVIII: No. 1, January-March, 2007.

2007 : "Indian Democracy: A Rethinking", **South Asia Politics**, Vol. 5: No. 9, December 2006.

2006 : "Potential for Social Transformation and Economic Prosperity through Decentralized Governance under New Dispensation", **The Grassroots Governance Journal,** Vol. IV: No. 2, December 2006.

2006 : "Role of Panchayats in Social Development: Excellence in Decentralised Administration", **The Indian Journal of Public Administration,** Special Number, Vol. LII: No. 3, July-September, 2006.

2006 : "Planning for Development at Panchayats", **Man in India,** Vol. 86: No. 182, January-June 2006.

2006 : "Participatory Democracy in Indian Political System", **Gandhi Marg,** Vol. 27: No. 384, October-December 2005 and January-March, 2006.

2006 : "Women in Governance at Grassroots", **Grassroots** (*Tamil*), Vol. 1: No. 12, February 2006.

2005 : "Role of Panchayats in Social Development", **Madhya Pradesh Journal of Social Sciences,** Vol. 10: No. 2, July-December 2005.

2005 : "Role of Youth in Governance at Grassroots", **Endeavour,** (*Journal of Youth Development*) Vol. No. 1, July-December 2005.

2005 : "Role of Elected Women Representatives in Evolving Alternative Governance at Grassroots," **Social Change and Development,** Vol. 3, July 2005.

2005 : "Good Governance at Grassroots", **The Indian Journal of Political Science**, Vol LXVI: No. 2, April-June 2005.

2005 : "Extension in Higher Education in India: The Missing Dimension", **University News**, Vol. 43:No. 17, April 25-May 1, 2005.

2005 : "Rajiv Gandhi's Framework for Devolution of Powers for Democracy and Development", **The Grassroots Governance Journal**, Vol. II: No. 2, December 2004.

2005 : "Elected Women Representatives and Emerging Alternative Governance", **Punjab Journal of Politics**, Vol. XXIX: No. 1.

2004 : "The Empowerment Process: Women Representatives in Grassroots Institutions in Tamil Nadu", **Indian Social Science Review**, Vol. 6: No. 1, January-June, 2004.

2004 : "Panchayats and Communities in Family Welfare", **Social Welfare**, Vol. 51: No. 7, October 2004.

2004 : "Water: Way to Good Governance", **Dawn to Earth**, Vol. 13: No. 11, October 31, 2004.

2004 : "Women in Governance for Development at Grassroots", **The Indian Journal of Public Administration**, Vol. L: No. 1, January-March 2004.

2004 : "Panchayats in Tamil Nadu: Achievements and Problems", **Social Science** (*in Tamil*) Vol. 1: No. 3, March 2004.

2004 : "Building Alliances and Capabilities among the Elected Women Representatives of Grassroots Institutions," **Women Link**, Vol. 10: No. 1, January-March 2004.

2003 : "Where Panchayats are Heading: Field Notes from Tamil Nadu", **The Grassroots Governance Journal**, Vol. No. 2, December 2003.

2003 : "Towards Participatory Governance at Grassroots: Synergization of Rural Communities and Institutions", **South Asian Journal of Socio Political Studies,** Vol. 4: No. 1, December 2003.

2003 : "Managing the Community: Synergization of Traditional Panchayat with Formal Panchayat Raj system in Tamil Nadu, India." **Loyola Journal of Social Sciences**, Vol. XVII: No. 2, July-December 2003.

2003 : "Role of Caste Groups in New Panchayati Raj System: A Case Analysis of Tamil Nadu", **Grassroots Governance**, Vol. I: No. 1, January-June, 2003.

2003 : "Dalit Leadership in Panchayats: Tamil Nadu", **Participation and Governance**, Vol. 9: No. 26, March 2003.

2002 : "Impediments to Empowerment of Women: Experiences of Elected Women Representatives in Panchayats in Tamil Nadu", **The Indian Journal of Political Science**, Vol. 63, No. 1 (March 2002).

2001 : "Role of Women in New Panchayati Raj System" (in Tamil) **Karuthukkalam,** Vol. 1: No. 4 December 2001.

2001 : "Women Leadership and Women Empowerment"(in Tamil) **Thittam**, 32:12, August 2001.

2001 : "New Panchayati Raj System in Tamil Nadu", **South Asian Journal of Socio-Political Studies**, Vol. 1: No. 2, January-June 2001.

2001 : "Genre of Women Leaders in Tamil Nadu", **Indian Journal of Public Administration**, Vol. XLVII: No. 1, (January-March, 2001).

2000 : "Understanding Indian Politics from the Perspective of Tamil Nadu Politics", **The Indian Journal of Public Affairs and Policy Research**, Vol. III: No. 1-4, January–December, 2000.

2000 : "Planning by the people in Tamil Nadu" (Tamil), **Thittam,** Vol. 32: No. 3, November 2000.

2000 : "Conflicting Roles in Representative Institutions: A case analysis of Tamil Nadu", **Journal of Extension and Research**, Vol. II: No. 2, January 2000.

1999 : "Importance of Understanding the power of the People", (Tamil), **Thittam**, Vol. 31: No. 1, September 1999.

1999 : "Gram Sabha: A Civil society at the Bottom", **Journal of Extension and Research**, Vol. 2: No. 1, July 1999.

1999 : "Emancipation of Women Leadership in Local Bodies", (Tamil), **Thittam**, Vol. 30: No. 10, June, 1999.

1999 : Evolving a new strategy to build the capacity of the Panchayat Women Leaders (in Tamil), **Thittam**, Vol. 31: No. 9, May 2000.

1999 : "Rural Reconstruction and Public Participation", **Journal of Extension and Research**, Vol. 1: No. 2, January 1999.

1999 : "An Approach of Decentralization of Power" (Tamil), **Special Issues on Local Bodies by Theekathir**, 1999.

1998 : "Planning in peoples Panchayat", (Tamil) **Thittam**, Vol. 30: No. 3, November 1998.

1998 : "New Panchayati Raj System in the Development Process of the World today" (Tamil), **Thittam,** Vol. 29: No. 11, July 1998.

1998 : "Sustaining Parliamentary Democracy", **ISDA Journal**, Vol. 8: No. 1, January-March 1998.

1997 : "Rural Economy in New Panchayati Raj" (Tamil), **Thittam**, 29:2, October 1997.

1997 : "Capacity Building Exercise for Elected Representatives in Tamil Nadu", **Journal of Rural Development**, 16:4, October-December 1997.

1997 : "Role of New Panchayati Raj System in Rural Economy", **Khadi Gramodyog**, XXXXIV: 1, October 1997.

1997 : "Resilience of Indian Democracy", **Kurukshetra**, XLV: 11, August 1997.

1997 : "Planning for a Village" (Tamil), **Thittam**, 28:10 (June 1997).

1997 : "A Status Report on the New Panchayati Raj System in Tamil Nadu", **Beyond Anubhav**, 1:2, May-June 1997.

1997 : "Empowering People: An Agenda for Immediate Action", **Gandhigram Golden Jubilee Souvenir 1947-97**, Gandhigram.

1995 : "Role of Women in New Panchayati Raj" (Tamil), **Thittam** Vol. 27: No. 3, November 1995.

1995 : "Mahatma Gandhi: Precursor of the Future", **Yojana**, 39:12, October 1995.

1995 : "New Panchayati Raj Structure" (Tamil), **XII Sarvodaya State Conference Souvenir** (21-05-95).

1995 : "National Integration: Dreams and Realities", **Review of Social Sciences,** 1: 2, January 1995.

1994 : "Salience of Development in Gandhian Framework", **Kurukshetra**, XLIII:1, October 1994.

1994 : "Empowerment of Women—A Novel Exercise", **Kurukshetra**, XLII: 9, June 1994.

1993 : "Need for Revitalizing Panchayati Raj Institutions in Tamil Nadu", **Southern Economist**, 32:7, August 1993.

1993 : "Needing Social Action for Effective Panchayati Raj Functioning", **Kurukshetra Special**, June 1993.

1993 : "Gandhian Approach towards Rural Development", **Southern Economist**, 31:22 and 24 1-15 April, 1993.

1993 : "An Analysis of Ethno-Politics in Tamil Nadu", **ISDA Journal**, 3:1, January-March 1993.

1992 : "Understanding the process of development through Natural Theory of Nationalism", **Gandhi Marg.** 14:3, (October-December 1992.

1992 : "Participatory Rural Appraisal and Rural Development", **Southern Economist** 31:8, 1992.

1992 : "Change in the Parliament Behaviour in India", **The Hindu,** Open Page 14-7-1992.

1992 : "Dynamics of National Integration and Ethnic Loyalty: A Symbiotic process in Indian Politics", **Journal of National Integration,** 1: 1, 1992.

1992 : "Linguistic Conflict, Ethnic Assertiveness and Political Mobilization in Canada and India", **ISDA Journal**, 2:1, 1992.

1992 : "Linguistic Conflict, Ethnic Assertiveness and Political Mobilization in Canada and India", **Indian Journal of Canadian Studies**, 1, 1992.

1991 : "Cultural Diversity, Uneven Development and Consociation Democracy: Integrative Process of Quebec in Canada and Tamil Nadu in India", **The Indian Journal of Political Science**, LII:2, 1991.

1990 : "Ethnic Identity and National Loyalty of an Ethnic Group in India", **The Indian Journal of Political Science**. LI:1, 1990.

1990 : "Legislative Institutions in India: Decline or Change", **The Indian Journal of Political Science**, LI: 3, 1990.

1989 : "Ethnic Conflict Management: A General Framework for Analysis", **Indian Journal of Political Studies**, 13, December, 1989.

1989 : "Qualitative Analysis of Resolutions of Massachusetts and Tamil Nadu State Legislatures on Ethnic Problems in Sri Lanka: A Comparative Study", **Kerala Journal of Political Studies**, II-IV: 4-8, 1987-89.

1989 : "Syndrome of Change in Legislative Behaviour", **Southern Economist**. 27:23-24, (1989).

1989 : "Ethnicity in Sri Lanka: A study in Ethnic Equalization", **Journal of Eelam Studies**, 2, 1989.

1989 : "Role orientation of the members of 8th Legislative Assembly of Tamil Nadu", **The Indian Journal of Political Science**. L: 2, 1989.

1989 : "Ethno methodology: An Appraisal", **Annamalai University Journal** (Humanities), 34, 1989.

1988 : "Impact of LTTE in Tamil Nadu Politics", **Tamil Voice International,** 1: 16, 1988.

1988 : Indo-Sri Lanka Accord and Ethnic Political Parties in Tamil Nadu, **Tamil Voice International,** 1:21, 1988.

1988 : "Ethnic Leadership and Social Change in Tamil Nadu", **The Indian Journal of Political Science,** XLIX: 4, 1988.

1987 : "Inculcating the values of Parliamentary Democracy", **Southern Economist,** 26:4, 1987.

1987 : "President under Indian Constitution: Myth and Reality", **Southern Economist,** 26:16, 1987.

1987 : "Comparative Analysis of Resolutions of State Legislatures", **Social Science Digest,** 5, 1987.

1986 : "Eclipse of the Second Chamber in Indian State Legislatures", **Southern Economist,** 25: 12, 1986.

1986 : "Evaluating Legislatures", **Annamalai University Journal** (Humanities) Part I: 32, 1986.

1986 : "Need of an academy for Legislators", **Southern Economist,** 24: 24, 1986.
1986 : "Tamil Nadu Legislature: A Qualitative Analysis of Questions", **Social Science Digest,** IV, 1986.
1984 : "Need for New Orientation in Analysis for Legislature", **Social Science Digest,** 2: 1-2, 1984.
1984 : "Tamil Nationalism as a factor in Indian Politics", **The Indian Journal of Political Science,** XLVI: 4, 1984.
1982 : "Political Awareness of the Students of Annamalai University", **Social Science Digest,** 1: 1, 1982.

25. Popular Articles (Total: 339)

2018 : "Students are carrier of certificates and not capacity and skill" **Kizhakkuvasal Udayam**, Vol. 10: No. 9, February, 2018.
2018 : "Religion and Secularism: Indian Perspective", **Omsakthi**, March, 2018.
2018 : "Have a big aim in your life" **Kanavu**, No. 10, Jan-March, 2018.
2018 : "New Age Politics", **Millennium Post**, 22nd February, 2018.
2018 : "Damaging Society by offering education through corrupt means", **Theekkadhir**, 19th February, 2018.
2018 : "Realign Modern Politics", **Millennium Post**, 7th February, 2018.
2018 : "Seriousness on the Job Front" **Millennium Post**, 2nd February, 2018.
2018 : "Message from R.K. Nagar By-election", **Millennium Post**, 25th January, 2018.
2018 : "R.K. Nagar By-election Blister" **Policy Pulse**, January 1-15 Vol. 3:No. 11, 2018.
2018 : "A Training Institute of Excellence and Eminence", **Kizhakkuvasal Udayam**, January, 2018.
2018 : "Development for Whom?" **Theekkadhir**. 10th January, 2018.
2017 : "Questioning is the basis of Democracy" **Theekkadhir**. 13th Dec., 2017.
2017 : "Ignorance in politics is dangerous for the country and the society", **Janasakthi**. 17th December, 2017.
2017 : "Disaster Management with People's Participation", **Dinamani**. 16th Dec, 2017.

2017 : "Stalwarts of the South", **Millennium Post**. 4th December, 2017.

2017 : "Let us understand the process of Vocational Education and Training", **Kizhakkuvasal Udayam**. December 2017.

2017 : "We are wasting our money and time in the name of skilling youth", **Dinamani.** 4th November, 2017.

2017 : "Transform the Graveyard and its Workers", **Theekkadir** 3rd November, 2017.

2017 : "Ashrams are for Transformation of Personality", **Kizhakku Vasal Udayam**, October 2017. Vol. 10:No. 5.

2017 : "How to Evaluate a Government?" **Dinamani**. 23rd October, 2017.

2017 : "Social Business", **Om Sakthi**, November 2017.

2017 : "Alternative to Dravidian Giants", **Millennium Post**. 23rd November, 2017.

2017 : "How to include the excluded in development and governance?" **Kanavu**. October 2017.

2017 : "Status of Dalits in Periyar lands", **Policy Pulse**. Vol. 3: No. 5, 1-5 October, 2017.

2017 : "We will Strengthen Gram Sabha to Empower the Poor", **Uzhavan Urimai**, October 2017.

2017 : "People will decide only in election", **Theekkadir**, 12th October, 2017.

2017 : "Creating a New India", **Dinamani**, 4th October, 2017.

2017 : "How to create a New India?" **Janasakthi**, Vol. 80: No. 35, 1st October, 2017.

2017 : "Peoples Movement for new Politics", **Millennium Post**, 30th September, 2017.

2017 : "Grama Sabha has to be strengthened", **Theekkadir**. 27th September, 2017.

2017 : "Where is the Prime Minister Candidate?" **Kizhakku Vassal Udayam**, Vol. 10: No. 4, September 2017.

2017 : "From Party Politics to People Politics", **Dinamani**, 1st August, 2017.

2017 : "Learn from Nature", **Kizhakku Vasal Udayam**, Vol. 10: No. 2, July 2017.

2017 : "No True Opposition", **Millennium Post**, 7th August, 2017.

2017 : "Accept the reality of Change", **Dinamani**, 17th August, 2017.

2017 : "Swiss farmers show the way to Indian farmers", **Kizhakku Vasal Udayam**, Vol. 10: No. 3, August, 2017.

2017 : "Where is the support for our farmers?" **Policy Pulse**, Vol. 2: No. 24, 16-31 July, 2017.

2017 : "Dr. Amedkar: More than a leader of the masses", **Policy Pulse**, Vol. 3: No. 1, 16-31, August 2017.

2017 : "Where are we heading? in higher education", **Policy Pulse**, Vol. 2:No. 20,16-31, May 2017.

2017 : "Underestimating the Change", **Millennium Post**, 5th September, 2017.

2017 : "A New Report for Policy Makers on Higher Education", **University News**, Vol. 55: No. 29, July 17-23, 2017.

2017 : "An Alternative Approach", **Dinamani**, 11th July, 2017.

2017 : "Waving the problems Away", **Policy Pulse**, 16-30 June, 2017, Vol. 2: No. 22.

2017 : "The Change faces of Indian Politics", **Millennium Post**, 24th June, 2017.

2017 : "Is Education a Business?" **Janasakthi**, 21st May, 2017.

2017 : "Where is Norway where is India?" **Kizhakkuvasal Udayam**, Vol. 9: No. 12, May, 2017.

2017 : "Higher Education Needs Higher Level Leadership", **Dinamani**, 19th May, 2017.

2017 : "Why Higher Education has gone down? **Dinamani**, 2nd June, 2017.

2017 : "Need of Skill Education", **Dinamani**, 16th June, 2017.

2017 : "Life Education in Usmania", **Kizhakkuvasal Udayam**, Vol. 10: No. 1, June, 2017.

2017 : "Rural Development from the perspective of M.K. Gandhi", **Sarvodayam** (*Tamil*), Vol. 11: No. 3, June, 2017.

2017 : "Rural Development from the perspective of M.K. Gandhi", **Sarvodayam** (*Tamil*), Vol. 11: No. 2, May 2017.

2017 : "New Narratives in Tamil Nadu Politics?" **Policy Pulse**, Vol. 2: No. 18, 16 to 30 April, 2017.

2017 : "Restrict Terms to Two: Election Reform", **Policy Pulse**, Vol. 2:No. 18, 16 to 30 April, 2017.

2017 : "Why not a World Class Rural Institute?" **Janasakthi**, 30th April, 2017.

2017 : "Perspectives for Future", **Kanavu**, April 2017.

2017 : "Unintended Consequences of MGNREGA", **Janasakthi**, 16th April, 2017.

2017 : "No new Narrative in Tamil Polity", **Millennium Post,** 14th April, 2017.

2017 : "Change has to start from you", **Dinamani**, 15th April, 2017.
2017 : "No Silage? Give them Cement", **Policy Pulse**, Vol. 2: No. 17, 1-15 April, 2017.
2017 : "The time to Act is now: Where we are in combating climate change wonders", **Policy Pulse**, Vol. 2: No. 17, 1-15 April 2017.
2017 : "Where are the Ministers of Kerala?" **The Tamil Hindu**, 5th April, 2017.
2017 : "Rural Development from the perspective of M.K. Gandhi", **Sarvodayam** (*Tamil*), Vol. 11: No. 1, April 2017.
2017 : "Listening to Voices not Noises", **Policy Pulse**, Vol. 2: No. 16, 16-31 March, 2017.
2017 : "Political Contradictions", **Janasakthi**, Vol. 80: No. 8, 26 March, 2017.
2017 : "Youth in India and Germany", **Kizhakkuvasal Udayam**, Vol. 9: No. 10, March 2017.
2017 : "A New Report for Policy Makers on Higher Education", **Policy Pulse**, Vol. 2: No. 16, 16-31 March, 2017.
2017 : "Where are our youth proceeding?" **Teekkadhir**, 24th March, 2017.
2017 : "Rural Development from the perspective of M.K. Gandhi". **Sarvodayam** (*Tamil*), Vol. 10, No. 12, March 2017.
2017 : "A Good scheme for the poor but not popular", **Dinamani,** March 2017.
2017 : "Rural Development from the perspective of M.K. Gandhi", **Sarvodayam** (*Tamil*), Vol. 10: No. 11, February 2017.
2017 : "The case of MGNREGS in India", **Policy Pulse**, Vol. 2: No. 14,16-28 February 2017.
2017 : "Japanese scholars interest in Indian State", **Kizhakku Vaasal Udhayam**, February, 2017.
2017 : "Stagnation leads to Disaster", **Dinamani**, 25th February, 2017.
2017 : "Jallikattu Protest: Symptom not Cause", **Policy Pulse**, Vol. 2: No. 13, 1-15 February, 2017.
2017 : "Deficit Democracy", **Dinamani**, 4th February, 2017.
2017 : "If not now when if not I who?" **Kanavu,** Vol. 6, January 2017.
2017 : "Peoples University", **Kizhakku Vaasal Udhayam**, Vol. 9: No. 8, January 2017.
2017 : "Deliberative Democracy is the need of the Hour", **Dinamani**, 21st January, 2017.

2017 : "Rural Development from the Perspective of M.K. Gandhi", **Sarvodayam** (Tamil), Vol. 10: No. 10, January 2017.

2017 : "Where is World Class Rural Institute?" **Millennium Post**, January 19, 2017.

2017 : "Panchayati Raj at Present", **Ungal Noolagam**, Vol. 8:No. 10, January 2017.

2016 : "Jaya showed how to make a pro-poor state", **Policy Pulse**, Vol. 2: No. 10, 16-31 December 2016.

2016 : "Lessons from Local Body Elections", **Om Sakthi**, December 2016.

2016 : "Brics Conference on Local Governance", **Kizhakku Vassal Udayam**, Vol. 9:No. 7, December 2016.

2016: "Twenty Years of Academic Works in Decentralization", **The Hindu** (*Tamil*), 30th November, 2016.

2016 : "A Tribute to a Gandhian Educationalist", **Sarvodaya Talisman,** Vol. 10:No. 5, November 2016.

2016 : "Green Growth and Social Development", **Ungal Noolagam**, Vol. 8: No. 8, November 2016.

2016 : "People's Institutions: Cooperative are Destroyed by Political Parties", **The Hindu Tamil**, 12th November, 2016.

2016 : "Social Education is Part of Higher learning Institutions", **The Hindu Tamil**, 5th November, 2016.

2016 : "Village Placement Programme", **Kizhakku Vassal Udayam**, Vol. 9:No. 5, October 2016.

2016 : "Call for the Youth to Local Governance", **Kanavu** (Tamil), Vol. 5, October.

2016 : "Think Differently for Politics" **Dinamani**, 10th October, 2016.

2016 : "Belgium to Sevapur: Services of Mother Leoprovo", **Kizhakkuvasal Udayam**, Vol. 9: No. 4, September 2016.

2016 : "Why our Higher Education has Drawn?" **Janasakthi**, 23rd September, 2016.

2016 : "Importance of Extension in Higher Education", **Policy Pulse,** Vol. 2: No. 4,16-30 September, 2016.

2016 : "No Eyes in Draft New Education Policy", **Janasakthi**, 15th September, 2016.

2016 : "Beyond Construction of Toilets", **Millennium Post**, 6th September, 2016.

2016 : "Awareness about Democracy", **Omsakthi**, September, 2016.

2016 : "Education: Will Javadekar Deliver?" **Policy Pulse**, Vol. 2: No. 2, 16-31 August, 2016.

2016 : Life is full of Bed of Roses if We Understand", **Kizhakkuvasal Udayam**, Vol. 9: No. 3, August 2016.

2016 : "Politicization of Skill Development", **Dinamalar**, 28th August, 2016.

2016 : "Is Varsity Research a Waste?" **Policy Pulse,** Vol. I: No. 23, July 1-15, 2016.

2016 : "Tiff over New Education Policy", **Policy Pulse**, Vol. I: No. 22, June 16-30, 2016.

2016 : "Find Ways to Curb Cash for Vote", **Policy Pulse**, Vol. I: No. 21, June 1-15, 2016.

2016 : "Summer Camp for Sensitivity Creation on Human Rights" **Kizhakku Vaasal Uthayam,** Vol. 9: No. 2, July 2016.

2016 : "Political Education through Election", **Janasakthi**, 29th July, 2016.

2016 : "Election and Democracy", **Theekadhir,** 29th July, 2016.

2016 : "Change in the Electoral Process and Democracy", **Dinamani**, 23rd July, 2016.

2016 : "Central Governments Outlook on Decentralization", **Janasakthi**, 22nd, July, 2016.

2016 : "Decentralize Now", **One India One People,** Vol. 20: No. 4, August 15, 2016.

2016 : "Training the Head and Heart", **Policy Pulse**, Vol. 1: No. 24, July 16th to 31st, 2016.

2016 : "For the attention of the leaders of our Government", **Ungal Noolagam**, Vol. 8: No. 4, July 2016.

2016 : "Reasons for Poverty and Prosperity, **Janasakthi**, 12th June, 2016.

2016 : "Minimal Democracy", **Dinamani**, 16th May, 2016.

2016 : "Importance of Reliable Data in Policy Making", **Policy Pulse**, 1st to 15th May, 2016.

2016 : "Scientific Data Management for Policy Making", **Policy Pulse**, 16th to 30th April, 2016.

2016 : "Alliance Parties are Arch Enemies", **Policy Pulse**, 16th to 30th May, 2016.

2016 : "Importing Skills: The German Way", **Policy Pulse**, 1st to 15th May, 2016.

2016 : "How People Decide In General Elections?" **Dinamani**, 26th April, 2016.

2016 : "They School", **Kizhakku Vaasal Uthayam,** Vol. 8: No. 11, April 2016.

2016 : "Can our cities become livable?" **Om Sakthai**, April 2016.
2016 : "Costly Elections: Interview, **Kalki**, April 2016.
2016 : "We need more Kankayakumars", **Janasakthi**, 27th March, 2016
2016 : "Health and Education", **Janasakthi**, 21st March, 2016.
2016 : "Tackling Democracy to Ward off and Remove Deficit", **Policy Pulse**, Vol. 1:No. 16, 16-31 March, 2016.
2016 : "Make Higher Learning Institutes People–Centric", **Policy Pulse**, Vol. 1:No. 15, 1-15 March, 2016.
2016 : "Reservation of Seats for Women in Local Bodies", **Dinamani**, 15th March, 2016.
2016 : "Responsibilities of Citizens beyond voting", **Dinamalar**, March, 13th, 2016
2016 : "The Education", **Kizhakku Vaasal Uthayam,** Vol. 8: No. 10 March, 2016.
2016 : "Limited Understanding of MGNREGA", **Desiya Murasu** Vol. 8: No. 3, February 15, 2016.
2016 : "Newness in Governance", **Dinamani**, 13th February, 2016.
2016 : "We have forgotten the 74th Amendment", **Janasakthi**, 12th February, 2016.
2016 : "Need of a Policy for Training to Grassroots Leaders", **Millennium Post**, 3rd February, 2016.
2016 : "A New Political Culture", **Janasakthi**, 3rd February, 2016.
2016 : "Newness comes in the New Year", **Kizhakku Vaasal Uthayam,** Vol. 8: No. 8, January, 2016.
2016 : "Unskilled Labourers: A Wrong Classification", **Janasakthi**, 20th January, 2016.
2016 : Learning Labour Lost, **Policy Pulse**, Vol. 1: No. 11, 1-15th January, 2016.
2015 : "Development is the outcome of a Struggle", **Kizhakku Vaasal Uthayam,** Vol. 8: No. 7. December, 2015.
2015 : "Have we Learned Lessons from the Past for Disaster Management?" **Dinamani,** 4th December, 2015.
2015 : Why we are not able to? **Kizhakku Vaasal Uthayam,** Vol. 8: No. 6, November 2015.
2015 : "A Day with Abdulkalam", **Dinamani** (Special Edition), 2015.
2015 : "Towards People Politics", **Janasakthi,** 2nd November, 2015.
2015 : "Message of the Government; where it goes? **Janasakthi,** 11th October, 2015
2015 : "Gap between our talk and action", **Kizhakku Vaasal Uthayam,** Vol. 8, September 2015.

2015 : "Higher Learning Institutions and Communities", **Millennium Post**, 3rd October, 2015.

2015 : "To Deeper Democracy", **Golden Jubilee Sovnir of Nadir Uravin Murai**, Dindigul, 2015.

2015 : "Development in the Responsibility of the State Government", **Dinamani,** 24th August, 2015.

2015 : "Belittling High offices in India", **Janasakthi,** 11th August, 2015.

2015 : "Social Science Research and Our Society", **Dinamani**, 17th July 2015.

2015 : "Politics on Waste Management", **Janasakthi,** 22nd July, 2015.

2015 : "The issues forgotten by the Middle Class", **Janasakthi,** 23rd June, 2015.

2015 : "Synergy between Research and Outreach", **Millennium Post,** 13th June, 2015.

2015 : "Unqualified Certificate", **Janasakthi,** 3rd June, 2015.

2015 : "Waste Business in a Society", **Kizhakku Vaasal Uthayam**, Vol. 7: No. 11, April, 2015.

2015 : "Village Adoption or Evolving Model Panchayat", **Dinamani** 27th April, 2015.

2015 : "Alternative Path for Development of Human Society", **Kizhakku Vaasal Uthayam**, Vol. 7: No. 9, February 2015.

2015 : "Water, Land and Forest", **Janasakthi**, 12th March, 2015.

2015 : "Outreach: Missing in Indian Higher Education", **Millennium Post**, 12th March, 2015.

2015 : "A New Development Perspective", **Janasakthi**, 22nd March, 2015.

2015 : "We need not Graduates but Skilled Persons", **Dinamalar**, 22nd March, 2015.

2014 : "Fourth Monkey Movement", **Kizhakku Vaasal Uthayam**, Vol. 7: No. 6, November 2014.

2014 : "Extension for Social Transformation", **Dinamani,** 13th October, 2014.

2014 : "Impact of Glocalization" (Tamil), **Indian Comparative Literature**, Vol. 19: No. 2, April–June, 2014.

2014 : "Skill Development in Germany through their School System" (Tamil), **Kizhakkuvasal Udayam**, Vol. 7: No. 5, October, 2014.

2014 : "Retrograde Politics", **Dinamalar,** 1st September, 2014.

2014 : "Role of Teachers in Higher Learning Institutions", **Dinamalar**, 31st August, 2014.

2014 : "For the Attention of the Educationalist", **Janasakthi,** Vol. 77: No. 196, 4th August, 2014.

2014 : "Sabha of the Poor", **Janasakthi**, Vol. 77: No. 166, 5th July, 2014.

2014 : "New Development Mantra", **Janasakthi**, Vol. 77: No. 147, 16th June, 2014.

2014 : "Can People get their Money?" **Paadam**, Vol. 57, 4th May, 2014.

2014 : "Corporate Democracy", **Janasakthi**, 4th May, 2014.

2014 : "Indian Voters", **Janasakthi**, 9th April, 2014.

2014 : "Insensitive Legislators", **Janasakthi**, 28th March, 2014.

2014 : "Transformative Leaders", **Paadam,** Vol. 56, April 2014.

2014 : "Way Shown by Arvind Kejrival", **Dinamalar,** 15th March, 2014.

2014 : "Payment for Political Parties", **Paadam,** Vol. 55, March 2014.

2014 : "If you can, you can in Panchayati Raj", **Paadam**, Vol. 53, January 2014.

2014 : "Path to Lead in Politics for the Youth in India", **Janasakthi**, 16th February, 2014.

2014 : "Message Given by Rahul Gandhi", **Desiya Murasu**, Vol. 6: No. 6, 16th–28th February, 2014.

2013 : "Has Devolution Happened?", **Janasakthi**, November 15th, 2013.

2013 : "The Ethical Angle" open page, **The Hindu**, August 21st, 2013.

2013 : "Nepal Election and Democracy", **Paadam**, Vol. 53, December 2013.

2013 : "Educational Needs for Rural Transformation", **Paadam,** Vol. 52, November 2013.

2013 : "Youth Development Struggle", **Janasakthi**, Vol. 76: No. 265, 12th October, 2013.

2013 : "Success of Thought", **Paadam,** Vol. 51, October 2013.

2013 : "Next Prime Minister", **Puthiya Thalaimurai,** Vol. 5: No. 2, 3rd October, 2013.

2013 : "Role of Panchayats in Disaster Management", **Paadam**, Vol. 50, September, 2013.

2013 : "Corruption become a Culture", **Paadam**, Vol. 50, September, 2013.

2013 : "Need of the Hour is Development Consciousness", **Om Sakthi**, August 2013.

2013 : "Serving the People, **Paadam**, Vol, 49, August, 2013.

2013 : "Politics in the Lowest", **Paadam**, Vol. 48, July 2013.

2013 : "Helping Srilankan Tamils" (in Tamil), **Dinamani,** 17th June, 2013.

2013 : "Expectation of a Citizen", **Janasakthi,** 10th June, 2013.

2013 : "Politics and Governance today", **Paadam,** Vol. 47, June 2013.

2013 : "Higher Learning Institutions and Social Transformation", **Paadam,** 45, April 2013.

2013 : "J.C. Kumarapa's Vision on Indian Democracy", **Paadam,** Vol. 44, March 2013.

2013 : "Our Search for Leadership", **Janasakthi,** May 25, 2013.

2013 : "Director Cash Transfer to the Poor", **Janasakthi,** May 12, 2013.

2013 : "New Politics", **Puthiya Thalaimurai**, 9th May, 2013.

2013 : "Citizenship Building", **Janasakthi,** July 6, 2013.

2013 : "Dalits in Tamil Nadu" **Mint**, 30th April, 2013.

2013 : "20 years of Decentralization in India", **Paadam**, Vol. 46, May, 2013.

2013 : "A Bold Step of Tamil Nadu Government", **Janasakthi,** 26th April, 2013.

2013 : "Democracy as envisioned by J.C. Kumarappa", **Janasakthi,** 18th March, 2013.

2013 : "We need courageous Governance Leader to end Corruption", **Janasakthi**, 1st February, 2013.

2013 : "Whether people are Assets or Liabilities?" **Puthiya Thalaimurai Kalvi**, Vol. 3: No. 22, 14th January, 2013.

2013 : "Whether Local Bodies are empowered?" **Paadam**, Vol. 43, February 2013.

2013 : "Who will tell the truth?" **Paadam,** Vol. 42, January 2013.

2013 : "Is our Legislature democratic?" **Janasakthi**, 2nd January, 2013.

2013 : "Deficit Democracy", **Janasakthi,** 26th January, 2013.

2013 : "Deficit Democracy", **Janasakthi,** 27th January, 2013.

2012 : "Who can be trusted?" (Tamil) **Paadam,** No. 41, December 2012.

2012 : "Will M.K. Gandhi guides us?" (Tamil) **Omsakthi,** December 2012.

2012 : "Anna's Team and it Anti-Corruption: An Analysis" Part–II (Tamil), **Paadam,** Vol. 40, November 2012.

2012 : "Leadership for the 21st Century India", **Janasakthi**, 8th November, 2012.

2012 : "Anna's Movement: An Analysis Part–I (Tamil), **Paadam,** Vol. 38, September 2012.

2012 : "Rejuvenating Rural Areas" (Tamil), **Paadam,** Vol. 37, August 2012.

2012 : "Grama Rajyam is not a Dream but an Actionable Framework" (Tamil), **Om Sakthi,** August 2012.

2012 : "New Alliance for Development" (Tamil), **Paadam,** Vol. 36, July 2012.

2012 : "Need for Educational Programme on Governance" (Tamil), **Paadam,** Vol. 35, June 2012.

2012 : "Will the Higher Learning Institutions Realize their Responsibilities?" (Tamil), **Paadam,** Vol. 34, May 2012.

2012 : "Rereading Gandhi" (Tamil), **Om Sakthi**, May 2012.

2012 : "What is need to India to-day?" (Tamil), **Dinamani,** 21st June, 2012.

2012 : "Role of Panchayats in MGNREGA" (Tamil), **Janasakthi,** 6th June, 2012.

2012 : "Need of Skill Development for our Youth in India" (Tamil), **Paadam,** Vol: 33, April 2012.

2012 : "Mobilizing People" (Tamil), **Paadam,** Vol. 32, March 2012.

2012 : "Democracy and Public Service" (Tamil), **Dinamani,** 15th February, 2012.

2012 : "Orienting the Citizens for Deliberative Democracy" (Tamil), **Paadam**, Vol. 31, February 2012.

2012 : "Who is a Leader and who is a Dealer", **Om Sakthi,** February 2012.

2011 : "Panchayats in Evolution" (Tamil), **Sarathy Vairam,** Vol. 2, No: 5, November 2011.

2011 : "Questions raised by Anna's Movement on Anti-Corruption in India" (Tamil), **Paadam,** Vol. 30, December 2011.

2011 : "Challenges to be responded in Local Bodies after the Local Body Election in 2011" (Tamil), **Paadam,** Vol. 28, November 2011.

2011 : "Whether to Honour or to Discredit, it is in your hands", (Tamil), **Paadam,** Vol. 29, December 2011.

2011 : "Local Bodies and Social Development, (Tamil), **Ezhaignar Muzhagam**, Vol. 3, No. 2, Oct. 2011.

2011 : "Challenges for the Local Bodies after the Election", **Paadam**, Vol. 27, October 2011.

2011 : "Reduce the Cost of Politics" (Tamil), **Paadam,** Vol. 22, September 2011.

2011 : "Doles and Self Respect of Citizens" (Tamil), **Paadam**, Vol. 21, April 2011.

2011 : "Cost of Virtues and Values" (Tamil), **Paadam**, Vol. 23, June 2011.

2011 : "For Whom We are Working" (Tamil), **Paadam**, Vol. 23, June 2011.

2011 : "Whatever is happening is good for Indian Democracy" (Tamil), **Paadam**, Vol. 24, July 2011.

2011 : "Participatory Democracy and Representative Democracy" (Tamil), **Paadam**, Vol. 25, August 2011.

2011 : "Political Capitalism" (Tamil), **Dinamani**, 29th August, 2011.

2011 : "Awake from deep Slumber" (Tamil), **Dinamani**, 3rd August, 2011.

2011 : "Need of Reform in Education" (Tamil), **Dinamani**, 13th July 2011.

2011 : "How to make our life more respectable?" (Tamil), **Dinamani**, 3rd October 2011.

2011 : "Gap between the Potentials and actual operation of Panchayati Raj", (Tamil), **Junior Vikadan**, 19th October 2011.

2011 : "We need Reforms in Governance and Administration" (Tamil) **Paadam**, Vol. 19, February, 2011.

2010 : "Villages are to be strengthened" (Tamil), **Paadam,** a monthly Development Politics Journal Vol. No. 17, December, 2010.

2010 : "Obama's Visit to India" (Tamil), **Paadam,** a monthly Development Politics Journal Vol. No. 17, December, 2010.

2010 : "Status of Panchayati Raj-To-day" (Tamil), **Kudimakkal Murasu,** Vol. 9: No. 7, October 2010.

2010 : "Strengthen Democracy" (Tamil), **Paadam,** a monthly Development Politics Journal Vol. No. 16, November, 2010.

2010 : "Save Democracy" (Tamil), **Paadam,** a monthly Development Politics Journal Vol. No. 15, October, 2010.

2010 : "Path for Development" (Tamil), **Paadam,** a monthly Development Politics Journal Vol. No. 14 September, 2010.

2010 : "Status of Decentralization Today" (Tamil), **Paadam,** a monthly Development Politics Journal, Vol. No. 13, August, 2010.

2010 : "Violation of Regulatory Authorities in Regulating the Violations and Peoples Vigilance" (Tamil), **Paadam,** a monthly Development Politics Journal, Vol. No. 12, July, 2010.

2010 : "Globalised Corruption: A Perspective" (Tamil), **Paadam,** a monthly Development Politics Journal, Vol. No. 11, June 2010.

2010 : "Small States or Panchayat Governments (Tamil), **Paadam,** a monthly Development Politics Journal, Vol. No. 10, May 2010.

2010 : "Understanding the Context" (Tamil), **Paadam,** a monthly Development Politics Journal, Vol. No. 9, April 2010.

2010 : "Power Shift is a Gradual Process", **One India One People**, Vol. 13: No. 10 March 2010.

2010 : "Review of the report of the World Bank on Global Warming and Climate Change" (Tamil), **Paadam,** a monthly Development Politics Journal" Vol. No. 7, February 2010.

2010 : "Contributions of Elinor Ostrom (Tamil), **Paadam,** a monthly Development Politics Journal Vol. No. 6 Jan., 2010.

2009 : "Organize for People Politics" (Tamil), **Paadam,** Vol. No. 4, December, 2009.

2009 : "What we need is an Ideology for Development?" (Tamil), **Paadam,** Vol. No. 5, November, 2009.

2009 : "Where Humanity Goes?" (Tamil), **Paadam,** Vol. No. 3, October 2009.

2009 : "Quality of the State depends on quality of Citizenship" (Tamil), **Paadam,** Vol. No. 2, September 2009.

2009 : "Our Money our Responsibility" (Tamil), **Paadam,** a monthly Development Politics Journal, Vol. No. 1, August, 2009.

2009 : "Still Politics of Political Parties" (Tamil) **Om Sakthi**, June 2009.

2009 : "Growth and equity" (Tamil), **Dinamani**, 19th May, 2009.

2008 : "Create a Good Society" (Tamil), **Dinamani,** 7th August, 2008.

2008 : "Pathways to Prosperity-I" (Tamil), **Tamil Ozai,** 1st August, 2008.

2008 : "Pathways to Prosperity-II" (Tamil), **Tamil Ozai,** 2nd August, 2008.

2008 : "People in the Clutches of the Commercialized Education" (Tamil), **Tamil Ozai,** 6th July, 2008.

2008 : "Need Administrative Reform at Grassroots" (Tamil), **Dinamani,** 5th May, 2008.

2008 : "When Autonomy for Panchayat?" (Tamil), **Tamil Ozai,** 4th May, 2008.

2008 : "Can you become a Yunus?", **Sarvodaya Talisman,** March-April 2008, Vol. 1: No. 6.

2008 : "Thought for Growth and Development" (Tamil), **Tamil Ozai,** 5th March, 2008.

2008 : "Who is with People?" (Tamil), **Tamil Ozai,** 13th January, 2008.

2007 : "Globalization of Economy and Decentralization of Powers-I" (Tamil), **Tamil Ozai**, 17th December, 2007.

2007 : "Globalization of Economy and Decentralization of Powers-II" (Tamil), **Tamil Ozai,** 18th December, 2007.

2007 : "Globalization of Economy and Decentralization of Powers-III" (Tamil), **Tamil Ozai,** 19th December, 2007.

2007 : "Where Are We Now?" (Tamil), **Tamil Ozai,** 13th November, 2007.

2007 : "To Achieve Success in Our Activities" (Tamil), **Tamil Ozai,** 18th November, 2007.

2007 : "Exporting Local Bodies" (Tamil), **Tamil Ozai,** 29th November, 2007.

2007 : "Changes Are Not Due to Magic" (Tamil), **Dinamani**, 20th October, 2007.

2007 : "Will the Schemes of the Central Government Reach the People" (Tamil), **Dinamani**, 15th November, 2007.

2007 : "Still we have not Understood Development", (Tamil), **Tamil Ozai**, 9th October, 2007.

2007 : "A New Approach to Poverty Reduction" (Tamil), **Tamil Ozai,** 22nd September, 2007.

2007 : "Why not we do Advocacy?" (Tamil), **Tamil Ozai,** 8th September, 2007.

2007 : "Government should Respect its Own Laws" (Tamil), **Tamil Ozai**, 30th August, 2007.

2007 : "In Search of an Alternative Governance" (Tamil), **Tamil Ozai,** 12th July, 2007.

2007 : "Political Murders in Panchayats", **India Today**, 18th July, 2007.

2007 : "India's Glore in Confusion" (Tamil), **Dinamani**, 29th March, 2007.

2007 : "Everyone needs perspective to protect people" (Tamil), **Tamil Ozai**, 22nd March 2007.

2007 : "Transformative Leaders for Critical Action" (Tamil), **Tami Ozai**, 7th March, 2007.

2006 : "Understanding the Panchayati Raj System" (Tamil), **Tamil Ozai**, 24th November, 2006.

2006 : "Removed our shame" (Tamil), **Dinamani**, 15th November, 2006.

2006 : "Different Roles in Democracy" (Tamil), **Tamil Ozai**, 7th December, 2006.

2006 : "Walk Towards Panchayat" (Tamil), **Tamil Ozai**.

2006 : "Have we achieved what we wanted to achieve?" **India Today,** 11th October, 2006.

2006 : "Belittling People by the Politicians" (Tamil), **Dinamani,** 12th August, 2006.

2006 : "Let Them Change by themselves or be changed by People" (Tamil), **Dinamani**, 18th January, 2006.

2005 : "Performance of Panchayat in Tamil Nadu" (Tamil), **Farmers Right**, October 2005.

2005 : "Build the Capacity of People and Empower them" (Tamil), **Kudimakkal Murasu**, December 2005.

2005 : "We do not realize our strength" (Tamil), **Dinamani**, 6th August, 2005.

2005 : "We are defeating ourselves" (Tamil), **Dinamani,** 29th April, 2005.

2005 : "Perception on Role and Responsibilities" (Tamil), **Dinamani,** 3rd March, 2005.

2004 : Silent Revolution for a New Liberation (Tamil), **Dinamani**, 29th December, 2004.

2004 : "A Good Scheme for the People" (Tamil), **Dinamani**, 31st October, 2004.

2004 : "New Qualification to Contest in Local Body Elections" (Tamil), **Dinamani**, 29th September, 2004.

2004 : "Democratizing the Indian Society" (Tamil), **Dinamani**, 19th August, 2004.

2004 : "Number or Member" (Tamil), **Dinamani,** 9th June, 2004.

2004 : "How is the performance of the members of Indian Parliament?" (Tamil), **Dinamani,** 19th April, 2004.

2003 : "Experience of Decentralization in Tamil Nadu", **Sarvodaya,** Vol. I: No. 4, September-October, 2003.

2003 : "Achievements of Panchayats", **Sarvodayam** (Tamil), Vol. I: No. 4, August, 2003.

2003 : "There is Justification for reservation of seats for women" (Tamil), **India Today**, 6th August, 2003.

2003 : "Interview to Down to Earth on Women Empowerment", **Down to Earth,** 15th August, 2003.

2003 : "Good Governance at Grassroots" (Tamil), **Dinamani,** 17th July, 2003.

2002 : Indian Paradox (in Tamil), **Dinamani,** (December 2002).

2002 : To whom the Government exists? (Tamil), **Dinamani**, (September 2002).

2002 : It is a basest treachery committed against the people (Tamil), **Dinamani**, August 2002.

2002 : Self Respect for Development (Tamil), **Dinamani,** (June 2002).

2002 : Refresher Course for Legislators (Tamil), **Dinamani**, May 2002.

2001 : "We will become citizens" (Tamil), **Tamil Murasu,** Vol. 2: No. 1, December, 2001.

2001 : "Will there be any change in attitude?" (Tamil), **Dinamani**, 11th May, 2001.

2001 : "There is a limit to the Passiveness of the People" (Tamil) **Dinamani**, 11th March, 2001.

2001 : "When we get Salvation" (Tamil), **Dinamani**, 13th February, 2001.

2001 : "Role of Panchayats in Primary Education" (in Tamil), **Panchayati Raj and Primary Education**, Chennai: TANPIC, 2001.

2000 : "How many tiers for Tamil Nadu Panchayats?" **Grama Rajyam**, Vol. 55: No. 31, 32, (11.08.2000).

2000 : "Role of Panchayats in strengthening of Primary Education" **Panchayat News**, Vol. 47: No. 20, 21, 2000.

1999 : "The Need for Viable Coalition understands" (Tamil), **Dinamani**, 10th September, 1999.

1999 : "Politicians Forgotten Issues" (Tamil), **Dinamani**, 15th July, 1999.

1999 : "People are pawns" (Tamil), **Dinamani**, 11th June, 1999.

1997 : "Review of World Bank Development Report 1997" (Tamil), **Puthiyakalvi**, 17:11, September 1997.

1996 : "Is New Panchayati Raj System an Administrative Reform or a Symbol of Culture" (Tamil), **Dinamalar,** 20th September, 1996.

1996 : "New Panchayati Raj System and Human Resource Development" (Tamil), **Vijaya Bharatham** special issue, 1996.

1995 : "Opportunities to Service", Rotary International Conference, **Souvenir**, January 1995.

1994 : "Education in New Panchayati Raj System" (Tamil), **Naazhai** 1: 4, January-June, 1994.

1993 : "Sri Aurobindo's thoughts on Education" (Tamil), **Naazhai** 1: 2 (Oct-Dec., 1993)

1993 : "73rd Constitutional Amendment and New Phase of Federalism in India, **IDARA News Letter** January-March, 1993.

1992 : "Parliamentary Behaviour in India; A Study", **The Hindu** open page 14th July, 1992.

26. Reports (Total: 42)

2016 : Report on "**The Assessment of THAI scheme in Tamil Nadu**" submitted to the State Planning Commission, Tamil Nadu.

2015 : Report on **Evaluating the Impact of MGNREGA in Kottayam District** submitted to SIRD Kerala.

2015 : Report on **Evaluating the Impact of MGNREGA in Thiruvanthapuram District** submitted to SIRD Kerala.

2015 : **Voluntarism among Youth** submitted to UNICEF, Chennai.

2014 : Report on **Critical Mass to Critical Action** submitted to ICSSR, New Delhi.

2010 : **Report of the Validation Workshop on Globalization and Decentralization** (Primary Education, Reforms in Drinking Water Sector, Primary Health Care, Democracy and Market, Special Economic Zone and Dalit in Tamil Nadu), Gandhigram, Rajiv Gandhi Chair for Panchayati Raj Studies, 2010.

2010 : **Report on National Seminar on Globalization, Decentralization and Gender,** Gandhigram, Rajiv Gandhi Chair for Panchayati Raj Studies, 2010.

2009 : **Report on the Study of Primary Education in Tamil Nadu,** sponsored by Ford Foundation, New Delhi.

2009 : **Report on the study of Reforms in Drinking Water Sector,** sponsored by Ford Foundation, New Delhi.

2009 : **Report on the Study of Primary Health Care in Tamil Nadu,** sponsored by Ford Foundation, New Delhi.

2009 : **Report on the Study of Special Economic Zone in Tamil Nadu,** sponsored by Ford Foundation, New Delhi.

2009 : **Report on the Study of Dalits in Tamil Nadu,** sponsored by Ford Foundation, New Delhi.

2009 : **Report on the study of Market and Democracy in Tamil Nadu,** sponsored by Ford Foundation, New Delhi.

2009 : **Citizens Report on Service Delivery in Tamil Nadu,** sponsored by Catalyst Trust, Chennai.

2009 : **District Human Development Report of Nagapattinam**, sponsored by UNDP and State Planning Commission.

2009 : **District Human Development Report of Dindigul**, sponsored by UNDP and State Planning Commission.

2008 : **Report on the Role of Panchayats in Disaster Preparedness and Disaster Management in the States of Gujarat, Odisha, Andhra Pradesh and Tamil Nadu,** sponsored by Action Aid, India.

2007 : **Report on Policy and Budget Analysis of Agriculture, Irrigation and Fertilizer Subsidy**, sponsored by the Ford Foundation.

2006 : **Report on the Study on the Handloom Sector in Tamil Nadu**, sponsored by the Ford Foundation.

2006 : **Report on the Study on Plantation Sector in Tamil Nadu,** sponsored by the Ford Foundation.

2006 : **Report on the Study on Water Sector in Tamil Nadu,** sponsored by the Ford Foundation.

2006 : **Report on the Study on Agriculture Sector in Tamil Nadu,** sponsored by the Ford Foundation.

2006 : **Report on the Study on Food Security in Tamil Nadu,** sponsored by the Ford Foundation.

2006 : **Report on the Study on Rural Artisans in Tamil Nadu,** sponsored by the Ford Foundation.

2004 : **Report on the Evaluation of Schemes Administered by the District Administration of Pudukkottai District.**

2004 : **Report of the Media Review Workshop to review 'Panchayat Malar'**, sponsored by The Hunger Project, New Delhi.

2004 : **Report of the Writers Workshop on Women in Panchayati Raj** held at Gandhigram on 1st and 2nd June, 2004.

2004 : **Report of the Regional Workshop on Networking of Elected Women Representatives** held at Salem on 20th May, 2004.

2003 : **Report on the Process and Performance of the Women and Dalit Gram Panchayat Presidents of Tamil Nadu,** sponsored by PRIA, New Delhi.

2003 : **Report on the Process and Performance of the Gram Panchayat Presidents of Tamil Nadu,** sponsored by UNICEF, Chennai.

2002 : **Report on Interface between the Self Help Group Leaders and the Panchayati Leaders** organized at Gandhigram on 4th and 5th January, 2002 sponsored by UNICEF, Chennai.

2002 : **A Report on the State Level Workshop on Primary Education and Panchayati Raj at Chennai on 11th January, 2002** sponsored by PRIA, New Delhi.

2001 : **A Report on the Evaluation of Anna Marumalarchi Thittam in Dindigul District** sponsored by DRDA, District Administration, Gandhigram: Rajiv Gandhi Chair for Panchayati Raj Studies, 2001.

2001 : **A Report on Comparative Analysis of the Performance of Panchayati Leaders in Social Development Issues,** sponsored by Population Foundation of India, New Delhi, Gandhigram: Rajiv Gandhi Chair for Panchayati Raj Studies, 2001.

2001 : **Capacity Building for Local Body Leaders and Functionaries and Incentives to Panchayats for their Effective Functioning,** a study conducted by Rajiv Gandhi Chair for Planning Commission, Government of India, Gandhigram: Rajiv Gandhi Chair for Panchayati Raj Studies, 2001.

2001 : **Community Action for Social Development through Panchayats: Deliberations of the two-day workshop held at Krishnagiri on 28th and 29th June, 2001,** sponsored by Population Foundation of India, New Delhi, Gandhigram: Rajiv Gandhi Chair for Panchayati Raj Studies, 2001.

2001 : **A Report on the workshop conducted in Gandhigram on 22nd June to evolve a performance scale to evaluate the performance of panchayats,** sponsored by UNICEF, Chennai, Gandhigram: Rajiv Gandhi Chair for Panchayati Raj Studies, 2001.

2000 : **A Report of the interface programme for the Cambodian High Level Delegation on "Devolution of Powers and Empowerment of Women",** Gandhigram: Rajiv Gandhi Chair for Panchayati Raj Studies, 2000.

2000 : **A Report of the State Level Consultation on Feminist Perspectives in Associating Women Representatives in Local Bodies**, sponsored by Singamma Sreenivasan Foundation, Bangalore, Gandhigram: Rajiv Gandhi Chair for Panchayati Raj Studies, 2000.

2000 : **A Report of the Research Methodology Course on Local Body Institutions and Rural Development**, sponsored by ICSSR, New Delhi, Gandhigram: Rajiv Gandhi Chair for Panchayati Raj Studies, 2000.

2000 : **A Report of the State Level NGOs Network Meet on Associating Women Representatives in Local Bodies**, sponsored by Singamma Sreenivasan Foundation, Bangalore, Gandhigram: Rajiv Gandhi Chair for Panchayati Raj Studies, 2000.

2000 : **A Report on A study on Functional Efficiency of Gram Sabha in Tamil Nadu,** sponsored by Second State Finance Commission, Gandhigram: Rajiv Gandhi Chair for Panchayati Raj Studies, 2000.

27. Book Reviews (Total: 21)

2014 : "Swaraj" Aravind Kejriwal, New Delhi: Harper Collins Publishers India, 2012, **Indian Journal of Public Administration**, Vol. LX: No. 2, April-June 2014.

2009 : Democracy and Human Development in India, Naresh Gupta, **The Indian Journal of Public Administration**, Vol. LV: No. 2, April-June, 2009.

2009 : "Governance Discourse: Reader (Eds) Bidyut Chakrabarty and Mohit Bhattacharya, **The Indian Journal of Public Administration**, Vol. LV: No. 2, April-June, 2009.

2009 : "Reshaping Economic Geography World Development Report–2009", **Sarvodaya Talisman**, Vol. 3: No. 2, May-June, 2009.

2009 : Social Research Methodologies in Action, Vols. I and II, **The Indian Journal of Public Administration**, Vol. LV: No. 1, January-March 2009.

2008 : "Decentralization Institutions and Politics in Rural India", **The Indian Journal of Public Administration,** April-June, 2008. Vol. LIV: No. 2.

2008 : "Indian Administration: Politics, Policies and Prospects", **The Indian Journal of Public Administration,** April-June, 2008, Vol. LIV: No. 2.

2008 : "Hind Swaraj, Gandhi's Challenge to Modern Civilization" (Ed.) R.P. Mishra, Vol. I, New Delhi: Concept Publishing Company, 2007, **The Indian Journal of Public Administration,** Vol. LIII:No. 4, October-December, 2007.

2005 : "Comparative Analysis of Political Systems" V.N. Khanna, Comparative Study of Government and Politics, New Delhi: R. Chand and Co, 2004 (II Edition), **University News**, 43:30, July 2005.

2003 : "Ethnic Politics in North East" Grin Phukon, Ethnicization of Politics in North East India, **Review Projector** (India), Vol. 6: No. 4, October-December 2003.

1998 : "Beyond the Summit: World Peace and Harmony", K. Hussain, Mumbai: Bharatiya Vidya Bhavan, 1996, **Review Projector (India)**, 1:1, 1998.

1992 : "Administrative Reforms in a Developing Society" edited by M. Kistiah, New Delhi: Sterling Publishers Private Limited, 1990, **The Indian Journal of Political Science**, LII: 4, 1991.

1991 : "State and Society in India: Studies in Nation Building" by T.K. Oommen, New Delhi: Sage Publications, 1990, **The Indian Journal of Political Science** LII: 1, 1991.

1990 : "Regionalism in Indian Politics" Chandrika Singh—Emergence of Arunachal Pradesh as a State, New Delhi: Mittal Publications, 1989, **Review Projector (India)** 10: 1-3 (1990).

1989 : "Machiavelli in a Modern Context", Sisir Bhattacharya, Machiavelli—a Study of his theory of the State. New Delhi: Gitanjali Publishing Company, 1988, **Review Projector (India)**, 9: 4-6 (1989).

1989 : "Development and Social Justice" By Anil Bhatt, New Delhi: Sage Publications, 1989. **The Indian Journal of Political Science**, L: 3 (1989).

1989 : "Political Development in South Asia". By Paramanand, New Delhi: Sterling Publishers Private Limited, 1989, **The Indian Journal of Political Science**. L: 4 (1989).

1988 : "Column of Communism", S.V. Sheshagiri Rao, End of A Scientific Utopia, Hyderabad: Nava Bharath Publication, 1986, **Review Projector (India)**, 8 (1988).

1988 : "Federal Authority Content and Reality", S.L. Verma, Federal Authority in the Indian Political System, Jaipur:R.B.S.A. Publishers, 1987: **Review Projector (India)**,8:1-3, (1988).

1988 : "Vision of A Leader", Bhagavan Singh, Pandit Govind Ballabh Pant: The Colossus Speaks, New Delhi: Sterling Publishers (P) Ltd., 1987, **Review Projector (India)**, 8: 4-6, (1988).

1987 : "Comparative Exploratory Political Discourse", Bhiku Pariekh and Thomas Pantham eds., Political Discourse: Explorations in Indian and Western Political Thought, New Delhi: Sage Publications, 1987, **Review Projector (India)**, 7:10-12 (1987).

28. Seminar/Workshops/Conferences Participated

International **(Total: 46)**

2016 : Chaired a session in the two day International seminar on State Politics, Governance and Development in India organized by ISEC, Bangalore in collaboration with Japanese Scholars on 27th and 28th December, 2016.

2016 : Presented a paper entitled "Ethnicity and Politics of Development in Tamil Nadu" in the International Seminar on State Politics, Governance and Development in India organized by ISEC, Bangalore in collaboration with Japanese Scholars on 27th and 28th December, 2016.

2016 : Delivered a Keynote address on Participatory Budgeting and Planning in Social Development in the 3rd Technical Session of the BRICS International Conference in Kochi, Kerala organized by Ministry of Panchayati Raj, Government of India from 3rd to 5th November, 2016.

2016 : Participated and chaired a session on Experience of Local Governance in Common wealth Countries in the International Conference on "Marginalization, Poverty Reduction and Decentralization" in Kerala Institute of Local Administration (KILA), Thirusur, Kerala from 19th to 22nd November, 2016.

2016 : Delivered a Keynote address in the International Conference on "Empowering Youth in the Era of Globalization" on 4th February 2016 in Periyar University, Salem.

2016 : Presented a paper on "Democracy Promotion through Decentralization: A Conceptual Discourse" in the International Conference on Understanding Contemporary India organized by Mahatma Gandhi University, Kottayam, Kerala on 14th and 15th January, 2016.

2015 : Delivered a lecture in the plenary session of the International Conference on "Decentralization of Powers and Rights Based Development" organsied by The Government of Kerala from 15th to 17th May, 2015 at Thiruvananthapuram.

2015 : Chaired a session as chairperson in the panel on "Decentralization and Rights of the differentially abled People" in the International Conference organzed by the Government of Kerala on 16th May, 2015 at Thiruvananthapuram.

2014 : Presented paper on "Trends in Decentralization in India" in the International Conference on Gram Swaraj through Decentralization in Trissur, Kerala from 27th to 29th November, 2014.

2014 : Participated and chaired a session on VET in India (A panel for Indian Scholars) in the International Conference on Comparative Vocational Education and Training in Cologne University, Germany from 22nd to 24th September, 2014 organized by GREAT of Cologne University.

2014 : Delivered a Special Lecture on Child Development and Panchayat in the International Conference on Deepening Democracy through Decentralization in special session organized by UNICEF on 21st January, 2014 in Trivandrum organized by KILA.

2014 : Presented a paper on "Democratization through Decentralization" in the International Conference on Deepening Democracy through decentralization organized by KILA in Trivandrum from 19th to 21st January, 2014.

2013 : Presented a paper on "Increasing Employability of the Students in Higher Learning Institutions through Increasing Social Responsibility and Higher Connectivities" in Indo–Nepal workshop on Strategic Planning and Development in Higher Education held in Kathmandu, Nepal from 21st to 24th November, 2013 organized by Edumatic Solutions

2013 : "Role of Local Bodies in Managing the Issues of Climate Change" A Lead Lecture delivered in VIII International Conference on Climate Change and Socio Economic Crisis in Bharathidasan University, Thiruchirapalli from 23rd to 27th April, 2013.

2012 : Delivered a panel lecture on "Democratic Decentralization" in the international conference on Democratic Decentralization in Trisur, Kerala organized by Kerala Institute of Local Administration from 20th to 23rd December, 2012.

2012 : Delivered a special lecture on "Democratization of Village Communities" in the International workshop on 'Decentralization Experience in India' in Alwar, Rajasthan from 17th to 19th December, 2012 organized by NCAER New Delhi sponsored by IDRC, Canada

2012 : Presented a Paper "VET for Rural Transformation" in the Indo-German international conference on "Vocational Education and Training in India and Germany in Cologne University, Germany from 13th to 17th November, 2012".

2012 : Presented a paper on "Transformative Leadership at Grassroots for Total Transformation" in the International Symposium organized in Coimbatore by Shanti Ashram on 30th and 31st January, 2012.

2012 : Delivered a Special Address on "The Role of Local Governance in Natural Resource Management" in the International Seminar on Sustainable Development and Environment Management on 4th March, 2012 organized by the Rural Technology Centre, Gandhigram Rural Institute, Gandhigram.

2012 : Participated as a Resource Person in the International Workshop on "Effective Vocational Education and Training in India and Germany" in New Delhi from 13th to 16th February, 2012 organized by Cologne University, Germany.

2011 : Presented a paper on "Governance at the Grassroots in India" in the Colloquium organized by the Department of Political Science in Leibniz University, Hannover, Germany on 27th July, 2011.

2011 : Presented a paper on "Higher Education in Germany with Special reference to Skill Building of Students" in the Workshop organized by the Business School, Cologne University on 22nd September, 2011.

2011 : Presented a paper on "The Impact of Globalization on the Poor in India" in the Business Colloquium organized by the Department of Economics in the School of Business, Cologne University on 27th June, 2011.

2011 : Participated in "Talk in the Walk Programme" on Economic Geography of Dusberg, Germany on 26th September, 2011.

2011 : Participated in World Trade Fair in Koln on 28th May, 2011.

2010 : Presented a theme paper on "Role of People in the Alternative Development Paradigm" in the International Seminar on Sustainable Technologies and Management in Gandhigram on 25th November, 2010 organized by the National Institute of Technical Teachers Training and Research.

2009 : Presented a paper on "Containing Corruption at Grassroots" in International Policy Dialogue organized by CODESRIA from 1st to 3rd October, 2009 in Senegal.

2008 : Presented a paper on "Reforming Governance at Grassroots" in the UGC sponsored International Seminar on Public Affairs and Governance: Challenges and Strategies organized by Madras University on 24th and 25th January, 2008.

2007 : Presented a theme paper on "Local Governance in the Framework of Federalism in India" in the 4th International Conference on Federalism at New Delhi from 3rd to 8th November, 2007 organized by the Interstate Council, Ministry of Home Affairs, Government of India.

2006 : Presented a theme paper on "The Role of Community Based Organizations and Panchayati Raj in Micro Level Planning in Tsunami Affected Areas" in the Asian Forum at Chennai on 16th to 18th December, 2006.

2006 : Delivered a lecture on Role of Communities and Panchayats in Disaster Management in Tsunami Affected Areas in India in the 3 UN Forum organized by UN-HABITAT in Vancouver Canada from 22nd to 26th June, 2006.

2005 : Presented a paper on "Grassroots Level Governance and Panchayati Raj Institutions in India" in the III International Conference on Rural India held at Hyderabad on 10th November, 2005, organized by Bhoovigyan Foundation, New Delhi.

2005 : Presented a paper on "Peoples Participation in Tsunami Reconstruction and its Implications" in the International Workshop on Government Budgets, Donor Aid and Natural

Disaster held at Colombo from 9th to 11th November, 2005, organized by International Budget Project, Washington DC.

2005 : Participated in the International Conference on "Human Centered Sustainable Development Paradigm" organized by M.S. Swaminathan Research Foundation at Chennai from 8th to 10th August, 2005.

2004 : Presented a paper on "Women Governance at Grassroots and Social Development" in the International Conference organized by PRIA at Hyderabad from 19th to 21st February, 2004.

2000 : Participated in the International Conference on Democratic Decentralization in Thiruvananthapuram from 23 to 28th May, 2000 organized by the State Planning Board.

2000 : Delivered a special lecture on "Role of New Panchayati Raj System in Land Resource Management" in the plenary session of the International Conference organized by the Ministry of Agriculture and Ministry of Rural Development in New Delhi on 11th November, 2000.

1998 : Presented a paper entitled "Marching towards the Next Millennium: A Grassroots perspective" in the Global Meet organized by World Academy of Art and Science in Vancouver, Canada from 3rd to 7th November, 1998.

1996 : Presented a paper entitled "Populism and Sustainable Ethnicity in India and Canada: A Comparative Analysis" in the XII International Conference on Canadian Studies in Kerala University, Trivandrum from 4th to 7th Jan. 1996.

1994: Presented a paper entitled "Ebb and Flow of Ethnic movement in India and Canada" in the X Canadian International Conference held in Goa University, Goa from 10th to 13th May, 1994.

1992 : Presented a paper entitled "Linguistic Conflict, Ethnic Assertiveness and Political Mobilization in Canada and India" in the Eighth International Seminar on Canadian Studies in the Department of English, Gujarat University, Ahmedabad from 6th to 9th January, 1992.

1991 : Presented a paper entitled "Ethnic Violence and State Terrorism in Sri Lanka", in 15th International Political Science Association's World Congress, Buenos Aires, Argentina, July 21-25, 1991.

1991 : Presented a paper entitled "Mixed Identity, Divided Loyalty and National Integration: Quebec in Canada and Tamil Nadu in India—A Comparison", in 7th International Seminar on Canadian Studies from 5th to 8th January,1991 at Trichy, Tamil Nadu, India.

1990 : Presented a paper entitled "Role of French Canadian women in Canadian National Integration" in the 6th International Seminar on Canadian Studies in the Department of Sociology, Poona University from 12th to 15th March, 1990.

1990 : Presented a paper with Professor V. Subramaniam (Canada) entitled "The Language Ethnicity Relation in Tamil Nadu and Sri Lanka: A Comparison" in the XII World Congress of Sociology at Madrid, Spain from 9th to 13th July, 1990.

1989 : Presented a paper entitled "Cultural Diversity, Uneven Development and Consociational Democracy: Integrative Process of Quebec in Canada and Tamil Nadu in India", in V International Seminar on Canadian Studies, M.S. University, Baroda from 13th to 16th March, 1989.

***National* (Total: 240)**

2017 : Delivered the Key Note address in the 57th All India Political Science Association Congress held at Chennai from 15th to 17th December, 2017.

2017 : Moderated a session of leaders of political parties on "Federalism in 21st Century" in the 57th All India Political Science Association Congress on 16th December, 2017 in the University of Madras.

2017 : Delivered the Chairperson Address on "Education should be made as an instrument of social transformation" in the 41st Annual Conference of the Indian Academy of Social Sciences held at Periyar University, Salem on 19th December, 2017.

2017 : Delivered a special lecture on "Transformational Leadership at the Grassroots" in the TOT programme conducted by SIRD, Mysore for National Level Master Trainers on 29th November, 2017.

2017 : Participated as a Resource Person in National Dissemination Workshop on "State Finance Commissions and Changing Fiscal Landscape in India: The Tamil Nadu Fifth State Finance Commission Report" on 13th November, 2017 organized by Madras Institute of Development Studies at Chennai.

2017 : Participated in the two days workshop on "Social Entrepreneurship" in Sri Aurobindo Society on 30th and 31st October, 2017 organized by Vivekananda Institute of Management, Mumbai.

2017 : Delivered a concluding remarks in the conference organized at New Delhi by Cologne University on "The Past, the Present and the Future of VET in India" on 24th and 25th October, 2017.

2017 : Presented a paper entitled "A Critical Analysis of the Functioning of the Rural Institutes in India" in the National Discussion Meet on "Educational Ideas of Gandhi in Policy Perspective" organized by NUPEA at Delhi on 3rd to 5th October, 2017.

2017 : Delivered a lecture on "The Need of Transformative Leadership to Transform the Communities" in the National Consultative Meeting organized by UNICEF, Chennai on 31st August, 2017.

2017 : Presented a theme paper on "Rights, Duties and Responsibilities of Citizens" in the National Workshop on curriculum development for school education on 21st and 22nd July, 2017 organized by the School Education Department, Government of Tamil Nadu.

2017 : Delivered a lecture on "Transformational Leadership at Grassroots" in the National Workshop on "Leadership and Capacity Building" organized by NIRD, Hyderabad from 19th to 22nd June, 2017.

2017 : Participated in the Training Assessment Programme as Resource Person to Identify Resource Persons for Panchayati Raj Training sponsored by NIRD and PR, Hyderabad and organized by SIRD, Kerala from 29th May to 1st June, 2017.

2017 : Presented an approach paper on "Capacity Building Approach" in the workshop organized by UN Women in New Delhi on 18th May, 2017.

2017 : Delivered a Lecture on Transformational Leadership in the Master Training Programme for Resource Persons for Panchayati Raj Training organized by SIRD, Kerala sponsored by NIRD & PR, Hyderabad 30th May, 2017.

2017 : Delivered a lecture on "the Importance of Multidisciplinary

Research in Social Sciences" in the capacity building workshop organized by Central University Puducherry sponsored by ICSSR, New Delhi on 27th May, 2017.

2017 : Participated in the National Workshop on "Certifying Resource Persons on PRI" organized by NIRD & PR on 19th and 20th April, 2017.

2017 : Participated in All India Vice-Chancellor's Conference in Osmania University on 27th and 28th April, 2017 at Hyderabad.

2017 : Delivered a Keynote Address in the National Seminar on Decentralized Participatory Development Plan: Opportunities and challenges" in National Institute of Rural Development and Panchayati Raj, Hyderabad on 9th and 10th February, 2017.

2016 : Participated as a Resource Person in a National Consultation to finalize a Diploma programme in the National Institute of Rural Development and Panchayati Raj on 21st November, 2016.

2016 : Participated as a Resource Person in the model syllabus preparation workshop for UGC on Public Administration in IGNOU, New Delhi on 25th and 26th October, 2016.

2016 : Chaired a session and delivered a lecture on "**Ambedkar in strengthing the state through the constitution against democracy"** in the VGC Sponsored National Seminar on relevance of Dr. B.R. Ambedkar's Thoughts on National Integration and Development in Gandhigram Rural Institute on 29th and 30th September, 2016.

2016 : Delivered a Keynote lecture on Creating Ideal People's village in the National Consultation on "**Smart City Creation**" organized by KAS a German Foundation in Visakhapattinam on 12th and 13th September, 2016.

2016 : Participated in the National Round Table on **"Towards Climate Compatible Green Growth Development: Achievements and Opportunities"** in New Delhi on 29th August, 2016 organized by Climate and Development Knowledge Network.

2016 : Participated as a resource person in the National Workshop to Validate the Training Modules to Train Women Rural Local Body Leaders organized by The TATA Institute of Social Sciences on 25th July, 2016 in Tiruvanduram.

2016 : Participated in Expert Committee Meeting to evolve a PG Diploma programme on Right to Information in Indira Gandhi National Open University, New Delhi on 28th April, 2016.

2016 : Participated in Expert Committee Meeting to evolve a PG Programme in Public Administration under the CBCS system for UGC in Indira Gandhi National Open University, New Delhi on 29th April, 2016.

2016 : Presented a Paper on "Democratization of Communities through Rural Local Governance" in National Seminar on The Question on Democracy organized by Centre for Studies on Developing Societies, New Delhi from March 14th to 16th March, 2016.

2016 : Delivered a Lecture on "The Role of Local Bodies in Disaster Preparedness and Management" in the national seminar on "Disaster Management Organized by Barathidasan University on 24th February, 2016.

2016 : Delivered a Special Lecture on "Financial Inclusion for Rural Transformation" in National Seminar on Financial Inclusion sponsored by Reserve Bank of India organized by Valluvar College of Arts and Science, Karur, 11th and 12th March, 2016.

2016 : Delivered a Key note address in a National seminar on "Man and Masculinities in South India" on 10th and 11th March, 2016 organized by Madurai Kamaraj University, Madurai

2016 : Delivered a lecture in the National Thinkers Conference on Decentralization on 20th and 21st January, 2016 in Kerala Institute of Local Administration, Trissur.

2016 : Presented a Paper on "Impact of Globalization in the life and livelihood of the poor in the National Seminar on Globalization and Religion organized by the Institute of Indian Culture, Mumbai on 27th and 28th January, 2016.

2016 : Participated in the National Level Consulting for creating Knowledge Network for Panchayati Raj organized by the Ministry of Panchayati Raj, Government of India in NIRD Hyderabad on 8th January 2016.

2015 : Delivered a Lecture on "Decentralization: Unfinished Agenda" in the National Conference on "Decentralization in the Context on 14th Finance Commission" organized by a Centre for development Studies Kolkata on 28th and 29th December, 2015.

2015 : Delivered a Special Lecture on "Nehru's Framework of Panchayati Raj in the Plenary Session of the National Seminar on Nehru's Legacy Revised in Bangalore University on 26th and 27th November, 2015.

2015 : Presented a Framework of Training Module to Train Elected Women Representatives of the Local Bodies in National Commission for Women in New Delhi on 4th December, 2015.

2015 : Delivered a Keynote Address in the National Colloquium on "Agricultural Scenario in India organized by Periyar University, Salem on 17th December, 2015.

2015 : Particiapted as Resource Person in National Workshop on "Case Study Research Method for Rural Development" in National Institute of Rural Developemnt, Hyderabad from 5th to 9th October, 2015.

2015 : Participated in the National review workshop on the report of devolution Index in Mumbai on 27th and 28th June, 2015. Organized by Tata Institute of Social Science, Mumbai.

2015 : Participated in the National Workshop on "New Research Paradigram in Social Science" organized jointly by Tata Institute of Social Sciences and Aurobindo Society, Pondicherry on 1st and 2nd May, 2015.

2015 : Delivered Presidential Address in the Inaugural Meeting of the National Seminar on "Social Exclusion of Dalit Women in 21st Century: Strategies for Inclusion" in Gandhigram Rural Institute on 13th March, 2015 sponsored by ICSSR, New Delhi.

2015 : Presented a lead paper on "Transformational Leadership from the Grassroots" in the UGC sponsored National Seminar on "Women Leadership" on 5th and 6th March, 2015 organized by the Centre for Women Studies, the Gandhigram Rural Institute, Gandhigram.

2015 : Participated and Delivered a Lecture on "Policy option for Deepening Democracy through Decentralization and Development" in Osmania University in the National Colloquium on "Centralized Government to Decentralized Governance" on 21st February, 2015.

2015 : Delivered a Lecture on "Role of Transformational Leaders in Participatory Educational Governance at the Grassroots" in the 2nd Anil Bodia Memorial Policy National Seminar in

National University of Educational Planning and Administration, New Delhi on 16th and 17th February, 2015.

2015 : Delivered the Inaugural Address in the National Conference on "Democratic Decentralization—Challenges of Women Governance in Kerala" organized by Vimala College, Trissur, Kerala on 3rd February, 2015 sponsored by State Council for Higher Education and KILA.

2014 : Delivered the Inaugural Address in the National Seminar on "Ideals of Dr. B.R. Ambedkar for Nation Building and Social Transformation" in PSGR Krishnammal College, Coimbatore on 29th December, 2014 sponsored by UGC.

2014 : Delivered a lecture on "Doing Socially Relevant Research" in the National Seminar on Social Science Research: Challenges and the way forward in Puducherry Central University on 19th and 20th November, 2014 organized by the Institute of Social Science, New Delhi.

2014 : Participated in the consulting workshop on preparation of devolution index for the Ministry of Panchayati Raj, Government of India in Tata Institute of Social Sciences, Mumbai on 14th October, 2014.

2014 : Participated in the Task Force Meeting organized by the Government of India for the preparation of report on "Status of Women in India" in New Delhi on 30th September, 2014.

2014 : Participated in the National Workshop on "Local Governance and Service Delivery" in IRMA. Anand, Gujarat on 27th May, 2014.

2014 : Delivered series of lectures on the possibility of working with rustic folk through the new local governance arrangements among the Prime Minister Rural Development Fellows on 14th and 15th April, 2014 in Tata Institute of Social Sciences, Mumbai.

2014 : Presented paper on "Transformative Leadership of M.K. Gandhi" in the National Seminar on "Gandhi and His Contemporary Issues Organized by the Department of Gandhian Thought and Ramalingar Philosophy, Madurai Kamaraj University on 28th March, 2014.

2014 : Presented a paper on "Relevance of Gandhi, Lincoln and Martin Luther King's Leadership today" in the National Seminar on "Globalizing Justice, Peace, Democracy and Development: Rediscovering of Gandhi, Abraham Lincoln and Martin Luther King Jr." in Gandhigram Rural Institute—Deemed University on 26th and 27th March, 2014.

2014 : Participated as a resource person in finalizing the training module to train transformative leaders among the youth in New Delhi on 22nd, 23rd February, 2014 organized by Jawaharlal Nehru Leadership Institute.

2014 : Participated in the workshop on "Panchayati Raj and Integrity in Accountability" in Tata Institute of Social Sciences, Mumbai on 26th February, 2014.

2014 : Delivered a lecture on "Democracy, Development and Peace" in the workshop on Theater for Democracy organized by CESSI, Madurai on 8th March, 2014.

2014 : Delivered a Key Note Address in the National Seminar on "Strategies to Human Development through Participation" in Ujjain organized by Madhya Pradesh Institute of Social Science Research on 12th and 13th February, 2014

2014 : Participated in the National Workshop on Preparing Manual for conducting Leadership Programme for Social Transformation on 22nd and 23rd February, 2014 organized by Rajiv Gandhi Foundation.

2014 : Participated as a Resource person to finalize the training module on Transformative Leaders Training Programme in New Delhi on 9th January, 2014 organized Nehru Leadership Institute, New Delhi.

2013 : Presented a paper on "Policy options for Empowerment of through Panchayati Raj: in National Policy Dialogue on Empowerment of Panchayati Raj organized by Global Development Network in New Delhi on 28th November, 2013.

2013 : Delivered a special lecture on "Relevance of Gandhi in Rural Development-Activities" in the National Conferences on rural development and Panchayati Raj on 17th and 18th August, 2013 in Gandhinagar organsied by the Government of Gujarat.

2013 : Delivered a plenary lecture in the National Seminar on "Centrally sponsored schemes and Panchayati Raj Institutions" organsied by Kerala Institute Local Administration on 6th and 7th of September, 2013.

2013 : Participated in the workshop on "Gramodoya—Role of Higher Learning Institutions in Preparing Rural Development Professionals" on 29th and 30th July, 2013 in Pondicherry organized by Sri Aurobindho Society.

2013 : Participated in the Workshop in evolving Masters Programme on Development Practice on 20th and 21st June, 2013 in Rajiv Gandhi National Institute of Youth Development, Chennai.

2013 : Presented the Policy Note on Decentralization on NCAER, New Delhi on 18th June, 2013.

2013 : Delivered an Inaugural Address in the National Seminar on "Post–Nehruvian Era: Socio–Economic and Political Developments" on 27th April, 2013 in Bharathidasan University, Thiruchirapalli.

2013 : Participated in the Research Committee Meeting in IRMA Anand on 29th April, 2013 jointly organized by IDRC & IRMA.

2013 : Participated in National Consultation meeting on Status of Women in India organized by the High Level Committee, Government of India on 21st and 22nd March, 2013 in Vigyan Bhavan, New Delhi.

2012 : Participated in the National Workshop on Perfecting Devolution Index in New Delhi on 5th October, 2012 organized by Indian Institute of Public Administration.

2012 : Presented a paper on "Transformation Leadership: Anna a Case Analysis" in the National Seminar on C.N. Annadurai's Leadership organized by Annamalai University on 12th October, 2012.

2012 : Presented a lead paper on "Reaching Excellence through three dimensional works in Higher Learning Institutions" in the National Seminar organized by Pollachi Nachimuthu Gounder Mahalingam College, sponsored by NAAC on 17th and 18th August, 2012.

2012 : Participated in National Seminar on "Governance in the 21st Centruy—Leadership Development in Civil Service" organized by UNDP in New Delhi on 6th and 7th September, 2012.

2012 : Delivered Valedictory Address in the UGC Sponsored National Seminar on "Empowerment of Women through Political Rights" in Mother Teresa Women's University, Kodaikkanal on 6th July, 2012.

2011 : Participated in the National Workshop to finalize the curriculum on Panchayati Raj Programme in New Delhi from 31st to 2nd November, 2011 organized by Vishwa Yuva Kendra.

2011 : Participated as a Resource Person to prepare a training module for panchayat functionaries organized by Vishwa Yuva Kendra in New Delhi from 13th to 15th February, 2011.

2011 : Participated in the National Workshop on "Preparing Training Modules for Transformative Leadership for Panchayat Leaders" organized by Viswa Yuvak Kendra on 31st October to 1st November 2011 in New Delhi.

2011 : Presented a paper on "Producing Quality Research Articles for Social Science Journals in the writers Workshop" organized by Loyola College, Chennai on 3rd December, 2011.

2011 : Delivered a lecture on "Decentralization of Powers from Management Perspective" to the Ph.D. Scholars on 10th November 2011 in Indian Institute of Business Management, Bangalore.

2011 : Delivered a lecture on "Resource Mobilization for Social Science Research Projects" in the Refresher Course organized by the Madurai Kamraj University on 16th November 2011.

2011 : Delivered inaugural address in the National Workshop on "Role of Panchayats in MNREGA in Tamil Nadu" on 19th December 2011 organized by Bharathidasan University, Trichy.

2011 : Delivered Valedictory address in the National Seminar on "Rural Marketing and Rural Consumerism" in Gandhigram Rural Institute on 18th December 2011 organized by the Department of Rural Industries and Management of Gandhigram Rural Institute.

2011 : Delivered a Keynote address in the Human Rights Day Seminar in Alagappa University, Karaikudi on 12th December 2011.

2010 : Participated in the National Conference on "National Rural Livelihood Mission and the Role of Panchayats" in Kochi from 16th to 18th December, organized by the Ministry of Rural Development, Government of India.

2010 : Participated in the National consultation on 12th Five Year Plan approach paper preparation in New Delhi on 6th December, 2010 organized by the UNDP.

2010 : Presented a paper on "Innovative practices in local governance and local development" in the National Colloquium on innovative approaches and practices in local governance in Chennai on 26th and 27th November, 2010 organized by Rajiv Gandhi National Institute for Youth Development.

2010 : Participated in the National consultation on "creating Institute of Excellence for Panchayati Raj Institutions" on 5th October, 2010 at New Delhi organized by the Ministry of Panchayati Raj, Government of India.

2010 : Participated in the National workshop on "Strengthening women leadership in Local governments through federations" in New Delhi from 7th to 9th September, 2010 organized by Swiss Agency for Development and Cooperation.

2010 : Participated and presented a paper on perspectives in "Decentralized Governance in Health Service Delivery" in the National Round Table Organized by the Gujarat Institute of Development Research in Ahmadabad on 31st July, 2010.

2010 : Presented a paper on the "Role of Governance in Peace Building" in the Sangaman Leadership Summit in Coimbatore on 19th April, 2010 organized by Shanthi Ashram and UNIFEM.

2010 : Presented a paper on "Extending the Extendable from the Universities to the Students" to the newly recruited teachers of Madurai Kamaraj University on 24th April, 2010.

2010 : Presented a paper on "Panchayats Communities and Communal Harmony" in the National Seminar at Chennai on 27th and 28th April, 2010 organized by the Centre for Study of Society and Secularism, Mumbai.

2010 : Participated in the Round Table on "Public Private Panchayat Partnership" at New Delhi on 29th April, 2010 organized by FAO, New Delhi.

2010 : Delivered Keynote Address in the National Workshop on "Negotiating the Politics of Presence: Rural Local Governance and Gendered Citizenship" in Kerala Institute of Local Administration, Trissur, Kerala on 3rd May, 2010.

2010 : Presented a paper on "Financial Devolution for Local Bodies in Tamil Nadu" in the National Workshop on Financial Devolution organized by Fourth State Finance Commission on 14th and 15th May, 2010 in Thiruvananthapuram.

2010 : Presented a paper on "Make the Citizens informed about Development Finance and Service Delivery: Simplify Governance and Administration" in the National Workshop on "Institutionalizing Social Accountability Practices" in Indian Institute of Management, Ahmedabad on 7th and 8th June, 2010 sponsored by the Ford Foundation.

2010 : Presented a paper on "Elite Capture in Rural Local Governance in Tamil Nadu" in the National Round Table organized by the Institute for Social and Economic Change, Bangalore on 28th June, 2010.

2010 : Participated in National Level consultation on "Local Governance—Issues and Challenges in India" held at New Delhi on 12th and 13th January, 2010, organized by PRIA, New Delhi.

2009 : Presented a paper on "Ensuring Accountability and Transparency in Development Activities at Grassroots" in Solution Exchange Annual Forum 2009 organized by UNDP at Lucknow from 22nd to 24th October, 2009.

2009 : Presented a paper on "Role of Panchayats in Implementing Programmes and Schemes of the Centre and State Governments" in the Madurai Symposium Organized by Institute of Rural Management Anand on 16th September, 2009 at Madurai.

2009 : Presented a paper on "Status of Dalit Gram Panchayat Leaders in Tamil Nadu" in the National Seminar on Social Mobility and in South India organized by Pondicherry University on 24th and 25th September, 2009.

2009 : Participated in UNDP workshop on "Performance Indicators for States on Devolution of Powers", in New Delhi on 13th and 14th July, 2009.

2009 : Participated in the National Workshop on "Performance Indicators for States on Devolution" in New Delhi on 13th and 14th July, 2009 organized by UNDP at IIPA.

2009 : Participated and presented a paper on "Status of Dalit Gram Panchayat Presidents in Tamil Nadu" in the National Seminar on the "Impact of 73rd Amendment on the Marginalized Communities" organized by the Regional Centre for Social Development in Hyderabad on 25th and 26th March, 2009.

2009 : Participated in the National Workshop on "Status of EWR in Local Bodies in India" in New Delhi on 2nd and 3rd March, 2009 organized by the University of Delhi and the Ministry of Panchayati Raj, Government of India.

2009 : Presented a paper on "The Role of Civil Society Organization in Local Bodies" in the Annual Meeting of Caritas India at Bangalore on 19th January, 2009.

2009 : Participated and delivered a lecture on "The Status of Service

Delivery of Public Institutions from the Perspective of the Citizens in the Report releasing function organized by the Catalyst Trust in Chennai on 26th February, 2009.

2009 : Delivered inaugural address in the Gram Panchayat Leaders Association's Meet at Villuppuram on 28th February, 2006.

2008 : Presented a paper on "Panchayat Finance in Tamil Nadu" in the National Conference on "Issues before the Finance Commission: Empowering the Panchayati Raj Institutions" on 22nd and 23rd December, 2008 in IRMA, Anand, Gujarat.

2008 : Presented a theme paper on "Creating Support Structure for Local Bodies" in the National Workshop organized by the Hunger Project, New Delhi on 28th November, 2008.

2008 : Presented a theme paper on "Role of Civil Society Organization in Creating Support Structure for Decentralised Governance at Grassroots" in the workshop organized for NGOs in New Delhi on 27th November, 2008 organized by German Agro Foundation.

2008 : Presented a paper on "The Role of Gram Panchayats in Land Reform and Land Management in the National Workshop on "Land Reform in India" organized by National Institute of Rural Development in Hyderabad on 4th and 5th October, 2008.

2008 : Presented a paper "Role of Panchayats in Climate Change Management" organized by M.S. Swaminathan Foundation at Chennai on 19th, 20th and 21st April, 2008.

2008 : Presented a theme paper on "The Potentials of Panchayats in Implementing the Policy on Farming and Helping the Farmers" in National Consultation on Operationalization of National Policy for Farmers 2007 at Vigyan Bhavan, New Delhi, on 16th and 17th March, 2008.

2008 : Presented a paper on "Empowering People through Grassroots Governance" in the National Seminar on "Second Freedom Struggle" organized by Gandhigram Rural University from 1st to 3rd February, 2008.

2008 : Presented a paper on "The Role of Panchayats in the Management of Climate Change" in the National Workshop on the Role of ICT in Management of Climate Change at Grassroots in Chennai organized by M.S. Swaminathan Research Foundation on 11th February, 2008.

2007 : Participated and shared the Indian Experience in Local

Governance with the Norwegian Team of Scholars and Officials in the National Symposium on "Experience of Local Self Government in India and Norway" organized by the Ministry of Panchayati Raj, Government of India at New Delhi on 29th and 30th October, 2007.

2007 : Participated in Two Days National Workshop on Backward Region Grant Fund Programme organized by Ministry of Panchayati Raj held at Vigyan Bhawan, New Delhi from 13th to 14th October, 2007.

2007 : Presented a paper on "Role of Panchayats in Ground Water Management in National Ground Water Congress" held at New Delhi on 11th September, 2007 organized by the Ministry of Water Resources, Government of India.

2007 : Presented a paper on "Critical Issues in Decentralization of Powers" in the National Workshop organized by Centre for World Solidarity at Hyderabad from 28th to 30th March, 2007.

2007 : Presented a paper on "Decentralization of Society and Governance in India" in the National Seminar organized by Bhartidasan University at Trichy on 16th to 17th March, 2007.

2007 : Delivered a Plenary Lecture on "Role of Panchayati Raj in Natural Resource Management and Implementing the Recommendations of National Commission on Farmers" in All India Agriculture Science Congress in Coimbatore on 16th February, 2007.

2006 : Presented a theme paper on "Grassroots Governance: Emerging Trends and Issues" in the National Seminar on "Indian Urban Governance: Emerging Trends and Issues" in the University of Madras on 8th and 9th December, 2006.

2006 : Presented a paper entitled "Role of Panchayat in Disaster Mitigation and Reconstruction" in the First Disaster Management Congress on 29th November, 2006 at New Delhi organized by National Institute of Disaster Management, New Delhi.

2006 : Delivered a Lecture on "Nehru and Democratization" in the National Seminar on Nehru and Contemporary World in Madurai Kamaraj University on 19th December, 2006.

2006 : Delivered a Keynote Lecture on "Synergy between Youth Clubs and Panchayats on Civic Engagement" in the Colloquium on Youth Development Issues and World Development Report at Chennai organized by the World Bank on 16th November, 2006.

2006 : Delivered a Lecture on "Role of Panchayats and Community Organizations in Water Management at Grassroots" NIRD Foundation Day Seminar on 10th and 11th November, 2006 at Hyderabad.

2006 : Delivered a Keynote Address in the National Seminar on "Panchayati Raj Institutions After 73rd Constitutional Amendment: A New Deal for Rural India" at Tirupathi organized by AGRASRI from 19th to 20th August, 2006.

2006 : Delivered a Keynote Address on Local Self Government and SHG Women in a National Seminar organized by Alagappa University on 27th July, 2006 sponsored by National Women Commission.

2006 : Delivered a Lecture on "Every Gram Panchayat a Knowledge Centre" in the Third Convention of the National Alliance for Mission 2007 at Chennai on 28th and 29th July, 2006 organized by M.S. Swaminathan Research Foundation.

2006 : Presented a paper on "The Process of Preparation of District Human Development Report" in the UNDP National Workshop on Preparation of Human Development Report at Bhopal on 1st and 2nd August, 2006.

2006 : Delivered a Keynote Address in the National Seminar on "India's Social, Economic and Political Development" sponsored by the Central Planning Commission and organized by Madhya Pradesh Institute of Social Science Research in Ujjain from 24th to 26th May, 2006.

2006 : Delivered a Lecture in the workshop on "Youth in Panchayat Raj Campaign" organized by Rajiv Gandhi National Institute of Youth Development, Sriperumbudur, Chennai on 22nd and 23rd May, 2006.

2006 : Participated in Interdisciplinary Dialogue on "Mission 2007: Hunger Free India" organised by Dr. M.S. Swaminathan Foundation from 20th to 22nd April, 2006.

2006 : Delivered Keynote Address in the National Seminar on "Pappapatti Syndrome and Panchayati Raj" sponsored by the Ministry of Panchayati Raj, Government of India and organized by the Annamalai University on 5th and 6th April, 2006.

2006 : Presented a paper on "Jawaharlal Nehru and Grassroots Democracy" in the National Seminar on Nehru's Contribution towards Modern India organized by the Bharathidasan University, Trichy on 24th March, 2006.

2006 : Delivered Keynote Address in the National Seminar on "Working of the Panchayati Raj System in India" organized by the University of Madras, 23rd and 24th February, 2006.

2006 : Delivered a Keynote Address in the National Seminar on "Women Empowerment: Experience of SHG" in the Presidency College, Chennai on 27th March, 2006.

2006 : Presented a paper on "Water Governance at Grassroots" in the Workshop on Food Security and Livelihood through Sustainable Water Resource Management in Tamil Nadu at Gandhigram on 9th and 10th January, 2006 organized by Oxfam, India.

2005 : Presented a paper on "Capacity Building for Grassroots Governance" in the National Workshop on Local Governance in Rural India, organized by German Agro Action Foundation at Bangalore on 1st December, 2005.

2005 : Participated in the National Workshop on "Strengthening the Role of Women in Grassroots Democracy", held at Delhi on 19th November 2005, organized by Rajiv Gandhi Foundation.

2005 : Presented a paper on "Participatory Planning and its Implications" in the National Conference on Panchayats at Present and Way Forward, organized by the Ministry of Panchayati Raj, Government of India from 16th to 18th December, 2005.

2005 : Presented a paper on "Role of Elected Women Representatives in Grassroots Governance" in Round Table of Media Leaders at Chennai on 9th December 2005 organized by the Hunger Project, New Delhi.

2005 : Participated in National Technical Workshop on "District Human Development Report"—on 15th and 16th September 2005 at Chennai organized by UNDP, New Delhi.

2005 : Participated in National Workshop as Resource Person on "Youth and Globalization" in Tata Institute of Social Sciences, Mumbai on 22nd and 23rd September, 2005.

2005 : Presented a paper on "Taking Colleges to Communities" in the National Conference on "Curricular Innovations and Quality Improvement in Autonomous Colleges" in Arulanandar College, Madurai on 30th September, 2005.

2005 : Participated in National Consultation Meeting of National Farmers Commission in New Delhi on 19th September, 2005.

2005 : Participated in the National Symposium on "Power to the

People"—Gram Sabha to Lok Sabha organized by the Ministry of Panchayati Raj, Government of India on 13th September, 2005 at SIRD of Mysore.

2005 : Participated in National Convention of the "National Alliance for Creating Virtual Academy for Rural Prosperity" at New Delhi on 11th and 12th July, 2005 organized by M.S. Swaminathan Research Foundation.

2005 : Presented a paper on "Role of Panchayats in Relief, Rehabilitation and Preparation of Micro plans for Reconstruction of Tsunami affected Areas" in the National Consultation on Post-Disaster Management organized by M.S. Swaminathan Foundation at Chennai on12th and 13th May, 2005.

2005 : Presented a paper on "Role of Panchayati Raj Institutions in Disaster Management in a National Level Consultation" organized by Rejuvenate India Movement at Chennai on 18th and 19th April, 2005.

2005 : Participated as a Resource Person in the discussion on the "Role of Panchayats in Tsunami Affected Areas" organized at Chennai on 29th January, 2005 by Institute of Social Science, New Delhi.

2005 : Delivered Keynote Address in a National Seminar on the "Performance Evaluation of Panchayati Raj Institutions" in Annamalai University on 17th February, 2005.

2004 : Participated in the National Workshop on Assessing Capacity Building Exercises carried out for Local Body Leaders and Functionaries in India organized by The Hunger Project, New Delhi on 17th and 18th November, 2004.

2004 : Presented a paper entitled "Good Governance at Grassroots" in the National Seminar on Good Governance in the New Millennium in the University of Madras on 31st December.

2004 : Presented a paper entitled "Emerging Alternative Governance at Grassroots" in the symposium organizer by IRMA, Anand on 14th, 15th and 16th December, 2004.

2004 : Participated in the Round Table on Capacity Building of Local Body Leaders at Jaipur on 17th and 18th December 2004, organized by The Ministry of Panchayati Raj, Government of India.

2004 : Presented a paper on "Participation, Governance and Poverty Reduction" in NIRD Seminar on Employment Generation and Poverty Reduction through Panchayat Raj held at Hyderabad on 27th through 29th October, 2004.

2004 : Participated in the Workshop on "Vulnerability Assessment and Enhancing Adaptive Capacity to Climate Change in Semi Arid Areas" organized at Delhi by M.S. Swaminathan Foundation from 21st to 22nd September, 2004.

2004 : Participated in Vice-Chancellors Conference on E-Learning and E-Content development at Goa from 24th to 26th September, 2004 organized by the UGC, New Delhi.

2004 : Participated in National Consultation on the Issues of Women Leaders of Panchayats held at SIRD, Chennai on 25th July, 2004, State Commission for Women, Chennai.

2004 : Participated in the National Consultation Meeting of Experts and Master Trainers to design a training strategy organized by Rajiv Gandhi Foundation at Delhi on 12th and 13th July, 2004.

2004 : Presented a paper on Researchable Areas in Decentralized Governance in the National Workshop on "The Latest Trends and Issues in Social Science Research Methodology" organized by Annamalai University from 23rd to 24th April, 2004.

2004 : Presented a theme paper entitled "Panchayats, Relevance and Potentials to Achieve Social Development" in National Consultation Organized by UNFPA at New Delhi on 16th and 17th February, 2004.

2004 : Presented a theme paper entitled "Globalization and Decentralization: Synergization or Polarization" in The Ford Foundation at New Delhi on 26th February, 2004.

2003 : Presented a paper on "Financial Devolution to Local Bodies in Tamil Nadu" in the workshop on Financial Devolution to Local Bodies" at Chennai on 7th April, 2003 in Madras Institute of Development Studies.

2003 : Presented a paper on "Possible Linkages between Panchayats and Civil Society" in the workshop organized by DHAN Foundation in Madurai on 10th March, 2003.

2002 : Presented a paper on "Local Democracy in Tamil Nadu at cross-roads in the Seminar on Local Democracy in India" organized by Europe India Rural Link at Madurai on 27th and 28th January, 2002.

2002 : Participated in the National Seminar on "Governance where people matter" organized by PRIA at New Delhi on 5th and 6th of February, 2002.

2002 : Presented a paper on "Possibilities for research in ethnic issues of Canada and India for theorization" in the National Seminar on Education in India and Canada: A Comparative Perspective organized by Pondicherry University from 27th February to 1st March, 2002.

2002 : Participated as a resource person in the National Workshop on "Reviewing the Recommendations of the Review Panel on 73rd and 74th Amendments to the Constitution of India in Goa from 11th to 12th March, 2002.

2002 : Participated as a resource person to review the training module in the National Workshop on "Strengthening of Panchayati Raj System—A Training Intervention" in Lal Bahadur Shastri National Academy of Administration, Mussoorie from 22nd to 23rd March, 2002.

2002 : Participated in the Expert Committee Meeting in Indira Gandhi Open University, New Delhi for the Preparation of a Course Programme for M.A. Political Science on 26th and 27th September, 2002.

2001 : Presented a paper entitled "Role of Caste Groups in New Panchayati Raj System: A case analysis of Tamil Nadu" in the UGC National Seminar organized in University of Madras, Chennai from 4th to 5th January, 2001.

2001 : Presented a paper entitled "Synergization of institutional arrangements for Development and Social Justice at the Grassroots: A case analysis" in the Foundation Day Seminar of National Institute of Rural Development, Hyderabad from 7th to 8th January, 2001.

2001 : Presented a paper entitled "Issues and Solutions in Governance at Grassroots for Development" in the National Seminar organized by ICSSR, New Delhi from 15th to 17th January, 2001.

2001 : Participated in the National Workshop on "Strengthening Panchayati Raj System—A Training Intervention", held at New Delhi from 8th to 9th February, 2001 organized by Rajiv Gandhi Foundation.

2001 : Participated in the National Council Meeting of The Hunger Project at New Delhi on 28th February, 2001 to evolve a strategy to end hunger in the rural areas through Panchayati Raj System.

2001 : Participated in the consultative committee meeting at New Delhi to finalize training module to conduct Capacity Building Exercises for Local Body Leaders and Functionaries, on 18th and 19th July, 2001 organized by Rajiv Gandhi Foundation.

2001 : Presented a paper on "Power Sharing and Participation in Decision Making" in the National Seminar on National Policy for the Empowerment of Women 2001, at Coimbatore organized by Avinashilingam Deemed University.

2001 : Presented a paper on "Issues and Problems of Elected Women Representatives in Tamil Nadu" in the National Workshop on Gender and Governance organized by the Alagappa University, Karaikudi from 15th to 16th September, 2001.

2000 : Presented a paper "Empowering Women Through the Local Bodies in India" in the National Seminar on Women in Local Governance organized by the Institute of Social Studies Trust in Bangalore from 1st to 2nd June, 2000.

2000 : Presented a paper "Problems of Women Representatives in rural Local Bodies in Tamil Nadu" in the National Seminar on Women in Panchayati Raj organized at Central University, Hyderabad from 29th to 31st March, 2000.

2000 : Presented a paper on "Role of State Finance Commissions in the Process of Decentralisation of Powers: A Case Analysis of Tamil Nadu" in the National Workshop organized by National Institute of Rural Development, Hyderabad on 3rd and 4th October, 2000.

2000 : Presented a paper on "Designing and Managing the District Panchayat in Tamil Nadu" in the National Seminar organized by the State Institute of Rural Development, Chennai from 5th to 8th September, 2000 sponsored by Ministry of Rural Development, Government of India.

2000 : Presented a paper on "Non-conventional Resource Mobilization Capacity of the Panchayati Raj Institutions in Tamil Nadu" in the National Seminar organized by Madras Institute of Development Studies, Chennai on 22nd and 23rd September, 2000.

1999 : Presented a paper entitled "Women Participation in Local Governance: A case analysis of Tamil Nadu", in the National Seminar on Women in Local Governance: Exploring New Frontiers", organized by the Institute of Social Studies Trust in Bangalore from 3rd to 5th February, 1999.

1999 : Served as a resource person in the National Workshop on "Local Bodies and Climate Management", organized by M.S. Swaminathan Foundation in Chennai on 6th February, 1999.

1999 : Presented a paper entitled "Need of an Amendment to the 73rd and 74th Amendments to the Constitution of India: A perspective analysis from the Experience of Tamil Nadu", in the National Conference on "Amendments to the Constitution (73rd and 74th Amendment) Acts, 1992 in Bangalore organized by the Institute of Social Sciences from 4th to 5th January, 1999.

1999 : Presented a paper entitled "Role and responsibility of Panchayati Raj Institutions: Training Needs and Training Methodology", in the National Workshop organized by the Department of Rural Development, Government of Tamil Nadu and UNICEF in Chennai on 18th and 19th March, 1999.

1999 : Participated and served as a resource person in the Workshop organized by the Ford Foundation to establish a network of Panchayati friendly organizations in India in Bangalore on 6th of January, 1999.

1999 : "Participated and Presented a paper on the utility of Report Card Methodology in Improving Governance in Local Bodies in National Workshop on Report Card Methodology" at Bangalore, organised by Public Affairs Centre from 25th to 27th October, 1999.

1999 : Presented a report of the functioning of Gram Sabha in Tamil Nadu in the National Conference on Gram Sabha held at NIRD, Hyderabad from 28th to 29th July, 1999.

1999 : Participated in the National Workshop organized by National Institute of Rural Development, Hyderabad to review the action research report entitled "Strategies for Strengthening Panchayati Raj Institutions in Karnataka" from 24th to 25th November, 1999.

1999 : Participated in the Hunger Project National Workshop on Panchayati Raj from 20th to 21st November, 1999 in Bangalore organized by the Hunger Project, USA.

1999 : Participated in the National Workshop on Bio-villages and Panchayats in Pondicherry from 29th November to 1st December 1999 organized by M.S. Swaminathan Research Foundation.

1998 : Presented a paper entitled "From Assimilation to Communalism: A Study in Dravidian Movement" in the UGC National Seminar on Dravidian Movement in the University of Madras, Chennai from 27th to 29th April, 1998.

1998 : Presented a paper entitled "Role of Panchayati Raj in Regenerating Rural Common Property Resources and Revival of Rural Industries" in the National Seminar on Development of Rural Industries in Fifty Years organized by Gandhigram Rural Institute and sponsored by KVIC Mumbai from 25th to 26th March, 1998.

1998 : Presented a paper entitled "Business Sadhaks and their Spirito Technology in Indian Entrepreneurial Movement" in the UGC sponsored National Seminar on Entrepreneurship Promotion and Development organized by Gandhigram Rural Institute from 16th to 17th April, 1998.

1998 : Presented a paper entitled "Grassroots Institutions in Tamil Nadu: Changes and Challenges" in the UGC National Seminar on Local Self-Government in South India organized by Madras University from 20th to 21st April, 1998 at Chennai.

1998 : Presented a paper entitled "Why this spurt on Corruption now?" in the UGC sponsored National Seminar on Corruption in Social Life organized by Gandhigram Rural Institute on 2nd February, 1998.

1998 : Presented a paper entitled "Corruption at Micro Level and ways to contain it" in the National Workshop on Corruption at the Grassroots, organized by Gandhigram Rural Institute from 3rd to 4th December 1998 at Chennai.

1998 : Presented a paper entitled "Devolution of Finance to Local Bodies: Issues before XI Finance Commission", in the National Workshop on "Issues before the XI Finance Commission—The case of Tamil Nadu", organized by the Madras Institute of Development Studies in Chennai on 8th December, 1998.

1997 : Participated and presented a training design in the workshop on Training and project design for Empowerment of Panchayati Raj Institutions in issues of population, Health and Social Development organized by Population Foundation of India from 27th to 29th January, 1997 in M.S.S.R. Foundation, Madras.

1997 : Participated in the National Conference on "Panchayats: Powers, Personnel and Finance" in Trivandrum from 3rd to 4th November, 1997 organized by the Institute of Social Sciences, New Delhi and Institute of Management in Government, Trivandrum.

1997 : Presented a paper on "Conflicting Perceptions of Panchayati System in Tamil Nadu" in National Consultation on 21st October, 1997 in New Delhi organized by the Institute of Social Sciences, New Delhi.

1997 : Presented a paper on New Panchayati Raj System and its Implications in the Projects of DANIDA in the workshop organized by Royal Danish Mission in Cochin from 17th to 18th September, 1997.

1997 : Participated in National Symposium on Welfare State in a Liberalized Economy from 26th to 27th September, 1997 in Madras organized by Satyamurthy Centre for Democratic Studies, Chennai.

1997 : Presented a paper entitled "New Federalism in the offing or Indian Federalism in the Fifth Decade" in the UGC sponsored National Seminar on Centre-State Relations in India in the University of Madras from 19th to 20th December, 1997 at Chennai.

1997 : Presented a paper entitled "Functioning of Gram Panchayat in Tamil Nadu" in the National Seminar on Panchayats organized by Rajiv Gandhi Foundation, New Delhi from 22nd to 23rd December, 1997.

1996 : Presented a paper on "Non-conventional Resource Mobilization and people participation" in Local Body Institutions in the National Conference on Local Body finance organized by the Government of Tamil Nadu at Madras from 14th to 15th March 1986.

1995 : Presented a paper titled "National Integration: Dreams and Realities" in the UGC National Seminar on "National Integration: Problems and Prospects" in Annamalai University from 6th to 8th March, 1995.

1995 : Presented a paper entitled "Evolving Indicators of Rural Development: Problems and Prospects", in the National Seminar on Indicators of Rural Development organized by the Department of Applied Research in Gandhigram Rural Institute, from 9th to 10th March, 1995.

1995 : Presented a paper entitled "Paradigmatic shift in the Analysis of Ethnic Conflict in Canada and India" in the Annual Conference of the Indian Association for Canadian Studies, from 22nd to 25th April, 1995 in New Delhi.

1995 : Presented a Paper entitled "Populism and Ethnicity in Tamil Province: A mythical past and uncertain Future" in the UGC National Seminar on Dravidian Movement: A Study in Reformulation in Madras University from 15th to 17th November, 1995.

1995 : Participated in National Symposium on "Rejuvenating Grassroots Democracy and Federalism" on 6th and 7th October, 1985 organized in Madras by Sathiyamurthi Centre for Democratic Studies and M.S. Swaminathan Foundation.

1995 : Presented a paper entitled "New Panchayati Raj System and Human Resource Development" in XVIII Annual Convention of State resource Centre from 27th to 29th October, 1995 in Trichy.

1995 : Participated in one day consultation to organise National Panchayati Raj convention on 13 October, 1995 in New Delhi under the auspices of Rajiv Gandhi National Institute of Youth Development.

1994 : Presented a paper entitled "Corruption—a deterrent in the process of power flow from state to local bodies in Tamil Nadu" in the Annual Xavier Institute Convention on Panchayati Raj and People's Empowerment at Ranchi from 17th to 18th February, 1995.

1994 : Presented a paper entitled "Gandhian Framework of Human Evolution: Revisited" in the National Seminar on Gandhism organized by Kerala Academy of Social Sciences in Trivandrum on 3rd October, 1994.

1993 : Presented a paper entitled "Politics of Development Administration in Tamil Nadu: Issues and Trends" in the XIV All India Public Administration Conference held at Madras from 28th to 29th March, 1993.

1993 : Presented a paper entitled "Alarmist or Development Approach towards Communal Harmony and National Integration" in the National Seminar on Communal Harmony and National Integration organized by World Conference at Religion for Peace (India) National Chapter in Coimbatore on 25th April, 1993.

1993 : Presented a paper entitled "Poly ethnicity in India and Canada: A Research Design for Comparative Analysis" in the National Seminar on "Religion and Literature in Canada and India" from 26th to 28th April, 1993 at Bharathidasan University, Tiruchirapalli.

1992 : Attended a workshop on "Agenda for Future" at the Institute for Social and Economic Change in Bangalore on 22nd May, 1992.

1992 : Presented a paper entitled "Value crisis and Mahatma Gandhi: A New Credo for Human Unisom" in XVth Annual Conference of Indian Society of Gandhian Studies from 27th-29th, December 1992 in the Department of Gandhian Studies and Ramalinga Philosophy, Madurai Kamaraj University, Madurai.

1991 : Presented a paper entitled "The Myth of Ethnicity and Human Unisom: An Unending Trail of Human Collectivities to Reach a New World Order" in the Anthropology section meeting of Indian Science Congress at Indore, 1991.

1990 : Presented a paper entitled "Ethnic Identity and National Loyalty of an Ethnic Group in India", in the UGC National Seminar on "India's Experience with Democracy", in the Department of Political Science, Madurai Kamaraj University, from 11th to 13th January, 1990.

1990 : Presented a paper entitled "Dynamics of National Integration and Ethnic Loyalty: A Symbiotic Process in Indian Politics" in the UGC National Seminar on "National Integration" in the Department of Political Science, Annamalai University from 1st to 3rd March, 1990.

1989 : Presented a paper entitled "Ethnic Conflict Management: A General Framework for Analysis", in XXIII Annual Conference of the Indian Association for American Studies, ASRC at Hyderabad from 19th to 22nd February, 1989.

1989 : Presented a paper entitled "Role orientations of the members of 8th Legislative Assembly of Tamil Nadu", in the National Seminar on "Legislative Behaviour in India", in the Department of Political Science, Nagpur University, from 24th to 26th March, 1989.

1989 : Presented a paper entitled "Ethnicity and Development: A New Formulation", in the 46th All India Political Science Conference held at Pune from 3rd to 5th November, 1989.

1988 : Presented a paper entitled "Ethno methodology: An Appraisal", in XXII Annual Conference of the Indian Association for American Studies at Patna University, Rajgir from 22nd to 26th August, 1988.

1988 : Participated in a Symposium on "Indian and U.S. Constitutions: Problems and Prospects", jointly organized by Annamalai University and USEFI at Annamalainagar, Tamil Nadu, from 22nd to 26th, August, 1988.

1987 : Presented a paper entitled "Comparative Study on Committee System in the US and India: An overview", in XXI Annual Conference of the Indian Association for American Studies at Poona University, Pune, from 2nd to 4th March, 1987.

1987 : Presented a paper entitled "Ethnic Leader and Social Change: A Study in Micromodelling", in 45th All India Political Science Conference from 22nd to 24th December, 1987, at Aligarh Muslim University, Aligarh.

1986 : Presented a paper entitled "Qualitative Analysis of Resolutions of Massachusetts and Tamil Nadu State Legislatures on Ethnic Problems of Sri Lanka", in XX Annual Conference of the Indian Association for American Studies at Madurai Kamaraj University from 24th to 26th April, 1986.

1985 : Attended the "Appreciation Course in Parliamentary Processes", from 22nd to 25th July, 1985, organized by the Bureau of Parliamentary studies and Training Lok Sabha Secretariat, New Delhi.

1985 : Presented a paper entitled: "Tamil Nationalism as a factor in Indian Politics", in 44th Annual Conference of the Indian Political Science Association from 26th to 28th December, 1985 at IIT Madras.

1984 : Attended the USEFI workshop on "American History and Politics", from 21st May to 2nd June, 1984, Annamalai University, Annamalai Nagar.

1982 : Attended the UGC Summer Institute in "Research Methodology in Political Science", from 20th May to 17th June, 1982 in the Department of Political Science, Annamalai University, Annamalai Nagar.

1981 : Attended the UGC Summer Institute in "Social Science Research Methodology", from July 20th to 25th 1981, in the Department of Sociology, Annamalai University, Annamalai Nagar.

Regional **(Total: 119)**

2018 : Delivered a lecture on "Youth and Democracy" in the Democratization programme organized by PRIA, in Gandhigram Rural Institute on 6th February, 2018.

2018 Delivered the inaugural address in the Birth Centenary Celebration of Indira Gandhi at Pudukkottai Raj's Government College on 9th February, 2018.

2018 : Delivered a lecture on "Leadership for Social Transformation" in the Book Fair Festival seminar at Thiruppur on 3rd February, 2018.

2017 : Delivered a special lecture on "Growth and Development in India" in the Book Fair Seminar on 4th December, 2017 at Dindigul.

2017 : Delivered a special lecture on "Democratizing the community through local governance" in the one day meet of the women leaders of SHG to explore the possibility of contesting in the local body election on 11th December, 2017.

2017 : Delivered Inaugural Address in the "National Panchayati Raj Day" in Rajiv Gandhi National Institute for Youth Development at Chennai on 24th April, 2017.

2017 : Delivered a lecture on "Globalization, Liberalization and Privatization" to the teachers in Bharatidasan University on 11th March, 2017.

2017 : Delivered a lecture on "Roles and Responsibilities of the teachers in Higher Learning Institutions" to the teachers in Bharatidasan University on 11th March, 2017.

2016 : Participated as an Expert Team Member for academic audit of Avinashilingam Institute on Women Education on 9th November, 2016.

2016 : Delivered a Valedictory address in the seminar on Moral and Value Education in Gandhigram Rural Institute—Deemed University on 6th October, 2016.

2016 : Delivered a talk on Remembering Gandhian Educationalist G.R. towards a New Education of Gandhi on Founders Birth Anniversary on 7th October, 2016 in Gandhigram Rural Institute—Deemed University, Gandhigram.

2016 : Participated in the "Regional Consultation on Land Alienation in Southern States" organsied by EKTA Parishad, at Madurai on 18th September, 2016.

2016 : Participated in the regional round table workshop on "Facing the Local Body Elections" for civil society organizational heads at IDEAS, Madurai on 3rd September, 2016.

2016 : Presented a concept note on "Integral Rural Development and Creation of Transformational Leaders at Grassroots" for the Rural Development officials in the Chamber of Secretary, Rural Development, Government of Tamil Nadu on 6th September, 2016 at Chennai.

2016 : Delivered a Keynote lecture on "Human Rights Education and Democracy Promotion" in one day orientation programme organized for Head Masters of Higher Secondary Schools in Tamil Nadu organzed by the Human Rights Education Foundation at Madurai, on 30th August, 2016.

2016 : Delivered a Lecture on "Importance of Review of Literature in the Research Methodology" course organized by the Department of Lifelong Learning in Gandhigram Rural Institute on 26th July, 2016 sponsored by Rajiv Gandhi National Institute of Youth Development.

2016 : Delivered a Special Lecture on "Development Politics" in the Seminar organized on World Book Day function by Dindigul Literary Association on 23rd April, 2016.

2016 : Delivered a lecture on "Preparedness of Article for inclusion in an Edited Volume" in the workshop organized by the State Institute of Rural Development, Kerala on 8th April, 2016 in Kottarakara.

2016 : Presented a paper on "Arulselvar in Tamil Nadu Legislative Assembly" in the two day seminar organized by Gandhi Museum, Madurai on 22nd and 23rd January, 2016.

2015 : Delivered a keynote address in the Regional Seminar on "Digital India" organized by Department of Computer Science on 9th July, 2015.

2014 : Delivered a lecture on "Use of Commons for the Poor through the Gram Panchayats" in the Regional consultation on status of Dalit women in Tamil society on 20th December, 2014 at Madurai organized by the Evidence.

2014 : Delivered a lecture on "Engaging Men and Boys Through Governance" in the Southern Regional Consultation organized by Forum to Engage Men in Madurai on 13th September, 2014.

2014 : Participated in the Consultative meeting for establishing collaboration with German University for Skill Development Academic Programmes in Bharathiar University, Coimbatore on 4th August, 2014.

2014 : Delivered the Inaugural Address in the Youth Model Parliament session of the Valluvar College of Science and Management Studies, Karur on 5th April, 2014.

2014 : Delivered a Foundation Day address in the Peace Trust on "The Role of Civil Society in Present Context" on 29th March, 2014 in Dindigul.

2014 : Delivered a lecture on the "Potentials on Panchayati Raj in Emancipating the Dalits" in the Dalit Conference in Sivagangai on 1st March, 2014.

2013 : Delivered a Lecture on "Capacity Enhancement for Educational Managers" in Kochin on 22nd December, 2013 organized by Edumatic solutions.

2013 : Presented a paper on "Three Dimensional Responsibilities of the Teachers of Higher Learning Institutions" in the Regional Workshop organized by Edumatic Solution in Coorg from 4th to 6th December, 2013.

2013 : Delivered a lecture on "Interface between Higher Learning Institutions and the Communities" in the Refresher course of the Bharathidasan University on 20th July, 2013.

2013 : "Sharing Experience in Evolving Micro Plan" in the Regional Workshop organized by the State Planning Commission on 1st July, 2013.

2013 : Delivered a Special Lecture on "Skill Education for Arts and Science Students" in Education Fair 2013 in Dindigul on 27th April, 2013.

2013 : Delivered a lecture on "New Methodological Nuances in Social Science Research" in the Social Science Research Methodology course organized by the UGC Academic Staff College in Bharatidasan University on 15th March, 2013.

2013 : Delivered a key note address in Regional Seminar on "Politics, Government and Society" organized by Mannar Thirumalai Naicker College, Madurai on 12th March, 2013.

2013 : Participated as a resource person in the Reorientation Workshop for field level functionaries in M.S. Swaminathan Foundation at Chennai on 8th and 9th of February, 2013.

2013 : Delivered key note address in the Capacity building for college teachers sponsored by the UGC conducted in

Palaniandavar College for Women on 2nd February, 2013.

2012 : Presented a paper on "Local Body Election in Tamil Nadu: An Analysis" in the Regional Training workshop organized by the State Election Commission on 21st August, 2012.

2012 : Presented a Paper on "Achieving Peace through Development" in the Regional Seminar on Communal Harmony organized by Saint Ramalinga Trust in Chennai on 3rd October, 2012.

2012 : Presented a Paper on "Writing Research Articles for Publication in International Journals in Social Science" in the Regional Workshop organized by Loyola College Chennai on 20th October, 2012.

2012 : Participated as Jury in Peoples Tribunal for Legal Redressal on "Voices of Dalit Victim—Land Rights Violation" in Madurai on 30th June, 2012 organized by Evidence.

2012 : Delivered Inaugural Address in the Kanyakumari District Panchayat Leaders Association Convention in Nagarcoil on 19th March, 2012.

2012 : Delivered an address to the Engineering College students of Kumaraguru College of Technology in an orientation programme on "Gandhian Framework for Governance" on 12th June, 2012 at Vedaranyam Kasthurba Gandhi Kanya Kurukulam.

2012 : Delivered Valedictory Address in the Regional Seminar on "Local Bodies in India" organized by left oriented Panchayat leaders organization at Kutralam on 2nd of June, 2012.

2012 : Delivered a keynote address in the Workshop on "Inclusion of Dalits in Governance in Local Bodies" organized by Dalit Federation in Thirunelveli on 28th April, 2012.

2012 : Delivered Valedictory Address in National Science Day Celebration in Salem Periyar University on 28th February, 2012.

2012 : Participated in the Regional Round Table on "Civil Society at Cross Roads" in Madurai, on 17th February, 2012 organized by PRIA, New Delhi.

2012 : Delivered a Special Lecture on "Relevance of Gandhi Today in Kumaraguru College of Technology, Coimbatore on 10th February, 2012.

2012 : Delivered a Special Lecture on the "Art of Text Book Writing" in the UGC sponsored Workshop on Writing Books in Islamiah College, Vaniyambadi on 19th February, 2012.

2010 : Presented a theme paper in the Regional workshop on "the role of Agriculture University in Micro level planning" in Coimbatore on 16th September, 2010 organized by Agriculture University, Coimbatore.

2010 : Participated in the Regional meeting of the Solution Exchange Community of the UNDP at Gandhigram on 7th October, 2010.

2010 : Presented a paper on "Writing thematic articles for publication in National Journals" in the Regional workshop for young writers and research scholars on 24th September, 2010 organized by Loyola College, Chennai.

2010 : Presented a paper on "Democratic Culture in Indian Democracy" in the R. Venkataraman Centenary Celebration held at Gandhigram on 4th October, 2010.

2010 : Presented a paper on "Rural Development Scenario in Tamil Nadu" in the Regional Seminar on Tamil Nadu in 2015 at Chennai on 29th June, 2010 organized by the Tamil Nadu Foundation Incorporated USA.

2010 : Delivered a lecture on "Understanding Democracy" in the Workshop on "Inclusive Democracy Secularism and Communal Harmony" in Gandhigram Rural University from 4th to 8th January, 2010 organized by the Centre for Study of Society and Secularism, Mumbai.

2009 : Participated in a panel discussion on "Higher Education 2020" and made a presentation on "Rural Higher Education in India in the Context of Globalization" in Arul Anandar College, Madurai on 12th December, 2009.

2009 : Delivered a Key note address on the contribution of Elinor Astrom in the workshop organized by the Department of Political Science, Gandhigram Rural University on 4th December, 2009.

2009 : Delivered a lecture on "Governance Structure in India with a focus on Local Governance" to the Japanese Team in Gandhigram Rural University on 29th August, 2009.

2009 : Delivered a lecture on "Potentials of Panchayats in delivering services to the marginalysed" to the partners of the funding agency HEKS in Dindigul on 29th July, 2009.

2009 : Delivered a special lecture on "Indian Political System" in the UNDP programme organized by Centre for Women

Studies, Bharathidasan University on 24th July, 2009 for the Elected Women Representatives of Tamil Nadu.

2008 : Delivered a key note lecture on "The Role of Panchayati in Communal Harmony" in the Regional Seminar organized by M.V.M. College for Women in Dindigul on 24th October, 2008.

2008 : Presented a paper on "The Role of Panchayat in Centre-State Relationship in India" in the Regional Workshop on Local Governments and Decentralized Governance organized by the Commission on Centre-State Relations in Thiruvananthapuram on 10th and 11th March, 2008.

2008 : Delivered a Lecture on "The Role of Panchayats in the Management of Climate Change" in the National Workshop on the Role of ICT in the Management of Climate Change organized by M.S. Swaminathan Research Foundation, Chennai on 11th February, 2008.

2007 : Presented a paper on "New Federalism in India after the Creation of Third Tier of Governance" in the Regional Round Table organized by the Inter State Council, Ministry of Home Affairs, Government of India, in Goa on 30th and 31st July, 2007.

2007 : Participated in the Working Group Meeting of the State Planning Commission to prepare a report on "Empowerment and Poverty Reduction in Tamil Nadu" at Chennai on 16th April, 2007.

2007 : Delivered a Lecture on the "Role of Dalit Leaders in Panchayati Raj System in India" at Madurai Kamaraj University on 24th February, 2007.

2006 : Delivered a Keynote address in the Local Body Leaders Conference on 24th November, 2006 at Madurai organized by Communist Party of India.

2006 : Delivered a Keynote address in the Local Body Leaders Conference at Chennai organized by Pattali Makkal Katchi (PMK) on 15th November, 2006.

2006 : Delivered a Lecture on "Bala Sabhas and Grama Sabhas" in the UNICEF Project Seminar at Coimbatore on 4th November, 2006.

2006 : Delivered a Lecture on "The Process of Women's Participation in Panchayati Raj Institutions" in the Regional Seminar on Women's Political Empowerment organized by UNICEF on 17th June, 2006.

2006 : Presented a paper on "Constitutional Sanctions and Community Practices" in the State Level Workshop on Pre Election Voters Awareness at Chennai organized by the Hunger Project on 19th May, 2006.

2006 : Presented an approach paper before the III State Finance Commission on Local Body Finance at Dindigul on 17th January, 2006.

2006 : Delivered a popular lecture on "Linkage between Self Help Groups and the Panchayati Raj System" in the Multi Media Campaign organized by the Government of India at Tirunelveli on 30th January, 2006.

2006 : Presented a paper on "Role of Gram Panchayat in Implementing National Rural Employment Scheme in Tamil Nadu" in the one day Workshop on National Rural Employment Scheme in Gandhigram, organized by the District Administration on 7th January, 2006.

2005 : Delivered a Valedictory address in the Regional Workshop on Youth and Hunger, organized by Shanti Ashram at Coimbatore on 27th November, 2005.

2005 : Delivered a Keynote address on 'Globalization of Economy and Decentralization of powers" in the V State Level Convention of the FEDCOT at Trichy on 31st May, 2005.

2005 : Delivered a Keynote Address on the symposium on "Information and Communication Strategies for Grassroots Development" held at Chennai organized by the University of Madras on 5th March, 2005.

2004 : Presented a paper on "Women Governance at Grassroots" in the UGC sponsored seminar on 'Women Empowerment' organized by Pasumpon Muthuramalinga Thevar College at Usilampatti on 22nd July, 2004.

2004 : Presented a paper entitled "Impact of training on Local Body Women Leaders" in the regional convention organized by Institute of Social Sciences, New Delhi at Chennai on 30th March, 2004.

2004 : Presented a paper on "Role of Women Leaders in Local Politics and Governance in Administering Development" in the convention on Empowerment of Women, organized by the British Council in Avinashi Lingam Institute of Home Science on 24th March, 2004 at Coimbatore.

2003 : Presented a paper on "Struggle and Strategies of Elected

Women Representatives in Local Bodies to Administer Development and Social Justice" in the workshop organized at Chennai on 24th April, 2003 by Institute of Social Sciences, New Delhi.

2003 : Participated and shared our DANIDA Project experience with the Participants of the workshop organized on "Water Supply and Sanitation" at Chennai on 9th January, 2003.

2002 : Presented a paper on "Role of Women and NGO in Strengthening Elected Candidates in Panchayats" in the Regional Consultative Meet of Centre for World Solidarity at Chennai on 15th and 16th February, 2002.

2002 : Presented a paper on "Role of NGOs on Women Empowerment" in Regional Assembly of CARITAS INDIA in Coimbatore on 29th July, 2002.

2002 : Presented a paper on "Systems Reforms and Speedier Redressal Mechanism for Good Governance" in the workshop on Empowerment of Civil Society in Strengthening Good Governance at Chennai on 23rd June, 2002 organized by Peace Trust sponsored by World Bank.

2002 : Participated in the Workshop on "Capacity Building Needs of Elected Representatives of Local Bodies in Tamil Nadu" at Chennai on 23rd and 24th August, 2002 organized by PRIA, New Delhi.

2001 : Presented a paper on "Role of Panchayati Raj Institutions in Continuing Education Programme" in the Seminar on Integration of NYK activities with Continuing Education at Gandhigram from 30th to 31st October, 2001 organized by the State Resource Centre, Chennai.

2000 : Presented a paper on "Role of Media in New Panchayati Raj System" in the Media workshop organized by the Government of India, Ministry of Rural Development in Gandhigram from 14th to 15th March, 2000.

2000 : Participated and chaired a session in the workshop for validation of training module organized by the Government of Tamil Nadu on 1st March, 2000 at Chennai.

2000 : Presented the States Report of Tamil Nadu Panchayati System in the advocacy consultation on Panchayati Government and the Budget Session 2000 organized by Human Rights Advocacy and Research Foundation at Chennai on 27th January, 2000.

2000 : Participated in the workshop on validation of training module to conduct training programme for Leaders and Officials on Multi Level Planning, at Chennai organized by the State Planning Commission on 30th May, 2000.

2000 : Participated in the meetings organized by II State Finance Commission to finalize the modalities of the work at Chennai on 27th April, 2000.

2000 : Participated in the seminar organized by State Planning Commission to finalize training module for Multi Level Planning at Chennai on 28th January, 2000.

2000 : Participated in the state level seminar on devolution of finance to local bodies on 10.8.2000 at Chennai organized by II State Finance Commission, Government of Tamil Nadu.

2000 : Presented a paper on "Panchayati Raj Institutions and Primary Education" in the one day seminar organized by Tamil Nadu Primary School Improvement Campaign at Chennai on 9th August, 2000.

2000 : Delivered series of special lectures on "Decentralization of Power" in Annamalai University on 21st March, 2000.

2000 : Participated in the Regional workshop on validation of training material for Local Body leaders, organized by the Department of Rural Development and sponsored by UNICEF, Chennai on 31st October and 1st November, 2000.

2000 : Presented a paper entitled "Interface between the Elected Women Representatives and the Bureaucracy in Tamil Nadu" in the Regional Seminar organized by Institute for the study of Developing Areas in Trivandrum on 3rd and 4th November, 2000.

1999 : Delivered Key note address in the programme organized for NGO "To build the Capacity of Trainers to Train the Women Leaders of Local Bodies", organised by Human Rights Advocacy and Research at Chennai on 29th October, 1999.

1999 : Presented a paper entitled "Role of Local Bodies in Continuing Education" in the Annual Conference of State Resource Centre at Anna University, Chennai from 17th to 18th September, 1999.

1999 : Participated and presented the theme paper on "Management of Common Property Resources, Empowerment of Women and Performance of Dalit Representatives" in the Round Table organized by Peoples Governance Cell, Chennai on 11th December, 1999.

1999 : Participated and moderated the Media Consultation Programme on Decentralized Democracy and Empowerment of Women in Panchayats on 4th December, 1999, organized by Human Rights Advocacy and Research Foundation, Chennai.

1997 : Presented paper on "Agenda for immediate action to empower people through the New Panchayat Raj System" in the seminar organized by Gandhigram Trust in Madras from 30th to 31st January, 1997.

1997 : Delivered valedictory address in the Training Programme organized by the Tamil University to village panchayati leaders on 10th January, 1997 in Thanjavur.

1997 : Presented a theme paper on "State of the Art: Status of the present state in welfare activities" in the seminar on Social Defence in Welfare State organized by the Department of Sociology in Gandhigram from 19th to 21st February, 1997.

1997 : Delivered a special lecture on "Linking NGOs with Panchayats at Grassroots Level" to the participants of the two-day refresher course on NGO Management organized by GRI-PRA Unit on 24th June, 1997 in Gandhigram.

1997 : Presented a paper on "Role and Responsibilities of the Members of a city corporation" in meet the members programme organized in Coimbatore on 17th October, 1997 by Tamil Nadu Institute of Urban Studies, Coimbatore.

1996 : Presented a paper entitled "Revolution in raising expectations in rural India" in the workshop on Uncommon Opportunities for India organized by Rajaji Institute of Public Affairs on March 2nd, 1996 at Madras.

1996 : Delivered a special Lecture on New Panchayati Raj System and Poverty Alleviation" in Bharathidasan University, Trichy on 24th January, 1996.

1995 : Presented a paper entitled "Panchayati Raj Institutes in India: History and Issues" in the Sub-Regional workshop in Panchayati Raj System in Avinashilingam Institute of Home Science and Higher Education for Women in Coimbatore from 6th to 7th February, 1995.

1995 : Delivered a special lecture on "Voluntary Organizations and Rural Development" in the UGC Refresher course in Public Administration on 14th January, 1995 in Institute of Social and Economic Change, Bangalore.

1995 : Delivered a special lecture on "Federalism in Indian and Canadian Constitutions" in the Canadian Studies Development Programme on 22nd February, 1995 in Bharathidasan University, Trichy.

1995 : Presented a paper entitled "Panchayati Raj Legislation in India" in the Regional Seminar on "Panchayati Raj and Education" from 23rd to 24th February, 1995 in Bharathidasan University, Thiruchirapalli.

1995 : Participated in the Seminar on "Panchayati Raj Institutions in Tamil Nadu: A Historical Review" organized by Madras Institute of Development Studies and Institute of Social Sciences in Madras on 15th June, 1995.

1995 : Presented a Paper entitled "New Panchayati Raj System: A Phenomenon in Indian Politics" in the Seminar on Panchayati Raj and People's aspirations organized by Madurai Branch of Indian Institute of Public Administration of 27th August, 1995 in Madurai.

1994 : Presented a paper entitled "Gandhian Framework of Politics: Revisited" in the Seminar on Gandhian Approach to Rural Development in Gandhigram Rural Institute from 3rd to 4th October, 1994.

1993 : Presented a paper entitled "Social Action for Effective Functioning of Panchayati Raj System in Tamil Nadu" in the Conference on "Present Status and Future Prospects of Panchayati Raj in Tamil Nadu" in the Centre for Entrepreneur Development, Madurai on 13th March, 1993.

1992 : Participated in the Seminar organised by Anna University and People's Power Movement on "Education for the next generation" in the Anna University campus on 2nd February, 1992.

1992 : Presented a paper entitled "A Policy Approach to the study of Reservation and its Political Implications" in the Seminar organized by the Department of Sociology, University of Madras on 20th March, 1992.

1992 : Participated in a Seminar on "Role of Members in Trade Unions" at IFPAAW Rural Workers Education Centre at Thirumangalam on 19th May, 1992.

1989 : Presented a paper entitled "Adolescent political Reasoning: A Theoretical Consideration" in the 5th Annual Convention of the Tamil Nadu Political Science Academy on 26th November, 1989 at Bharathidasan University, Tiruchirapalli.

1988 : Presented a paper entitled "Electoral Alliances in Tamil Nadu since 1952", in the Annual Convention of the Tamil Nadu Academy of Political Science on 11th December, 1988 in Central Law College at Salem.

1986 : Presented a paper entitled "Eclipse of the Second Chamber in Indian State Legislature", in the II Annual Conference of the Tamil Nadu Academy of Political Science at Madras on 20th September, 1986.

1986 : Attended the UGC Zonal Workshop in Advanced Research Methodology in Political Science", from November 24th to 14th December, 1986 in the Department of Political Science, Osmania University, Hyderabad.

29. Endowment Lectures (Total:10)

2015 : Delivered the Thevar Centenary Memorial Lecture on "Transformational Leadership" in the Bharathidasan University on 23rd February, 2015.

2013 : Delivered Arulselvar Pollachi Dr. N. Mahalingam Endowment Lecture in Avinasilingam University on 25th February, 2013 on "Decentralization and Development."

2008 : Delivered P. Seenivasa Rao Centenary Lecture on "Role of Agriculture in Rural Economy" in the Indian School of Social Sciences, Chennai on 25th July, 2008.

2008 : Delivered a Special Address in the National Seminar on "The Politics of Inclusion and Exclusion" in Mother Teresa Women's University, Kodaikanal on 5th July, 2008.

2007 : Delivered Kalvivallal Kalasalingam Endowment Lecture on "Constitutional Law *Vs.* Community Law" in Madurai Kamaraj University on 7th September, 2007.

2006 : Delivered Dr. V.C. Kulandaisamy Educational and Research Foundation Day Special Lecture on 1st July, 2006 at Karur.

2005 : Delivered Nehru Memorial Lecture on "The Paradox of Indian Democracy" in Bharathidasan University on 26th September, 2005.

2005 : Delivered Sardar Vedarathinam Endowment Lecture on "The Role of Gandhian Institutions in Empowering Women" in Kasthurba Kanya Gurukulam at Vedaranyam on 24th August, 2005.

2005 : Delivered Dr. S. Bhaskaran's Endowment Lecture on

"Participatory Democracy in Indian Political System" in Annamalai University on 22nd February, 2005.

2003 : Delivered Rathnasamy Samiammal Endowment Lecture on "Empowerment of Women" in Avinashilingam Deemed University Coimbatore on 9th December, 2003.

30. Workshop/Conference/Seminar Organized

***International* (Total: 2)**

2005 : Organized a Toolkit Workshop on "Citizens Participation Process in Local Government in Reconstruction Process following Natural Disaster with Special Reference to Tsunami" from 24th to 26th October, 2005, sponsored by Toolkit Foundation, The Netherlands.

2000 : Organized an interface programme at Gandhigram for the Cambodian Team of Members of Parliament to study the impact of reservation of seats for women in Local Bodies in India, on 19th April, 2000.

***National* (Total: 25)**

2017 : Organized a National Validation Workshop on "The Report on Impact of MGNREGA on the Livelihood of the Rural Households in India" at Chennai on 28th January 2017 sponsored by ICSSR and IRMA.

2014 : Organized a National Seminar on "Deliberative Democracy through Democratic Decentralization" on 12th and 13th March, 2014 sponsored by the UGC, New Delhi.

2013 : Organized a National Seminar on Decentralization, Development and Social Harmony from 29th November to 1st December, 2013 sponsored by Third World Studies South Asian Chapter.

2013 : Organized a Ten-Day Research Methodology Course to the Ph.D. Scholars drawn from various States of India from 1st to 10th August, 2013 sponsored by ICSSR, New Delhi.

2013 : Organized a National Seminar on "Two Decades of Decentralization of Powers Experience in Southern States of India" sponsored by the UGC from 11th to 13th March, 2013 in Gandhigram Rural Institute.

2013 : Organized a National Seminar on "Governance and Development" sponsored by the UGC from 26th and 27th February, 2013 in Gandhigram Rural Institute.

2012 : Organized a National Seminar on "The Role of Panchayats in MGNREGA" in Gandhigram Rural Institute on 24th and 25th February, 2012.

2011 : Organized a National Seminar on "Status of Dalits and Dalit Leaders in Rural Local Governance in Gandhigram Rural Institute on 12th and 13th March, 2012.

2010 : Organized a two-day National Seminar on "Globalization, Decentralization and Gender" at Chennai on 18th and 19th October, 2010 supported by the Ford Foundation.

2010 : Organized a National Seminar on "Critical Mass to Critical Action" on 13th and 14th March, 2010 in Gandhigram Rural Institute—Deemed University, Gandhigram sponsored by UGC-Special Assistance Programme.

2009 : Organized a National Validation Workshop on the studies conducted on the Life and Livelihood of the poor in Tamil Nadu" on 7th and 8th November, 2009 in Dr. M.S. Swaminathan Research Foundation, Chennai sponsored by the Ford Foundation.

2008 : Organized a Regional Workshop jointly with IRMA, Anand at Chennai on 14th and 15th of March 2008 to validate the Status Report of Devolution of Powers in Tamil Nadu prepared by IRMA for the Ministry of Panchayati Raj, Government of India.

2007 : Organized a National Workshop to Validate a Research Study on the Role of Panchayats in Disaster Preparedness and Management in Odisha, Gujarat, Andhra Pradesh and Tamil Nadu in Chennai on 27th and 28th December, 2007, sponsored by Action Aid India.

2006 : Organized a National Workshop on "Role Panchayats in Disaster Mitigation and Management" at Chennai on 25th November, 2006 sponsored by All India Institute of Disaster Mitigation, Ahmedabad.

2006 : Organized a National Workshop on "Globalization and Decentralization" at Chennai from 7th to 9th August, 2006 sponsored by the Ford Foundation, New Delhi.

2005 : Organized the XXVIII Indian Social Science Congress on "The Crisis of Modern Civilization" from 16th to 20th

January 2005, sponsored by Indian Academy of Social Sciences and UGC.

2003 : Organized a National Workshop on "Panchayati Raj: Trials and Triumphs" at Chennai on 22nd and 23rd August, 2003 sponsored by the Hunger Project, New Delhi.

2002 : Organized a National Workshop on Rural Higher Education towards Sustainable Rural Development and Gram Swaraj at Chennai on 21st and 22nd June, 2002 sponsored by National Council of Rural Institutes, Hyderabad.

2002 : Organized a National Seminar on Rural Development: Retrospect and Prospects sponsored by UGC at Gandhigram on 2nd and 3rd August, 2002.

2001 : Organized a Refresher Course on New Panchayati Raj System in India for College and University teachers sponsored by the UGC from 12th November to 2nd December, 2002.

2000 : Organized a ten day Social Science Research Methodology Course for the Researchers pursuing Ph.D. programmes in Rural Development and Panchayati Raj System in Gandhigram from 11th to 20th September, 2000 sponsored by ICSSR, New Delhi.

1999 : Organized a Refresher Course on New Panchayati Raj System for College Teachers from 6th to 26th January, 1999, sponsored by the UGC, New Delhi.

1999 : Organized a National Workshop on "Curriculum Development in Human Rights and Duties Education", sponsored by UGC, New Delhi and held in Gandhigram from 28th to 29th September, 1999.

1997 : Organized a UGC sponsored National Seminar on "Redefining Individual Governance Society" in Gandhigram from 3rd to 5th October, 1997.

1996 : Organized a Refresher Course on New Panchayati Raj System to college teachers from 15th November to 5th December, 1996 sponsored by UGC, New Delhi.

1995 : Organized a National Workshop on "New Panchayati Raj System: Problems and Prospects", sponsored by CAPART, Ministry of Rural Development from 26th to 28th May, 1995.

Regional **(Total: 69)**

2017 : Organized a "Pre Election Candidate Awareness Campaign" in GRI on 2nd April, 2017.

2015 : Organized the validation workshop to validate the report on "Impact of MGNRGA in Thiruvanduram District in Kerala" on 22st July, 2015, sponsored by SIRD Kerala.

2015 : Organized the validation workshop to validate the report on "Impact of MGNRGA in Kottayam District in Kerala on 21st July 2015, sponsored by SIRD Kerala.

2015 : Organized an Interface workshop on the Representatives of People: National Parliament, State Legislature and Local Bodies in Gandhigram Rural Institute, Gandhigram on 23rd March, 2015.

2012 : Organized a two day Workshop to test the "New Module for Leadership Training" in Gandhgiram on 10th and 11th April, 2012 sponsored by Madras Management Association, Chennai.

2010 : Organized one-day regional workshop on "Evolving Disaster preparedness and Management policy for Tamil Nadu" in Gandhigram on 30th July, 2010.

2010 : Organized a Regional Media Workshop on the "Role of Local Bodies in Disaster Preparedness and Management" at Cuddalore on 20th July, 2010 sponsored by Action Aid International.

2010 : Organized a Regional Media Workshop on "Role of Local Bodies in Disaster Preparedness Plan" in Nagapattinam on 24th July, 2010 sponsored by Action Aid International.

2009 : Organized a Validation and Dissemination workshop on the study conducted and training manual evolved on "Disaster Preparedness and Management" in Gandhigram on 14th November, 2009 supported by the Action Aid India International, Chennai.

2009 : Organized a Training of Trainers programme for the NGO leaders on "Disaster Preparedness and Disaster Management" from 17th to 19th September, 2009 in Gandhigram Rural Institute—Deemed University sponsored by the Action Aid India International, Chennai.

2009 : Organized a Validation Workshop on Dindigul District Human Development Report on behalf of the State Planning Commission and UNDP on 27th January, 2009.

2009 : Organized a Validation Workshop on Nagapattinam District Human Development on behalf of the State Planning Commission and UNDP on12th February, 2009.

2008 : Organized a training workshop for the Coordinators of Citizens Centre from 4th to 6th January, 2008 sponsored by the Ford Foundation through Catalyst Trust.

2008 : Organized a training workshop to Panchayat leaders emerging as models in Governance, Administration and Development in Gandhigram Rural University, Gandhigram from 29th to 31st January, 2008.

2007 : An experience sharing session was organized to Sri Lankan delegation of lawyers on "Local Governance in India" at Gandhigram on 19th October, 2007.

2007 : An experience sharing session was organized to Bangladesh Development Managers on "Local Governance in India" at Gandhigram on 29th November, 2007.

2007 : Organized a Panchayat leaders meet on "Global-Local Dialogue" in Gandhigram on 10th and 11th April 2007 sponsored by the Ford Foundation.

2007 : Organized an NGO Meet on "Global-Local Dialogue" in Gandhigram on 4th and 5th May, 2007 sponsored by the Ford Foundation.

2007 : Organized a programme to Launch Panchayat Yuva Shakti Abhiyan in Tamil Nadu on 24th and 26th February, 2007 in Gandhigram Rural University.

2006 : Organized a short term training programme on "Governance at Grassroots" to the MSW students of the Institute of Social Sciences and Research, Bhuvaneswar, Odisha from 20th to 24th May, 2006.

2006 : Organized a Media Workshop for Reporters at Madurai "The Importance of Capturing the Struggles and Success of Elected Women Representatives of Grassroots Institutions" in Madurai on 5th June, 2006.

2006 : Organized a Visioning Workshop on the Methodology of Preparing District Human Development Report at Nagapattinam on 24th January, 2006 sponsored by UNDP, New Delhi.

2005 : Organized a Travelling Media Workshop for the senior staff Reporters of the National and Regional Dailies from Chennai on 22nd and 23rd November, 2005 in Gandhigram, sponsored by the Hunger Project.

2005 : Organized a Visioning Workshop on the Methodology of Preparing District Human Development Report at Dindigul on 21st October, 2005 sponsored by UNDP, New Delhi.

2005 : Organized Media Workshop for Journalists and Reporters of Media on "Women Leadership at Grassroots" in Tirunelveli on 4th August, 2005 sponsored by the Hunger Project.

2005 : Organized Dissemination Workshop on "Micro Plan" for Gram Panchayat Presidents of Tuticorin District on 3rd and 4th August, 2005 sponsored by the Hunger Project.

2005 : Organized two day Refresher Course on Namathu Gramam Scheme for Gram Panchayats of Dindigul District in three batches from 24th August to 2nd September, 2005, sponsored by the Government of Tamil Nadu.

2005 : Organized a Orientation Programme for Members of Legislative Assembly of Communist Party of India (Marxist) on "Current status of Devolution of powers in India" on 18th March, 2005.

2005 : Organized a Mela of Women Leaders of Grassroots Institutions at Gandhigram on 15th May, 2005, sponsored by Singamma Sreenivasan Foundation.

2005 : Organized one day Refresher Course on "Panchayat Management" for Women Gram Panchayat Leaders at Cuddalore on 2nd June, 2005.

2004 : Organized a Workshop on Micro Level Planning at Grassroots at Pudukkottai on 11th September, 2004, sponsored by the Hunger Project.

2004 : Organized a Orientation Programme on "Capacity Building for Decentralized Governance" for State Coordinators of the Hunger Project at Kodaikanal from 1st to 3rd September, 2004.

2004 : Organized a Media Workshop at Trichy for media representatives on Women Governance and Women Leaders on 31st July, 2004, sponsored by the Hunger Project.

2004 : Organized a media Workshop for media reporters on Women Leadership and Women Governance at Salem on 21st May 2004, sponsored by the Hunger Project.

2004 : Organized a Regional Workshop for Elected Women Representatives of Salem Region at Salem on 20th May, 2004, sponsored by SSF, Bangalore.

2004 : Organized a TOT to develop master trainers among the Women Leaders of Panchayats at Gandhigram from 14th to 16th May 2004, sponsored by the Hunger Project.

2004 : Organized a Regional Workshop on "Media Review on Panchayat Malar" a supplement brought out in partnership with *Dinamalar* by the Hunger Project on 6th May, 2004.

2004 : Organized a Writers Workshop on Women in Panchayati Raj at Gandhigram on 1st and 2nd June, 2004.

2004 : Organized a Media Workshop on Women in Panchayati Raj at Salem on 21st May, 2004.

2004 : Organized a Regional Workshop for Networking Elected Women Representatives at Salem on 20th May, 2004.

2003 : Organized a three day workshop on "Decentralization and Child Care" for the CRY Staff from 21st to 23rd November, 2003 sponsored by CRY, Chennai.

2003 : Organized a three day workshop on "Decentralization of Power and Grassroots Development" for the FEDCOT field staff from 2nd to 4th December, 2003 sponsored by FEDCOT, Chennai.

2003 : Organized a Regional Workshop of Elected Women Representatives of Local bodies at Thiruvarur on 27th December, 2003.

2002 : Organized a state level workshop on "Non-Formal Education and Panchayati Raj" on 8th and 9th January, 2002 sponsored by State Resource Centre, Chennai.

2002 : Organized a state level workshop on "Primary Education and Panchayati Raj" at Chennai on 11th January, 2002 sponsored by PRIA, New Delhi.

2002 : Organized a state level workshop on Capacity Building for Local Body Leaders in Tamil Nadu on 14th February, 2002 at Chennai sponsored by PRIA, New Delhi.

2002 : Organized a state level interface meet of Self Help Group leaders and Panchayat Leaders on 4th and 5th January, 2002 at Gandhigram sponsored by UNICEF, Chennai.

2002 : Organized a media workshop on "Women and Decentralized Governance" on 30th January, 2002 at Chennai sponsored by the Hunger Project, New Delhi.

2002 : Organized a state level Elected Women Representatives of Local Bodies Meet on 20th February, 2002 sponsored by Singamma Sreenivasan Foundation, Bangalore.

2002 : Organized a state level workshop to review the action project on "Community Participation in Social Development through Panchayats" on 21st and 22nd March, 2002 sponsored by Population Foundation of India, New Delhi.

2002 : Organized the State Council Meeting of the Tamil Nadu Council of the Hunger Project at Chennai on 13th April, 2002.

2002 : Organized an interface meet of the panchayati leaders held at Kerala on 21st, 22nd and 23rd of April, 2002 sponsored by Singamma Sreenivasan Foundation, Bangalore.

2002 : Organized a Media Workshop at Coimbatore on 28th April, 2002 sponsored by the Hunger Project.

2002 : Organized the Second Annual Convention of Elected Women Representatives in Local Bodies on 3rd May, 2002 sponsored by Singamma Sreenivasan Foundation, Bangalore.

2002 : Organized a Leadership Training Programme for women leaders of panchayats from 27th to 31st May, 2002 sponsored by the Hunger Project.

2002 : Organized a Leadership Training Programme for women leaders of panchayats from 10th to 14th June, 2002 sponsored by the Hunger Project.

2002 : Organized a Regional Seminar on "Micro Level Participatory Development Plan" at Gandhigram on 26th and 27th October, 2002 sponsored by the Hunger Project, New Delhi.

2001 : Organized a Regional Seminar on Administrative Reform in Gandhigram on 17th and 18th March, 2001 sponsored by the Ministry of Tourism, Government of India.

2001 : Organized a Regional Workshop on "Globalization, Identity Politics and Rising Violence" in Gandhigram on 24th and 25th March, 2001 sponsored by Indian Association for Women's Studies.

2001 : Organized a workshop on "Evolving Indicators of Performance to Evaluate the Performance of Panchayati Leaders" in Gandhigram on 22nd June, 2001 sponsored by UNICEF, Chennai.

2001 : Organized a "Annual Convention of Elected Women Representatives of Rural Local Bodies in Tamil Nadu" in Gandhigram on 5th August, 2001 sponsored by Ford Foundation, New Delhi.

2001 : Organized a workshop on "Evolving Strategies to Create

Voters Awareness" sponsored by PRIA, New Delhi on 10th September, 2001.

2001 : Organized a workshop on Media and Panchayati Raj at Madurai on 5th October, 2001 sponsored by the Hunger Project, New Delhi.

2001 : Organized a test run programme to test the training modules evolved to conduct capacity building to local body leaders from 3rd to 7th December, 2001 sponsored by Rajiv Gandhi Foundation, New Delhi.

2000 : Organized a NGOs meet to create Peoples Forum and People Information Centre in Village Panchayats on 24th September, 2000 sponsored by Catalyst Trust, Chennai.

1996 : Organized a workshop to evolve a manual for Leadership Training in New Panchayati Raj System from 20th to 22nd December, 1996 sponsored by CSRDS, Madras.

1995 : Organized a sub-regional workshop on "Panchayati Raj System and Prosperity movement", sponsored by Rajiv Gandhi Foundation, New Delhi from 26th to 28th December, 1995.

1995 : Organized a workshop on "Review of Tamil Nadu Panchayati Act, 1994" sponsored by Centre for Socio-Legal Research and Documentation Service, Chennai from 28th to 30th March, 1996.

1993 : Organized a conference jointly with the Institute of Social Sciences, New Delhi on "Present Status and Future Prospects of Panchayati Raj in Tamil Nadu" in the Centre for Entrepreneurship Development, Madurai on 13th March, 1993.

1991 : Organized a workshop on Alcoholism and its consequences to the Drivers and Conductors of RMTC (State owned Transport Corporation) from 26th to 27th September, 1991 at Dindigul.

31. Interview to the Press

2006 : Interview to the **Frontline,** September 22, 2006, p. 27.

2004 : Interview to the **Down to Earth**, 29th February, 2004.

2003 : Interview to the **Down to Earth**, 15th August, 2003.

2001 : Interview to the **Frontline**, 26th October, 2001, p. 34.

2001 : Interview to the **Frontline,** 23rd November, 2001, p. 38.

2001 : Interview to the **Frontline**, 29th March, 2002, p. 52.
1995 : Interview to **Junior Post** on Rural Entrepreneurship (28-4-1995) p. 17.
1995 : Interview to **Thuglak Tamil Fortnightly** on New Panchayati Raj System (May 1995) p. 15.
1994 : Interview to **Junior Post** on New Panchayati Raj (25-11-1994) p. 6.
1994 : Interview to **Thuglak Tamil Fortnightly** on New Panchayati Raj System (15-2-1994) p. 26.
1994 : Interview to **Thuglak Tamil Fortnightly** on Need for Capacity Building Exercise for Legislators (1-6-1994) p. 15.

32. Preparation of Training Tool

Transformational Women Leadership Training Module for National Commission for Women through Tata Institute of Social Sciences, Mumbai.

Disaster Preparedness and Management Trainers Manual Gandhigram: Rajiv Gandhi Chair for Panchayati Raj Studies, 2009.

Prepared a Training Module on Globalization and Decentralization" to orient Panchayat leaders in the issues of Globalization sponsored by the Ford Foundation.

Prepared a video cassette on New Panchayati Raj System and Social Development: A Documentary sponsored by Population Foundation of India.

Evolved a Training Manual to offer Leadership Training to Urban Local Body Women Leaders—sponsored by Tamil Nadu Institute of Urban Studies, Coimbatore.

Evolved Training Manual to conduct Capacity Building Exercise to Gram Panchayati Leaders of Tamil Nadu—sponsored by CAPART, New Delhi.

Evolved a Training Module on "Empowerment of Panchayati Raj Institutions on Issues of Population, Health and Social Development", sponsored by Population Foundation of India, New Delhi.

Prepared a training module on "Urban Governance issues and the role of Management of Information System" for the Executives and Elected Leaders of Urban Local Bodies organized by the Anna Institute of Management, Chennai.

Prepared a comprehensive training module to train panchayati leaders and officials in Tamil Nadu sponsored by Rajiv Gandhi Foundation, New Delhi and it is published by Rajiv Gandhi Chair for Panchayati Raj Studies.

Prepared a training module to conduct leadership training to women leaders of the Panchayats sponsored by the Hunger Project, New Delhi and it is published by Rajiv Gandhi Chair for Panchayati Raj Studies.

Prepared and published a guide book containing Powers and Responsibilities of Ward Members of Gram Panchayat, Block Panchayat and District Panchayat and Presidents of Gram Panchayat, Block Panchayat and District Panchayat (totally four guide books).

Prepared a guide book for Gram Panchayati leaders to prepare a perspective plan for the development of the Village Panchayat area based on the pilot project works carried out in 56 Panchayats in four districts of Tamil Nadu.

33. Radio Programmes

Voter Awareness programme conducted for 15 days through FM (Pasumai) Radio from 25th April to 10th May, 2009.

Series of ten lecture programmes on New Panchayati Raj System over All India Radio, Madurai.

Series of Lectures on the Functioning of Grassroots Democracy over All India Radio, Chennai and Madurai.

Occasional Lectures on Issues of Grassroots Democracy over All India Radio, Chennai, Madurai, Tuticorin.

Do you want development? (In Tamil) 5 Minutes talk in Kodai FM from 1st to 30th November, 2017.

34. TV Programmes

Participated in a Panel Discussion with Manisankar Aiyar, Rajasthan Panchayati Raj Minister and Managing Editor of *India Today* for UTV, Mumbai on Panchayati Raj and Human Development.

Exclusive Programmes on Local Democracy were given to SUN TV and SUN News.

Exclusive programme on Parliamentary Democracy was given to STAR VIJAY TV (a live telecast for one hour). On important issues on grassroots democracy views are expressed through these channels in regular News programmes.

Exclusive Programmes on Democratizing the Society and Empowering People especially Women in JAYA TV.

35. Extension Activities

2015 organized a training programme for Gram Panchayat leaders of Kariapatti Blocks of Virudunagar district on 22rd and 23rd August, 2015 sponsored by Sarvodaya Mandel in Gandhigram.

Organizing Awareness Camps in the villages to create awareness among the rural masses about the New Panchayati Raj System.

Organizing training programmes to Local Body leaders and others functionaries. Nearly 8000 Gram Panchayat leaders have been trained. Duration of the training programme is five days per batch.

Organizing leadership training programmes to elected women and Dalit representatives. Nearly 5000 Gram Panchayat leaders are trained by adopting leadership module. Duration of the programme is five days.

Helping Civil Society Organizations to conduct training programme to Gram Panchayat leaders on Disaster Preparedness and Risk Reduction by evolving training modules.

Helping Civil Society Organizations to evolve micro plan for Gram Panchayats by evolving guidelines.

Worked with 73 Gram Panchayats to evolve micro plan with active participation of people in Tamil Nadu.

Worked with 17 Gram Panchayats to evolve micro plan in Tsunami affected Gram Panchayats to manage disaster.

Periodically organizing media workshop on Local Governance to media representatives.

Assisting the Women and Dalit leaders at grassroots to form Federation at State level to address their issues and problems.

Assisting NGOs to create awareness among the people about the self-governance.

Assisting Anna Institute of Management by serving as Resource Person to take classes for the orientation workshop organized for leaders and functionaries of Urban Local Bodies in Tamil Nadu.

Assisting NGOs to conduct training programmes to Local Body Leaders.

Assisting District Administration to carry out effectively Rural Development Schemes through Panchayats.

Rajiv Gandhi Chair has been designated as a support structure to help the women and Dalit Panchayat leaders.

36. Curriculum Development

Evolved curriculum for a New M.A. Programme in Governance and Development (It is an innovative programme and hence UGC has sanctioned Rs. 41 lakhs).

Evolved Curriculum for a New two-year M.A. Programme in Development Administration and Panchayati Raj System.

Evolved Curriculum for a Five-year Integrated M.A. Programme in Development Administration.

Evolved Curriculum for a new two-year M.A. Programme in Human Rights and Duties Education.

Evolved Curriculum for M.Phil programme in Development Administration.

Evolved Curriculum for Diploma Programme in Panchayat Management through Distance Education.

37. Endowment Creation

Initiated and created eight endowments on eminent personalities—Tamil Scholar TKC, Justice Bagawati, Justice V.R. Krishna Iyer, Si.Pa. Aditanar, M.G. Ramachandran, G. Venkatachalapathy, A.K. Venkatasubramaniam, and T.V. Rama Subbaiyar with the liberal donations of philanthropists and activist NGOs.

38. Professional Membership and Related Activities

Member in Solution Exchange Committee of UNDP
Life Member in Indian Political Science Association
Life Member in Indian Association for American Studies
Life Member in American Studies Research Centre, Hyderabad
Life Member in Indian Association for Canadian Studies
Life Member in Social Science Research Council
Life Member in Indian Academy of Social Sciences
Life Member in Tamil Nadu Academy of Political Science
Life Member in Indian Public Administration Association

Life Member in Indian Institute of Public Administration, New Delhi
General Senetary of the Indian Association for Vocational Educational and Training Studies
Member, Faculty of Social Science, Annamalai University for three years

References

Available on request.

Personal

Born	:	August 9, 1953
Married	:	Yes
Wife	:	Mrs. P. Mala, B.Sc.
Health	:	Excellent
Children	:	Two
		(D) P. Senthil Vadivu (Married), M. Tech. (Bio Technology)
		(S) P. Aurobindh, B.E. (Computer Engineering) Software Engineer in Infinite

Index